MINNESOTA
MIDDLE LEVEL MATHEMATICS (5-8)

By: Sharon Wynne, M.S.

XAMonline, INC.
Boston

To obtain permission(s) to use the material from this work for any purpose including workshops or seminars, please submit a written request to:

XAMonline, Inc.
25 First Street, Suite 106
Cambridge, MA 02141
Toll Free 1-800-509-4128
Email: info@xamonline.com
Web: www.xamonline.com
Fax: 1-617-583-5552

Library of Congress Cataloging-in-Publication Data

Wynne, Sharon A.
   Minnesota Middle Level Mathematics (5-8) Exam / Sharon A. Wynne 1st ed.
   ISBN 978-1-60787-078-4
   1. Middle Level Mathematics (5-8)
   2. Study Guides
   3. Minnesota
   4. Teachers' Certification & Licensure
   5. Careers

Disclaimer:
The opinions expressed in this publication are the sole works of XAMonline and were created independently from the National Education Association, Educational Testing Service, or any State Department of Education, National Evaluation Systems or other testing affiliates.

Between the time of publication and printing, state specific standards as well as testing formats and Web site information may change and therefore would not be included in part or in whole within this product. Sample test questions are developed by XAMonline and reflect content similar to that on real tests; however, they are not former test questions. XAMonline assembles content that aligns with state standards but makes no claims nor guarantees teacher candidates a passing score. Numerical scores are determined by testing companies such as NES or ETS and then are compared with individual state standards. A passing score varies from state to state.

Printed in the United States of America   œ-1

Minnesota Middle Level Mathematics (5-8)
ISBN: 978-1-60787-078-4

Table of Contents

DOMAIN II
PATTERNS, RELATIONS, AND FUNCTIONS

DOMAIN III
SHAPE AND SPACE

COMPETENCY 8
APPLY PRINCIPLES OF MEASUREMENT AND GEOMETRY TO SOLVE PROBLEMS

COMPETENCY 9
ANALYZE FIGURES AND SHAPES IN TWO AND THREE DIMENSIONS

COMPETENCY 10
ANALYZE FIGURES AND SHAPES USING COORDINATE AND TRANSFORMATIONAL GEOMETRY

DOMAIN IV
DATA, RANDOMNESS, AND UNCERTAINTY

COMPETENCY 11
APPLY KNOWLEDGE OF DATA INVESTIGATIONS

COMPETENCY 12
UNDERSTAND THE PRINCIPLES OF PROBABILITY 170

DOMAIN V
DISCRETE MATHEMATICS AND READING 181

COMPETENCY 13
UNDERSTAND THE PROCESSES AND APPLICATIONS OF DISCRETE MATHEMATICS 183

COMPETENCY 14
UNDERSTAND THE CONTENT AND METHODS FOR DEVELOPING STUDENTS' CONTENT-AREA READING SKILLS TO SUPPORT THEIR READING AND LEARNING IN MIDDLE LEVEL MATHEMATICS 194

SAMPLE TEST

MINNESOTA
MIDDLE LEVEL
MATHEMATICS (5-8)

SECTION 1
ABOUT XAMONLINE

XAMonline—A Specialty Teacher Certification Company

Created in 1996, XAMonline was the first company to publish study guides for state-specific teacher certification examinations. Founder Sharon Wynne found it frustrating that materials were not available for teacher certification preparation and decided to create the first single, state-specific guide. XAMonline has grown into a company of over 1,800 contributors and writers and offers over 300 titles for the entire PRAXIS series and every state examination. No matter what state you plan on teaching in, XAMonline has a unique teacher certification study guide just for you.

XAMonline—Value and Innovation

We are committed to providing value and innovation. Our print-on-demand technology allows us to be the first in the market to reflect changes in test standards and user feedback as they occur. Our guides are written by experienced teachers who are experts in their fields. And our content reflects the highest standards of quality. Comprehensive practice tests with varied levels of rigor means that your study experience will closely match the actual in-test experience.

To date, XAMonline has helped nearly 600,000 teachers pass their certification or licensing exams. Our commitment to preparation exceeds simply providing the proper material for study—it extends to helping teachers **gain mastery** of the subject matter, giving them the **tools** to become the most effective classroom leaders possible, and ushering today's students toward a **successful future**.

SECTION 2
ABOUT THIS STUDY GUIDE

Purpose of This Guide

Is there a little voice inside of you saying, "Am I ready?" Our goal is to replace that little voice and remove all doubt with a new voice that says, "I AM READY. **Bring it on!**" by offering the highest quality of teacher certification study guides.

Organization of Content

You will see that while every test may start with overlapping general topics, each is very unique in the skills they wish to test. Only XAMonline presents custom content that analyzes deeper than a title, a subarea, or an objective. Only XAMonline presents content and sample test assessments along with **focus statements**, the deepest-level rationale and interpretation of the skills that are unique to the exam.

Title and field number of test

→Each exam has its own name and number. XAMonline's guides are written to give you the content you need to know for the specific exam you are taking. You can be confident when you buy our guide that it contains the information you need to study for the specific test you are taking.

Subareas

→These are the major content categories found on the exam. XAMonline's guides are written to cover all of the subareas found in the test frameworks developed for the exam.

Objectives

→These are standards that are unique to the exam and represent the main subcategories of the subareas/content categories. XAMonline's guides are written to address every specific objective required to pass the exam.

Focus statements

→These are examples and interpretations of the objectives. You find them in parenthesis directly following the objective. They provide detailed examples of the range, type, and level of content that appear on the test questions. **Only XAMonline's guides drill down to this level.**

How Do We Compare with Our Competitors?

XAMonline—drills down to the focus statement level.
CliffsNotes and REA—organized at the objective level
Kaplan—provides only links to content
MoMedia—content not specific to the state test

Each subarea is divided into manageable sections that cover the specific skill areas. Explanations are easy to understand and thorough. You'll find that every test answer contains a rejoinder so if you need a refresher or further review after taking the test, you'll know exactly to which section you must return.

How to Use This Book

Our informal polls show that most people begin studying up to eight weeks prior to the test date, so start early. Then ask yourself some questions: How much do you really know? Are you coming to the test straight from your teacher-education program or are you having to review subjects you haven't considered in ten years? Either way, take a **diagnostic or assessment test** first. Also, spend time on sample tests so that you become accustomed to the way the actual test will appear.

This guide comes with an online diagnostic test of 30 questions found online at *www.XAMonline.com*. It is a little boot camp to get you up for the task and reveal things about your compendium of knowledge in general. Although this guide is structured to follow the order of the test, you are not required to study in that order. By finding a time-management and study plan that fits your life you will be more effective. The results of your diagnostic or self-assessment test can be a guide for how to manage your time and point you toward an area that needs more attention.

After taking the diagnostic exam, fill out the **Personalized Study Plan** page at the beginning of each chapter. Review the competencies and skills covered in that chapter and check the boxes that apply to your study needs. If there are sections you already know you can skip, check the "skip it" box. Taking this step will give you a study plan for each chapter.

Week	Activity
8 weeks prior to test	Take a diagnostic test found at www.XAMonline.com
7 weeks prior to test	Build your Personalized Study Plan for each chapter. Check the "skip it" box for sections you feel you are already strong in. ✗ SKIP IT ☐
6-3 weeks prior to test	For each of these four weeks, choose a content area to study. You don't have to go in the order of the book. It may be that you start with the content that needs the most review. Alternately, you may want to ease yourself into plan by starting with the most familiar material.
2 weeks prior to test	Take the sample test, score it, and create a review plan for the final week before the test.
1 week prior to test	Following your plan (which will likely be aligned with the areas that need the most review) go back and study the sections that align with the questions you may have gotten wrong. Then go back and study the sections related to the questions you answered correctly. If need be, create flashcards and drill yourself on any area that you makes you anxious.

SECTION 3
ABOUT THE MINNESOTA MIDDLE LEVEL MATHEMATICS (5-8) EXAM

What is the Minnesota Middle Level Mathematics (5-8) Exam?

The Minnesota Middle Level Mathematics (5-8) exam is meant to assess mastery of the content knowledge required to teach middle school mathematics in Minnesota public schools.

Often **your own state's requirements** determine whether or not you should take any particular test. The most reliable source of information regarding this is your state's Department of Education. This resource should have a complete list of testing centers and dates. Test dates vary by subject area and not all test dates necessarily include your particular test, so be sure to check carefully.

If you are in a teacher-education program, check with the Education Department or the Certification Officer for specific information for testing and testing timelines. The Certification Office should have most of the information you need.

If you choose an alternative route to certification you can either rely on our website at *www.XAMonline.com* or on the resources provided by an alternative certification program. Many states now have specific agencies devoted to alternative certification and there are some national organizations as well, for example:
National Association for Alternative Certification
http://www.alt-teachercert.org/index.asp

Interpreting Test Results

Contrary to what you may have heard, the results of the Minnesota Middle Level Mathematics (5-8) test are not based on time. More accurately, your score will be based on the raw number of points you earn in each section, the proportion of that section to the entire subtest, and the scaling of the raw score. Raw scores are converted to a scale of 100 to 300. It is likely to your benefit to complete as many questions in the time allotted, but it will not necessarily work to your advantage if you hurry through the test.

Scores are available by email if you request this when you register. Score reports are available 21 days after the testing window and posted to your account for 45 days as PDFs. Scores will also be sent to your chosen institution(s).

What's on the Test?

The Minnesota Middle Level Mathematics (5-8) exam is a computer-based test and consists of two subtests, each lasting one hour. You can take one or both subtests at one testing appointment. A scientific calculator and a formulas page are provided with your test. The breakdown of the questions is as follows:

Category	Approximate Number of Questions	Approximate Percentage of the Test
SUBTEST 1	48	
I: Number Sense		43%
II: Patterns, Relations, and Functions		57%
SUBTEST 2	48	
I: Shape and Space		43%
II: Data, Randomness, and Uncertainty		29%
III: Discrete Mathematics and Reading		28%

Question Types

You're probably thinking, enough already, I want to study! Indulge us a little longer while we explain that there is actually more than one type of multiple-choice question. You can thank us later after you realize how well prepared you are for your exam.

1. **Complete the Statement.** The name says it all. In this question type you'll be asked to choose the correct completion of a given statement. For example:

> **The Dolch Basic Sight Words consist of a relatively short list of words that children should be able to:**
>
> A. Sound out
>
> B. Know the meaning of
>
> C. Recognize on sight
>
> D. Use in a sentence

The correct answer is C. In order to check your answer, test out the statement by adding the choices to the end of it.

2. **Which of the Following.** One way to test your answer choice for this type of question is to replace the phrase "which of the following" with your selection. Use this example:

> **Which of the following words is one of the twelve most frequently used in children's reading texts:**
>
> A. There
>
> B. This
>
> C. The
>
> D. An

Don't look! Test your answer. _____ is one of the twelve most frequently used in children's reading texts. Did you guess C? Then you guessed correctly.

3. **Roman Numeral Choices.** This question type is used when there is more than one possible correct answer. For example:

> **Which of the following two arguments accurately supports the use of cooperative learning as an effective method of instruction?**
>
> I.   Cooperative learning groups facilitate healthy competition between individuals in the group.
>
> II. Cooperative learning groups allow academic achievers to carry or cover for academic underachievers.
>
> III. Cooperative learning groups make each student in the group accountable for the success of the group.
>
> IV. Cooperative learning groups make it possible for students to reward other group members for achieving.
>
> A. I and II
>
> B. II and III
>
> C. I and III
>
> D. III and IV

Notice that the question states there are **two** possible answers. It's best to read all the possibilities first before looking at the answer choices. In this case, the correct answer is D.

4. **Negative Questions.** This type of question contains words such as "not," "least," and "except." Each correct answer will be the statement that does **not** fit the situation described in the question. Such as:

> **Multicultural education is not**
>
> A. An idea or concept
>
> B. A "tack-on" to the school curriculum
>
> C. An educational reform movement
>
> D. A process

Think to yourself that the statement could be anything but the correct answer. This question form is more open to interpretation than other types, so read carefully and don't forget that you're answering a negative statement.

5. **Questions that Include Graphs, Tables, or Reading Passages.** As always, read the question carefully. It likely asks for a very specific answer and not a broad interpretation of the visual. Here is a simple (though not statistically accurate) example of a graph question:

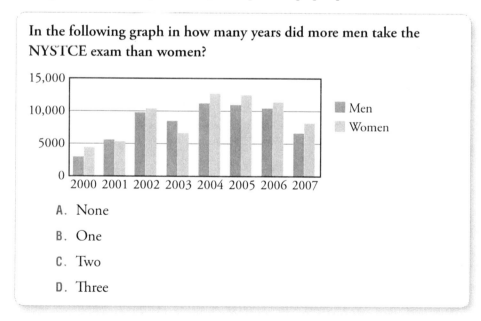

> **In the following graph in how many years did more men take the NYSTCE exam than women?**
>
> A. None
>
> B. One
>
> C. Two
>
> D. Three

It may help you to simply circle the two years that answer the question. Make sure you've read the question thoroughly and once you've made your determination, double check your work. The correct answer is C.

SECTION 4
HELPFUL HINTS

Study Tips

1. **You are what you eat.** Certain foods aid the learning process by releasing natural memory enhancers called CCKs (cholecystokinin) composed of tryptophan, choline, and phenylalanine. All of these chemicals enhance the neurotransmitters associated with memory and certain foods release memory enhancing chemicals. A light meal or snacks of one of the following foods fall into this category:

   - Milk
   - Rice
   - Eggs
   - Fish
   - Nuts and seeds
   - Oats
   - Turkey

   The better the connections, the more you comprehend!

2. **See the forest for the trees.** In other words, get the concept before you look at the details. One way to do this is to take notes as you read, paraphrasing or summarizing in your own words. Putting the concept in terms that are comfortable and familiar may increase retention.

3. **Question authority.** Ask why, why, why? Pull apart written material paragraph by paragraph and don't forget the captions under the illustrations. For example, if a heading reads *Stream Erosion* put it in the form of a question (Why do streams erode? What is stream erosion?) then find the answer within the material. If you train your mind to think in this manner you will learn more and prepare yourself for answering test questions.

4. **Play mind games.** Using your brain for reading or puzzles keeps it flexible. Even with a limited amount of time your brain can take in data (much like a computer) and store it for later use. In ten minutes you can: read two paragraphs (at least), quiz yourself with flash cards, or review notes. Even if you don't fully understand something on the first pass, your mind stores it for recall, which is why frequent reading or review increases chances of retention and comprehension.

5. **Get pointed in the right direction.** Use arrows to point to important passages or pieces of information. It's easier to read than a page full of yellow highlights. Highlighting can be used sparingly, but add an arrow to the margin to call attention to it.

6. **The pen is mightier than the sword.** Learn to take great notes. A by-product of our modern culture is that we have grown accustomed to getting our information in short doses. We've subconsciously trained ourselves to assimilate information into neat little packages. Messy notes fragment the flow of information. Your notes can be much clearer with proper formatting. **The Cornell Method** is one such format. This method was popularized in *How to Study in College*, Ninth Edition, by Walter Pauk. You can benefit from the method without purchasing an additional book by simply looking up the method online. Below is a sample of how *The Cornell Method* can be adapted for use with this guide.

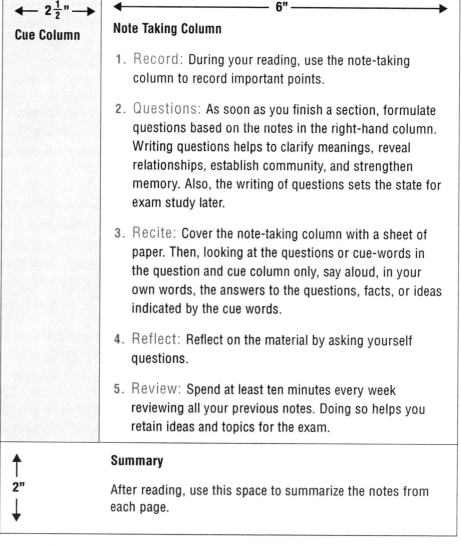

← 2½" →	← 6" →
Cue Column	**Note Taking Column**
	1. Record: During your reading, use the note-taking column to record important points.
	2. Questions: As soon as you finish a section, formulate questions based on the notes in the right-hand column. Writing questions helps to clarify meanings, reveal relationships, establish community, and strengthen memory. Also, the writing of questions sets the state for exam study later.
	3. Recite: Cover the note-taking column with a sheet of paper. Then, looking at the questions or cue-words in the question and cue column only, say aloud, in your own words, the answers to the questions, facts, or ideas indicated by the cue words.
	4. Reflect: Reflect on the material by asking yourself questions.
	5. Review: Spend at least ten minutes every week reviewing all your previous notes. Doing so helps you retain ideas and topics for the exam.
↑ 2" ↓	**Summary** After reading, use this space to summarize the notes from each page.

Adapted from How to Study in College, Ninth Edition, by Walter Pauk, ©2008 Wadsworth

The proctor will write the start time where it can be seen and then, later, provide the time remaining, typically fifteen minutes before the end of the test.

7. Place yourself in exile and set the mood. Set aside a particular place and time to study that best suits your personal needs and biorhythms. If you're a night person, burn the midnight oil. If you're a morning person set yourself up with some coffee and get to it. Make your study time and place as free from distraction as possible and surround yourself with what you need, be it silence or music. Studies have shown that music can aid in concentration, absorption, and retrieval of information. Not all music, though. Classical music is said to work best

8. Check your budget. You should at least review all the content material before your test, but allocate the most amount of time to the areas that need the most refreshing. It sounds obvious, but it's easy to forget. You can use the study rubric above to balance your study budget.

Testing Tips

1. Get smart, play dumb. Sometimes a question is just a question. No one is out to trick you, so don't assume that the test writer is looking for something other than what was asked. Stick to the question as written and don't overanalyze.

2. Do a double take. Read test questions and answer choices at least twice because it's easy to miss something, to transpose a word or some letters. If you have no idea what the correct answer is, skip it and come back later if there's time. If you're still clueless, it's okay to guess. Remember, you're scored on the number of questions you answer correctly and you're not penalized for wrong answers. The worst case scenario is that you miss a point from a good guess.

3. Turn it on its ear. The syntax of a question can often provide a clue, so make things interesting and turn the question into a statement to see if it changes the meaning or relates better (or worse) to the answer choices.

4. Get out your magnifying glass. Look for hidden clues in the questions because it's difficult to write a multiple-choice question without giving away part of the answer in the options presented. In most questions you can readily eliminate one or two potential answers, increasing your chances of answering correctly to 50/50, which will help out if you've skipped a question and gone back to it (see tip #2).

5. Call it intuition. Often your first instinct is correct. If you've been studying the content you've likely absorbed something and have subconsciously retained the knowledge. On questions you're not sure about trust your instincts because a first impression is usually correct.

6. **Graffiti.** Sometimes it's a good idea to mark your answers directly on the test booklet and go back to fill in the optical scan sheet later. You don't get extra points for perfectly blackened ovals. If you choose to manage your test this way, be sure not to mismark your answers when you transcribe to the scan sheet.

7. **Become a clock-watcher.** You have a set amount of time to answer the questions. Don't get bogged down laboring over a question you're not sure about when there are ten others you could answer more readily. If you choose to follow the advice of tip #6, be sure you leave time near the end to go back and fill in the scan sheet.

Do the Drill

No matter how prepared you feel it's sometimes a good idea to apply Murphy's Law. So the following tips might seem silly, mundane, or obvious, but we're including them anyway.

1. **Remember, you are what you eat, so bring a snack.** Choose from the list of energizing foods that appear earlier in the introduction.

2. **You're not too sexy for your test.** Wear comfortable clothes. You'll be distracted if your belt is too tight or if you're too cold or too hot.

3. **Lie to yourself.** Even if you think you're a prompt person, pretend you're not and leave plenty of time to get to the testing center. Map it out ahead of time and do a dry run if you have to. There's no need to add road rage to your list of anxieties.

4. **Bring sharp number 2 pencils.** It may seem impossible to forget this need from your school days, but you might. And make sure the erasers are intact, too.

5. **No ticket, no test.** Bring your admission ticket as well as **two** forms of identification, including one with a picture and signature. You will not be admitted to the test without these things.

6. **You can't take it with you.** Leave any study aids, dictionaries, notebooks, computers, and the like at home. Certain tests **do** allow a scientific or four-function calculator, so check ahead of time to see if your test does.

7. **Prepare for the desert.** Any time spent on a bathroom break **cannot** be made up later, so use your judgment on the amount you eat or drink.

8. Quiet, Please! Keeping your own time is a good idea, but not with a timepiece that has a loud ticker. If you use a watch, take it off and place it nearby but not so that it distracts you. And **silence your cell phone**.

To the best of our ability, we have compiled the content you need to know in this book and in the accompanying online resources. The rest is up to you. You can use the study and testing tips or you can follow your own methods. Either way, you can be confident that there aren't any missing pieces of information and there shouldn't be any surprises in the content on the test.

If you have questions about test fees, registration, electronic testing, or other content verification issues please visit *www.mtle.nesinc.com*.

Good luck!

Sharon Wynne
Founder, XAMonline

DOMAIN I
NUMBER SENSE

PERSONALIZED STUDY PLAN

✗ **KNOWN MATERIAL/ SKIP IT**

PAGE	COMPETENCY AND SKILL		
3	**1:**	**Understand numbers and number systems**	☐
	1.1:	Demonstrating knowledge of magnitude, mental mathematics, place value, and the reasonableness of results	☐
	1.2:	Demonstrating knowledge of the properties and relations of number systems	☐
	1.3:	Translating among equivalent representations of numbers, including representations of complex numbers	☐
9	**2:**	**Understand number theory and operations on numbers**	☐
	2.1:	Recognizing prime numbers, prime factorizations, greatest common factors, and least common multiples	☐
	2.2:	Demonstrating knowledge of basic number operations, including alternative computational algorithms	☐
	2.3:	Applying the properties of number operations	☐
17	**3:**	**Apply principles of problem solving**	☐
	3.1:	Analyzing methods of estimation and the reasonableness of estimates	☐
	3.2:	Selecting the best problem-solving approach to apply in a particular situation	☐
	3.3:	Solving problems using different strategies and representations	☐
	3.4:	Selecting expressions that model problem situations	☐

COMPETENCY 1
UNDERSTAND NUMBERS AND NUMBER SYSTEMS

> **SKILL 1.1** **Demonstrating knowledge of magnitude, mental mathematics, place value, and the reasonableness of results**

Place Value

In a number, every digit has a face value and a place value. The face values of the digits in the number 3467 are 3, 4, 6, and 7. The place value of a digit depends on its position in the number.

Whole number place value is determined by the relative positions of the digits to the left of the decimal point. Consider the number 792: reading from left to right, the first digit (7) represents the hundreds place. Thus, there are seven sets of 100 in the number 792. The second digit (9) represents the tens place, i. e., nine sets of ten. The last digit (2) represents the ones place.

Decimal place value is determined by the relative positions of the digits to the right of the decimal point. Consider the number 4.873: reading from left to right, the first digit (4) is in the ones place. The first digit after the decimal (8) is in the tenths place and indicates that the number contains eight tenths. The next digit (7) is in the hundredths place and tells us the number contains seven hundredths. The same pattern applies to the rest of the number, with each successive digit to the right of the decimal point decreasing progressively by powers of ten.

Example: The positions of the digits in the number 12345.6789 indicate the following powers of ten:

10^4	10^3	10^2	10^1	10^0		10^{-1}	10^{-2}	10^{-3}	10^{-4}
1	2	3	4	5	.	6	7	8	9

Mental Math and Estimates of Magnitude

Mental calculations may be used to estimate and check the reasonableness of answers. The highest place value in a number can be used to make a mental estimate of its "order of magnitude." For instance, if the highest place value of a number is 10^6, one can say that the number is in the millions. This will place the estimate within a factor of 10 of the exact answer. Although this is a very rough estimate, it can be useful in many situations. This is particularly important when calculators are used. Students need to be able to verify that the answer they are getting by punching in numbers is in the correct range and makes sense in the given context. Another simple check for reasonableness is to ask whether the answer expected is more or less than a given number. It is astonishing how many errors of computation can be avoided using this method. For instance, when converting 20 km to meters, asking whether the expected answer is greater than or less than 20 will help decide whether one should multiply or divide by 1,000 (a common point of confusion in conversion problems).

For further discussion of estimation methods and reasonableness of estimates, see Skill 3.1.

SKILL 1.2 **Demonstrating knowledge of the properties and relations of number systems** *(e.g., integer, rational, complex)*

Real Numbers

The following chart shows the relationships among the subsets of the real numbers.

Real Numbers

REAL NUMBERS: numbers that can be represented by an infinite decimal representation

REAL NUMBERS are denoted by $\mathbb{R}$ and are numbers that can be shown by an infinite decimal representation such as 3.286275347 . . . . Real numbers include rational numbers, such as 242 and $\frac{-23}{129}$, and irrational numbers, such as $\sqrt{2}$ and π, and can be represented as points along an infinite number line. Real numbers are also known as "the unique complete Archimedean *ordered field*." Real numbers are to be distinguished from imaginary numbers, which involve a factor of $\sqrt{-1}$.

Real numbers are classified as follows:

CLASSIFICATIONS OF REAL NUMBERS	
Natural Numbers Denoted by $\mathbb{N}$	The counting numbers. 1, 2, 3, . . .
Whole Numbers	The counting numbers along with zero. 0, 1, 2, 3, . . .
Integers, Denoted by $\mathbb{Z}$	The counting numbers, their negatives, and zero. . . . , -2, -1, 0, 1, 2, . . .
Rationals, Denoted by $\mathbb{Q}$	All of the fractions that can be formed using whole numbers. Zero cannot be the denominator. In decimal form, these numbers will be either terminating or repeating decimals. Simplify square roots to determine if the number can be written as a fraction.
Irrationals	Real numbers that cannot be written as a fraction. The decimal forms of these numbers neither terminate nor repeat. Examples include π, e and $\sqrt{2}$.

Complex Numbers

The set of complex numbers is denoted by $\mathbb{C}$. The set $\mathbb{C}$ is defined as $\{a + bi : a, b \in \mathbb{R}\}$ ($\in$ means "element of"). In other words, complex numbers are an extension of real numbers made by attaching an imaginary number i, which satisfies the equality $i^2 = -1$. COMPLEX NUMBERS are of the form $a + bi$, where a and b are real numbers and $i = \sqrt{-1}$. Thus, a is the real part of the number and b is the imaginary part of the number. When i appears in a fraction, the fraction is usually simplified so that i is not in the denominator. The set of complex numbers includes the set of real numbers, where any real number n can be written in its equivalent complex form as $n + 0i$. In other words, it can be said that $\mathbb{R} \subseteq \mathbb{C}$ (or $\mathbb{R}$ is a subset of $\mathbb{C}$).

> **COMPLEX NUMBERS:** numbers of the form $a + bi$, where a and b are real numbers and $i = \sqrt{-1}$

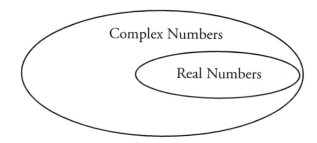

The number $3i$ has a real part 0 and imaginary part 3; the number 4 has a real part 4 and an imaginary part 0. As another way of writing complex numbers, we can express them as ordered pairs:

Complex Number	Ordered Pair
$3 + 2i$	$(3, 2)$
$\sqrt{3} + \sqrt{3}i$	$(\sqrt{3}, \sqrt{3})$
$7i$	$(0, 7)$
$\dfrac{6 + 2i}{7}$	$\left(\dfrac{6}{7}, \dfrac{2}{7}\right)$

The basic operations for complex numbers can be summarized as follows, where $z_1 = a_1 + b_1 i$ and $z_2 = a_2 + b_2 i$. Note that the operations are performed in the standard manner, where i is treated as a standard radical value. The result of each operation is written in the standard form for complex numbers. Also note that the **COMPLEX CONJUGATE** of a complex number $z = a + bi$ is denoted as $z^* = a - bi$.

> **COMPLEX CONJUGATE:**
> for a complex number
> $z = a + bi$, this is denoted
> as $z^* = a - bi$

$$z_1 + z_2 = (a_1 + a_2) + (b_1 + b_2)i$$
$$z_1 - z_2 = (a_1 - a_2) + (b_1 - b_2)i$$
$$z_1 z_2 = (a_1 a_2 - b_1 b_2) + (a_1 b_2 - a_2 b_1)i$$
$$\frac{z_1}{z_2} = \frac{z_1}{z_2}\frac{z_2^*}{z_2^*} = \frac{a_1 a_2 + b_1 b_2}{a_2^2 + b_2^2} + \frac{a_2 b_1 - a_1 b_2}{a_2^2 + b_2^2}i$$

Note that, because the division operation above is defined, the multiplicative inverse of any complex number $z \neq 0$ is also defined (where z_1 is 1 and z_2 is z) in the set of complex numbers.

In addition to these operations, the absolute value of a complex number, $z = a + bi$ (written $|z|$ or $|a + bi|$), is also defined. (The absolute value may also be termed the "magnitude" or the "modulus" of the number.)

$$|z| = \sqrt{zz^*} = \sqrt{a^2 + b^2}$$

> **SKILL 1.3** Translating among equivalent representations of numbers, including representations of complex numbers

If we compare numbers in various forms, we see that:

The integer $4 = \frac{8}{2}$ (fraction) $= 4.0$ (decimal) $= 400\%$ (percent)

From this, you should be able to determine that fractions, decimals, and percents can be used interchangeably within problems.

- To change a percent into a decimal, move the decimal point two places to the left and drop off the percent sign.

- To change a decimal into a percent, move the decimal two places to the right and add on a percent sign.

- To change a fraction into a decimal, divide the numerator by the denominator.

- To change a decimal number into an equivalent fraction, write the decimal part of the number as the fraction's numerator. As the fraction's denominator, use the place value of the last column of the decimal. Reduce the resulting fraction as far as possible.

Example: J.C. Nickels has Hunch jeans for sale at 25% off the usual price of $36.00. Shears and Roadster have the same jeans for sale at 30% off their regular price of $40. Find the cheaper price.

$\frac{1}{4} = .25$, so $.25(36) = \$9.00$ off; $\$36 - 9 = \$27$ sale price

$30\% = .30$, so $.30(40) = \$12$ off; $\$40 - 12 = \$28$ sale price

The price at J.C Nickels is $1 lower.

To convert a fraction to a decimal, as we did in the example above, simply divide the numerator (top) by the denominator (bottom). Use long division if necessary.

If a decimal has a fixed number of digits, the decimal is said to be a TERMINATING DECIMAL. To write such a decimal as a fraction, first determine what place value the digit farthest to the right has (for example: tenths, hundredths, thousandths, ten-thousandths, hundred-thousandths, etc.). Then drop the decimal point and place the string of digits over the number given by the place value.

> **TERMINATING DECIMAL:** a decimal that has a fixed number of digits

If a decimal continues forever by repeating a string of digits, the decimal is said to be a REPEATING DECIMAL. To write a repeating decimal as a fraction, follow these steps:

> **REPEATING DECIMAL:** a decimal that continues forever by repeating a string of digits

1. Let $x =$ the repeating decimal (Ex. $x = .716716716...$)

2. Multiply x by the multiple of 10 that will move the decimal just to the right of the repeating block of digits (Ex. $1000x = 716.716716...$)

3. Subtract the first equation from the second (Ex. $1000x - x = 716.716716... - .716716...$)

4. Simplify and solve this equation. The repeating block of digits will subtract out (Ex. $999x = 716$ so $x = \frac{716}{999}$)

5. The solution will be the fraction for the repeating decimal

COMMON EQUIVALENTS				
$\frac{1}{2}$	$=$	0.5	$=$	50%
$\frac{1}{3}$	$=$	$0.33\frac{1}{3}$	$=$	$33\frac{1}{3}\%$
$\frac{1}{4}$	$=$	0.25	$=$	25%
$\frac{1}{5}$	$=$	0.2	$=$	20%
$\frac{1}{6}$	$=$	$0.16\frac{2}{3}$	$=$	$16\frac{2}{3}\%$
$\frac{1}{8}$	$=$	$0.12\frac{1}{2}$	$=$	$12\frac{1}{2}\%$
$\frac{1}{10}$	$=$	0.1	$=$	10%
$\frac{2}{3}$	$=$	$0.66\frac{2}{3}$	$=$	$66\frac{2}{3}\%$
$\frac{5}{6}$	$=$	$0.83\frac{1}{3}$	$=$	$83\frac{1}{3}\%$
$\frac{3}{8}$	$=$	$0.37\frac{1}{2}$	$=$	$37\frac{1}{2}\%$
$\frac{5}{8}$	$=$	$0.62\frac{1}{2}$	$=$	$62\frac{1}{2}\%$
$\frac{7}{8}$	$=$	$0.87\frac{1}{2}$	$=$	$87\frac{1}{2}\%$
1	$=$	1.0	$=$	100%

See Skill 1.2 for representations of complex numbers as ordered pairs of real numbers.

COMPETENCY 2
UNDERSTAND NUMBER THEORY AND OPERATIONS ON NUMBERS

SKILL Recognizing prime numbers, prime factorizations, greatest
2.1 common factors, and least common multiples

Prime and Composite Numbers

PRIME NUMBERS are numbers that can be factored only into 1 and the number itself. When factoring into prime factors, all the factors must be numbers that cannot be factored again (without using 1). Initially, numbers can be factored into any two factors. Check each resulting factor to see if it can be factored again. Continue factoring until all of the remaining factors are prime, and these are the prime factors. Regardless of what way the original number was factored, the final list of prime factors will always be the same. Examples of prime numbers are 2, 3, 5, 7, 11, 13, 17, or 19. Note that 2 is the only even prime number.

Example: Factor 30 into prime factors.

Factor 30 into any two factors:

5×6	Now factor the 6.
$5 \times 2 \times 3$	These are all prime factors.

Factor 30 into any two factors:

3×10	Now factor the 10.
$3 \times 2 \times 5$	These are the same prime factors even though the original factors were different.

Example: Factor 240 into prime factors.

Factor 240 into any two factors:

24×10	Now factor both 24 and 10.
$4 \times 6 \times 2 \times 5$	Now factor both 4 and 6.
$2 \times 2 \times 2 \times 3 \times 2 \times 5$	These are prime factors.

This can also be written as $2^4 \times 3 \times 5$.

COMPOSITE NUMBERS are whole numbers that have more than two factors. For example, 9 is composite because in addition to the factors 1 and 9, it has factor

PRIME NUMBERS: numbers that can be factored only into 1 and the number itself

COMPOSITE NUMBERS: whole numbers that have more than two factors

3. Seventy is also composite because in addition to the factors of 1 and 70, it has factors 2, 5, 7, 10, 14, and 35.

Remember that the number 1 is neither prime nor composite.

Factors and Multiples

GCF

> **GREATEST COMMON FACTOR:** the largest number that is a factor of all the numbers given in a problem

> **Note:** There can be other common factors besides the GCF.

GCF stands for the **GREATEST COMMON FACTOR**, which is the largest number that is a factor of all the numbers given in a problem. The GCF can be no larger than the smallest number given in the problem. If no other number is a common factor, then the GCF will be the number 1. To find the GCF, list all of the possible factors of the smallest number given (include the number itself). Starting with the largest factor (which is the number itself), determine if it is also a factor of all the other given numbers. If so, that is the GCF. If that factor does not work, try the same method on the next smaller factor. Continue until a common factor is found. That is the GCF.

Example: Find the GCF of 12, 20, and 36.
The smallest number in the problem is 12. The factors of 12 are 1, 2, 3, 4, 6, and 12. The largest factor is 12, but it does not divide evenly into 20. Neither does 6, but 4 will divide into both 20 and 36 evenly.

Therefore, 4 is the GCF.

Example: Find the GCF of 14 and 15.
The factors of 14 are 1, 2, 7, and 14. The largest factor is 14, but it does not divide evenly into 15. Neither does 7 or 2. Therefore, the only factor common to both 14 and 15 is the number 1, which is the GCF.

LCM

> **LEAST COMMON MULTIPLE:** the smallest number into which all of the given numbers will divide

LCM is the abbreviation for **LEAST COMMON MULTIPLE**. The least common multiple of a group of numbers is the smallest number into which all of the given numbers will divide. The least common multiple will always be the largest of the given numbers or a multiple of the largest number.

Example: Find the LCM of 20, 30, and 40.
The largest number given is 40, but 30 will not divide evenly into 40. The next multiple of 40 is 80 (2 × 40), but 30 will not divide evenly into 80 either. The next multiple of 40 is 120. 120 is divisible by both 20 and 30, so 120 is the LCM (least common multiple).

Example: Find the LCM of 96, 16, and 24.

The largest number is 96. The number 96 is divisible by both 16 and 24, so 96 is the LCM.

SKILL 2.2 **Demonstrating knowledge of basic number operations, including alternative computational algorithms**

Operations on Whole Numbers

Mathematical operations include addition, subtraction, multiplication, and division. Addition can be indicated by these expressions: *sum, greater than, and, more than, increased by, added to.* Subtraction can be expressed by the phrases *difference, fewer than, minus, less than, and decreased by.* Multiplication is shown by *product, times, multiplied by,* and *twice.* Division is indicated by *quotient, divided by,* and *ratio.*

Addition and subtraction

There are two main procedures used in addition and subtraction: adding or subtracting single digits and "carrying" or "borrowing."

Example: Find the sum of 346 + 225 using place value.

PLACE VALUE		
100	**10**	**1**
3	4	6
2	2	5
5	6	11
5	7	1

Standard algorithm for addition check:

```
   3 ¹4 6
 + 2  2 5
   5  7 1
```

Example: Find the difference of 234 − 46 using place value.

PLACE VALUE		
100	**10**	**1**
1	13 4	4 6

PLACE VALUE		
100	**10**	**1**
1	12 4	14 6
1	**8**	**8**

Standard algorithm for subtraction check:

```
  2 3 4
−   4 6
  1 8 8
```

Multiplication and division

Multiplication is one of the four basic number operations. In simple terms, multiplication is the addition of a number to itself a certain number of times. For example, 4 multiplied by 3 is the equal to 4 + 4 + 4 or 3 + 3 + 3 + 3. Another way of conceptualizing multiplication is to think in terms of groups. For example, if we have 4 groups of 3 students, the total number of students is 4 multiplied by 3. We call the solution to a multiplication problem the PRODUCT.

PRODUCT: a solution to a multiplication problem

Example: A student buys 4 boxes of crayons. Each box contains 16 crayons. How many total crayons does the student have?

The number of crayons is 16 × 4.

```
    16
×    4
    64        Total number of crayons equals 64 crayons.
```

Division, the inverse of multiplication, is another of the four basic number operations. When we divide one number by another, we determine how many times we can multiply the divisor (number divided by) before we exceed the number we are dividing (dividend). For example, 8 divided by 2 equals 4 because we can multiply 2 four times to reach 8 (2 × 4 = 8 or 2 + 2 + 2 + 2 = 8). Using the grouping conceptualization we used with multiplication, we can divide 8 into 4 groups of 2 or 2 groups of 4. We call the answer to a division problem the QUOTIENT.

QUOTIENT: the answer to a division problem

If the divisor does not divide evenly into the dividend, we express the leftover amount either as a remainder or as a fraction with the divisor as the denominator. For example, 9 divided by 2 equals 4 with a remainder of 1 or $4\frac{1}{2}$.

Example: Each box of apples contains 24 apples. How many boxes must a grocer purchase to supply a group of 252 people with one apple each?

The grocer needs 252 apples. Because he must buy apples in groups of 24, we divide 252 by 24 to determine how many boxes he needs to buy.

$$
\begin{array}{r}
10 \\
24\overline{)252} \\
-24 \\
\hline
12 \\
-0 \\
\hline
12
\end{array}
$$

$\rightarrow$ The quotient is 10 with a remainder of 12.

Thus, the grocer needs 10 full boxes plus 12 more apples. Therefore, the minimum number of boxes the grocer must purchase is 11 boxes.

Adding and Subtracting Decimals

When adding and subtracting decimals, we align the numbers by place value as we do with whole numbers. After adding or subtracting each column, we bring the decimal down, placing it in the same location as in the numbers added or subtracted.

Example: Find the sum of 152.3 and 36.342.

$$
\begin{array}{r}
152.300 \\
+\ 36.342 \\
\hline
188.642
\end{array}
$$

Note that we placed two zeroes after the final place value in 152.3 to clarify the column addition.

Example: Find the difference of 152.3 and 36.342.

$$
\begin{array}{r}
2\ 9\ 10 \\
152.300 \\
-\ 36.342 \\
\hline
58
\end{array}
\qquad
\begin{array}{r}
(4)11(12) \\
152.300 \\
-\ 36.342 \\
\hline
115.958
\end{array}
$$

Note how we borrowed to subtract from the zeros in the hundredths and thousandths place of 152.300.

Operations with Signed Numbers

When adding and subtracting numbers with the same sign, the result will also have the same sign. When adding numbers that have different signs, subtract the smaller number from the larger number (ignoring the sign) and then use the sign of the larger number. When subtracting a negative number, change the sign of the number to a positive sign and then add it (i.e., replace the two negative signs with a positive sign).

Examples:

$(3) + (4) = 7$
$(-8) + (-4) = -12$
$(6) - (5) = 1$
$(3) - (6) = -3$
$(-4) - (2) = -6$
$(-6) - (-10) = 4$

When we multiply two numbers with the same sign, the result is positive. If the two numbers have different signs, the result is negative. The same rule follows for division.

Examples:

$(5)(5) = 25$
$(5)(-6) = -30$
$(-19)(-2) = 38$
$16 \div 4 = 4$
$(-34) \div 2 = -17$
$(-18) \div (-2) = 9$
$27 \div (-3) = -9$

Order of Operations

The Order of Operations is to be followed when evaluating expressions with multiple operations. Remember the mnemonic PEMDAS (Please Excuse My Dear Aunt Sally) to follow these steps in order:

1. Simplify inside grouping characters such as parentheses, brackets, radicals, fraction bars, etc.

2. Multiply out expressions with exponents.

3. Do multiplication or division from left to right.

   Note: Multiplication and division are equivalent even though multiplication is mentioned before division in the mnemonic PEMDAS.

4. Do addition or subtraction from left to right.

   Note: Addition and subtraction are equivalent even though addition is mentioned before subtraction in the mnemonic PEMDAS.

Example:

Evaluate: $\dfrac{12(9-7)+4\times5}{3^4+2^3}$

$$\dfrac{12(9-7)+4\times5}{3^4+2^3}$$

$$=\dfrac{12(2)+4\times5}{3^4+2^3} \qquad \text{Simplify within parentheses.}$$

$$=\dfrac{12(2)+4\times5}{81+8} \qquad \text{Multiply out exponent expressions.}$$

$$=\dfrac{24+20}{81+8} \qquad \text{Do multiplication and division.}$$

$$=\dfrac{44}{89} \qquad \text{Do addition and substraction.}$$

SKILL 2.3 Applying the properties *(e.g., associative, distributive)* of number operations

Real numbers exhibit the following addition and multiplication properties, where *a*, *b*, and *c* are real numbers.

Note: Multiplication is implied when there is no symbol between two variables. Thus,

   $a \times b$ can be written ab.

Multiplication can also be indicated by a raised dot $\cdot$ $(a \cdot b)$.

Closure

The Closure Property for Whole-Number Addition states that the sum of any two whole numbers is a whole number.

Example: Since 2 and 5 are both whole numbers, 7 is also a whole number.
The Closure Property for Whole-Number Multiplication states that the product of any two whole numbers is a whole number.

Example: Since 3 and 4 are both whole numbers, 12 is also a whole number.
The sum or product of two whole numbers is a whole number.

For any set of numbers to be closed under an operation, the result of the operation on two numbers in the set must also be included within that set.

Commutativity

$a + b = b + a$

Example: $5 + -8 = -8 + 5 = -3$

$ab = ba$

Example: $-2 \times 6 = 6 \times -2 = -12$

The order of the addends or factors does not affect the sum or product.

Associativity

$(a + b) + c = a + (b + c)$

Example: $(-2 + 7) + 5 = -2 + (7 + 5)$
  $5 + 5 = -2 + 12 = 10$

$(ab)c = a(bc)$

Example: $(3 \times -7) \times 5 = 3 \times (-7 \times 5)$
  $-21 \times 5 = 3 \times -35 = -105$

The grouping of the addends or factors does not affect the sum or product.

Distributivity

$a(b + c) = ab + ac$

Example: $6 \times (-4 + 9) = (6 \times -4) + (6 \times 9)$
  $6 \times 5 = -24 + 54 = 30$

To multiply a sum by a number, multiply each addend by the number, and then add the products.

Additive Identity (Property of Zero)

$a + 0 = a$

Example: $17 + 0 = 17$

The sum of any number and zero is that number.

Multiplicative Identity (Property of One)

$a \times 1 = a$

Example: $-34 \times 1 = -34$

The product of any number and 1 is that number.

COMPETENCY 3
APPLY PRINCIPLES OF PROBLEM SOLVING

> **SKILL 3.1** **Analyzing methods of estimation and the reasonableness of estimates**

There are several different ways of estimating. A common estimation strategy involves replacing numbers with simpler numbers that make for simpler computations. These methods include rounding, front-end digit estimation, and compensation.

Front-End Estimation

Although rounding is done to a specific place value (e.g., the nearest ten or hundred), front-end estimation involves rounding or truncating to the place value of the first digit in the number. The following example uses front-end estimation.

Example: Estimate the result of the calculation $\frac{58 \times 810}{1989}$.

To simplify the calculation, round each number to the highest place value. Thus, the calculation becomes

$$\frac{58 \times 810}{1989} \approx \frac{60 \times 800}{2000} = \frac{48000}{2000} = 24.$$

A more precise result is 23.62. In this case, the estimated value is close to the exact result.

Compensation

Another estimation technique, compensation, involves replacing different numbers in different ways so that one change can more or less compensate for the other.

Example: Calculate 32 + 53.

Although this example is simple, it is noteworthy that compensation can make the numbers easier to handle mentally.

$$32 + 53 = 30 + 55 = 85$$

Here both numbers are replaced in a way that minimizes the change; one number is increased and the other is decreased. This technique can also be applied

Estimation and approximation can be used to check the reasonableness of answers or to speed up a calculation where exact answers are not required. Estimation can be particularly important when calculators are used. Estimation also requires good mental math skills.

to algebraic expressions. In such cases, compensation or other similar forms of reorganization of numbers can drastically simplify certain operations.

Calculating a Range

A third estimation strategy calculates a range for the result.

Example: Estimate 458 + 873.

Again, this is a very simple example, but the principle can be applied to a range of different calculations. A simple range containing the answer can be found as follows.

$$458 + 873 > 400 + 800 = 1200$$
$$458 + 873 < 500 + 900 = 1400$$

Thus, the correct answer is in the following range:

$$1200 < 458 + 873 < 1400.$$

Various other estimation techniques can be applied as well, depending on the problem being solved.

Reasonableness

The reasonableness of an estimate can be judged in various ways, depending on the context of the problem. For instance, if the exact result of a calculation or the exact solution to a problem is known, then the estimated value can be considered reasonable if it varies from the exact value by a sufficiently small percentage.

The reasonableness of an estimate can be judged in various ways, depending on the context of the problem. For instance, if the exact result of a calculation or the exact solution to a problem is known, then the estimated value can be considered reasonable if it varies from the exact value by a sufficiently small percentage. Often, a variation of a few percent is acceptable; in some contexts, up to 10% variation is likewise acceptable. Large variations, however, may indicate that the estimate is not reasonable.

If the exact result or solution is not known, the reasonableness of an estimate can be judged to some extent by the expected effect of the procedure used in the estimate. For example, if a number is rounded in a calculation and the process of rounding has a small effect on the value of the number (only a percent or two, for instance), it may be likely that the estimate is reasonable.

The particular operations involved in a calculation are important to making a good judgment, however. Consider the calculation $10.4929 - 10.5103$. If these numbers are rounded to the nearest one, or even to the nearest tenth, then the estimated result is zero instead of -0.0174. In some contexts, this difference may be negligible, but in other contexts, it may be very important. Thus, estimating the reasonableness of an estimate requires consideration of not only the numbers and the operations involved in the problem but also the context of the problem.

SKILL 3.2 Selecting the best problem-solving approach to apply in a particular situation

The process of problem solving in mathematics is similar to that in other disciplines. One of the first steps is to identify what is known about the problem. Each problem for which a solution can be found should provide enough information to form a starting point from which a valid sequence of reasoning leads to the desired conclusion: a solution to the problem. Between identification of known information and identification of a solution to the problem is a gray area that, depending on the problem, could potentially involve a myriad of different approaches. Two potential approaches that do not involve a "direct" solution method are discussed below.

Each problem for which a solution can be found should provide enough information to form a starting point from which a valid sequence of reasoning leads to the desired conclusion: a solution to the problem.

Guess-and-Check

The guess-and-check strategy calls for making an initial guess of the solution, checking the answer, and using the outcome of this check to inform the next guess. With each successive guess, one should get closer to the correct answer. Constructing a table from the guesses can help organize the data.

Example: There are 100 coins in a jar: 10 are dimes, and the rest are pennies and nickels. If there are twice as many pennies as nickels, how many pennies and nickels are in the jar?

Based on the given information, there are 90 total nickels and pennies in the jar (100 coins − 10 dimes = 90 nickels and pennies). Also, there are twice as many pennies as nickels. Using this information, guess results that fulfill the criteria and then adjust the guess in accordance with the result. Continue this iterative process until the correct answer is found: 60 pennies and 30 nickels. The table below illustrates this process.

NUMBER OF PENNIES	NUMBER OF NICKELS	TOTAL NUMBER OF PENNIES AND NICKELS
40	20	60
80	40	120
70	35	105
60	30	90

Working Backward

Another indirect approach to problem solving is working backwards. If the result of a problem is known (for example, in problems that involve proving a particular result), it is sometimes helpful to begin from the conclusion and attempt to work backwards to a particular known starting point. A slight variation of this approach involves both working backwards and working forwards until a common point is reached somewhere in the middle. The following example from trigonometry illustrates this process.

Example: Prove that $\sin^2 \theta = \frac{1}{2} - \frac{1}{2} \cos^2 \theta$.

If the method for proving this result is not clear, one approach is to work backwards and forwards simultaneously. The following two-column approach organizes the process. Judging from the form of the result, it is apparent that the Pythagorean identity is a potential starting point.

$$
\begin{array}{l|l}
\sin^2 \theta + \cos^2 \theta = 1 & \sin^2 \theta = \frac{1}{2} - \frac{1}{2} \cos^2 \theta \\[2mm]
\sin^2 \theta = 1 - \cos^2 \theta & \sin^2 \theta = \frac{1}{2} - \frac{1}{2}(2\cos^2 \theta - 1) \\[2mm]
 & \sin^2 \theta = \frac{1}{2} - \cos^2 \theta + \frac{1}{2} \\[2mm]
 & \sin^2 \theta = 1 - \cos^2 \theta
\end{array}
$$

Thus, a proof is apparent based on the combination of the reasoning in these two columns.

Reasonableness

When solving any problem, it is helpful to evaluate the reasonableness of the solution. Often, errors in the solution lead to final results that do not make any sense in the context of the problem. Thus, checking the reasonableness of the solution can be a fast way to help determine if an error was made at some point in the process. Although such checks help to raise confidence in a solution, they do not necessarily guarantee that a solution is correct.

For instance, an error can result in a relatively small deviation in a numerical result; although the answer may still seem reasonable, it could still be incorrect. Thus, the reasonableness of a solution is a necessary but not sufficient check of its correctness.

Two characteristics of a numerical answer that can be quickly evaluated are sign and magnitude. If a problem calls for determining the length of a side of some

Selection of an appropriate problem-solving strategy depends largely on the type of problem being solved and the particular area of mathematics with which the problem deals. For instance, problems that involve proving a specific result often require different approaches than do problems that involve finding a numerical result.

Two characteristics of a numerical answer that can be quickly evaluated are sign and magnitude.

geometric figure, for example, then a negative number should indicate an error at some point in the solution. Similarly, a result that is magnitudes larger than would seem appropriate to the other aspects of the problem (such as the lengths of other measurements) could also indicate an error.

Additionally, the problem may provide information that limits the answer to a certain range. For example, if a problem asks for the average speed of an automobile over some distance and range of speeds, it is clear that the average speed should not exceed the maximum speed, nor should it be less than the minimum speed. Again, although this type of evaluation does not necessarily help to judge answers that fall within this range, it does help rule out results containing particularly egregious errors. On the other hand, if a speed distribution is shown that is weighted heavily toward faster speeds than slower speeds, it would then be reasonable to assume that the correct solution should be at the higher end of the speed range of the car. Similar types of qualitative evaluation or rough estimation for judging the reasonableness of a solution can be applied to other problems as well.

SKILL 3.3 Solving problems using different strategies and representations (e.g., ratio and proportions, percents, scientific notation)

Consumer Applications

The UNIT RATE when purchasing an item is its price divided by the number of units of measure (pounds, ounces, etc.) in the item. The item with the lower unit rate has the lower price.

> **UNIT RATE:** the price of an item divided by the number of units of measure

Example: Find the item with the best unit price:
  $1.79 for 10 ounces
  $1.89 for 12 ounces
  $5.49 for 32 ounces

$\frac{1.79}{10} = 0.179$ per ounce $\frac{1.89}{12} = 0.1575$ per ounce $\frac{5.49}{32} = 0.172$ per ounce

The best price is $1.89 for 12 ounces.

A second way to find the better buy is to make a proportion with the price under the number of ounces (or whatever). Cross-multiply the proportion, writing the products above the numerator that is used. The better price will have the smaller product.

Example: Find the better buy: $8.19 for forty pounds or $4.89 for twenty-two pounds. Find the unit costs.

$$\frac{40}{8.19} = \frac{1}{x}$$
$$40x = 8.19$$
$$x = 0.20475$$

$$\frac{22}{4.89} = \frac{1}{x}$$
$$22x = 4.89$$
$$x = 0.2222\overline{7}$$

Since $0.20475 < 0.2222\overline{7}$, $8.19 is the lower price and a better buy.

To find the amount of sales tax on an item, change the percent of sales tax into an equivalent decimal number. Then multiply the decimal number times the price of the object to find the sales tax. The total cost of an item will be the price of the item plus the sales tax.

Example: A guitar costs $120.00 plus 7% sales tax. How much are the sales tax and the total cost?

$7\% = .07$ as a decimal
$(.07)(120) = \$8.40$ sales tax
$\$120.00 + \$8.40 = \$128.40 \leftarrow$ total price

An alternative method to find the total cost is to multiply the price times the factor 1.07 (price + sales tax):

$\$120 \times 1.07 = \$8.40$

This gives you the total cost in fewer steps.

Example: A suit costs $450.00 plus $6\frac{1}{2}$% sales tax. How much are the sales tax and the total cost?

$6\frac{1}{2}\% = .065$ as a decimal
$(.065)(450) = \$29.25$ sales tax
$\$450.00 + \$29.25 = \$479.25 \leftarrow$ total price

An alternative method to find the total cost is to multiply the price times the factor 1.065 (price + sales tax):

$\$450 \times 1.065 = \$479.25$

This gives you the total cost in fewer steps.

Ratios

A RATIO is a comparison of two numbers. If a class has 11 boys and 14 girls, the ratio of boys to girls could be written one of three ways:

$11:14$ or 11 to 14 or $\frac{11}{14}$.

RATIO: a comparison of two numbers

The ratio of girls to boys is

14:11   or   14 to 11   or $\frac{14}{11}$.

Ratios can be reduced when possible. A ratio of 12 cats to 18 dogs would reduce to 2:3, 2 to 3, or $\frac{2}{3}$.

Note: Read ratio questions carefully. Given a group of 6 adults and 5 children, the ratio of children to the entire group would be 5:11.

Proportions

A PROPORTION is an equation in which one fraction is set equal to another. To solve the proportion, multiply each numerator by the other fraction's denominator. Set these two products equal to each other and solve the resulting equation. This is called CROSS-MULTIPLYING the proportion.

Example: $\frac{4}{15} = \frac{x}{60}$ *is a proportion.*
To solve this, cross-multiply:

$(4)(60) = (15)(x)$
$240 = 15x$
$16 = x$

Example: $\frac{x + 3}{3x + 4} = \frac{2}{5}$ *is a proportion.*
To solve, cross-multiply:

$5(x + 3) = 2(3x + 4)$
$5x + 15 = 6x + 8$
$7 = x$

Example: $\frac{x + 2}{8} = \frac{2}{x - 4}$ *is another proportion.*
To solve, cross-multiply:

$(x + 2)(x - 4) = 8(2)$
$x^2 - 2x - 8 = 16$
$x^2 - 2x - 24 = 0$
$(x - 6)(x + 4) = 0$
$x = 6 \text{ or } x = -4$

Both answers work.

SCIENTIFIC NOTATION is a convenient method for writing very large and very small numbers. It employs two factors: The first factor is a number greater than zero and less than 10, and the second factor is a power of 10. This notation is a shorthand way to express large numbers (like the weight in kilograms of 100 freight cars) or small numbers (like the weight in grams of an atom).

> **PROPORTION:** an equation in which one fraction is set equal to another

> **CROSS-MULTIPLYING:** multiplying each fraction's numerator by the other fraction's denominator

> **SCIENTIFIC NOTATION:** a convenient method for writing very large and very small numbers

For example, 356.73 can be written in various forms.

$$356.73 = 3567.3 \times 10^{-1} \quad (1)$$
$$= 356.73 \times 10^{0} \quad (2)$$
$$= 35.673 \times 10^{1} \quad (3)$$
$$= 3.5673 \times 10^{2} \quad (4)$$
$$= 0.35673 \times 10^{3} \quad (5)$$

Only (4) is written in proper scientific notation format.

Example: A particular material has a mass of 0.01 grams in one liter. What is the material's density in grams per milliliter?

A cursory examination of this problem shows that it will be necessary to divide a small number (0.01 grams) by a large number (1000 milliliters = 1 liter) to get the density. Thus, scientific notation is a helpful representation of the numbers in the problem. The density d is

$$d = \frac{1 \times 10^{-2}\, \text{g}}{1 \times 10^{3}\, \text{mL}} = 1 \times 10^{-5}\, \frac{\text{g}}{\text{mL}}.$$

The calculation and the result in this case are simplified considerably through the use of scientific notation. The solution is in a much neater form than 0.00001.

SKILL 3.4 Selecting expressions that model problem situations

See Skill 3.3 for problem situations modeled using numbers.

DOMAIN II
PATTERNS, RELATIONS, AND FUNCTIONS

PERSONALIZED STUDY PLAN

COMPETENCY 4
RECOGNIZE, DESCRIBE, AND GENERALIZE PATTERNS

SKILL Identifying and extending a variety of patterns
4.1

For a discussion of arithmetic and geometric sequences, see Skill 4.4.

Even though arithmetic and geometric sequences are the most common patterns, one can have series based on other rules as well. In some problems, the student will not be given the rule that governs a pattern but will have to inspect the pattern to find out what the rule is.

Example: Find the next term in the series 1, 1, 2, 3, 5, 8, …
Inspecting the terms in the series, one finds that this pattern is neither arithmetic nor geometric. Every term in the series is a sum of the previous two terms. Thus, the next term $= 5 + 8 = 13$.

This particular sequence is a well-known series named the Fibonacci sequence.

Just like arithmetic and geometric sequences, other patterns can be created using algebraic variables. Patterns may also be pictorial. In each case, one can predict subsequent terms or find a missing term by first discovering the rule that governs the pattern.

Example: Find the next term in the sequence ax^2y, ax^4y^2, ax^6y^3, …
Inspecting the pattern we see that this is a geometric sequence with common ratio x^2y.

Thus, the next term $= ax^6y^3 \times x^2y = ax^8y^4$.

Example: Find the next term in the pattern:

Inspecting the pattern, one observes that it has alternating squares and circles that include a number of hearts that increases by two for each subsequent term.

Hence, the next term in the pattern will be as follows:

The following table represents the number of problems Mr. Rodgers is assigning his math students for homework each day, starting with the first day of class.

Day	1	2	3	4	5	6	7	8	9	10	11
Number of Problems	1	1	2	3	5	8	13				

If Mr. Rodgers continues this pattern, how many problems will he assign on the eleventh day?

If we look for a pattern, it appears that the number of problems assigned each day is equal to the sum of the problems assigned for the previous two days. We test this as follows:

Day 2 = 1 + 0 = 1
Day 3 = 1 + 1 = 2
Day 4 = 2 + 1 = 3
Day 5 = 3 + 2 = 5
Day 6 = 5 + 3 = 8
Day 7 = 8 + 5 = 13

Therefore, Day 8 would have 21 problems; Day 9, 34 problems; Day 10, 55 problems; and Day 11, 89 problems.

Suppose we have an equation $y = 2x + 1$. We construct a table of values in order to graph the equation to see if we can find a pattern.

X	-2	-1	0	1	2
Y	-3	-1	1	3	5

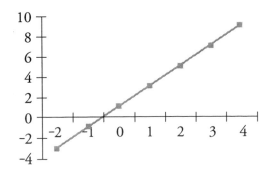

The pattern formed by the points is that they all lie on a line. We, therefore, can determine any solution of y by picking an x-coordinate and finding the corresponding point on the line. For example, if we want to know the solution of y when x is equal to 4, we find the corresponding point and see that y is equal to 9.

Example: Conjecture about pattern presented in tabular form.

Kepler discovered a relationship between the average distance of a planet from the sun and the time it takes the planet to orbit the sun. The following table shows the data for the six planets closest to the sun:

	MERCURY	VENUS	EARTH	MARS	JUPITER	SATURN
Average distance, x	0.387	0.723	1	1.523	5.203	9.541
x^3	0.058	.378	1	3.533	140.852	868.524
Time, y	0.241	0.615	1	1.881	11.861	29.457
y^2	0.058	0.378	1	3.538	140.683	867.715

Looking at the data in the table, we see that $x^3 = y^2$. We can conjecture the following function for Kepler's relationship: $y = \sqrt{x^3}$.

SKILL 4.2 **Recognizing an algebraic expression that describes the terms in a sequence of numbers and using it to predict other terms**

Representation of Patterns Using Symbolic Notation

Example: Find the recursive formula for the sequence 1, 3, 9, 27, 81...

We see that any term other than the first term is obtained by multiplying the preceding term by 3. Then, we may express the formula in symbolic notation as

$$a_n = 3a_{n-1}, a_1 = 1$$

where a represents a term, the subscript n denotes the place of the term in the sequence and the subscript $a - 1$ represents the preceding term.

Identification of Patterns of Change Created by Functions (e.g., Linear, Quadratic, Exponential)

A **LINEAR FUNCTION** is a function defined by the equation $f(x) = mx + b$.

> **LINEAR FUNCTION:** a function defined by the equation $f(x) = mx + b$

Example: A model for the distance traveled by a migrating monarch butterfly looks like f(t) = 80t, where t represents time in days. We interpret this to mean that the average speed of the butterfly is 80 miles per day and distance traveled may be computed by substituting the number of days traveled for t. In a linear function, there is a constant rate of change.

The standard form of a **QUADRATIC FUNCTION** is $f(x) = ax^2 + bx + c$.

QUADRATIC FUNCTION: the standard form of a quadratic function is $f(x) = ax^2 + bx + c$

Example: What patterns appear in a table for y = x² − 5x + 6?

X	0	1	2	3	4	5
Y	6	2	0	0	2	6

We see that the values for *y* are symmetrically arranged.

An **EXPONENTIAL FUNCTION** is a function defined by the equation $y = ab^x$, where *a* is the starting value, *b* is the growth factor, and *x* tells how many times to multiply by the growth factor.

EXPONENTIAL FUNCTION: a function defined by the equation $y = ab^x$, where *a* is the starting value, *b* is the growth factor, and *x* tells how many times to multiply by the growth factor

Example: y = 100(1.5)ˣ

X	0	1	2	3	4
Y	100	150	225	337.5	506.25

This is an exponential or multiplicative pattern of growth.

Iterative and Recursive Functional Relationships

A **RECURRENCE RELATION** is an equation that defines a sequence recursively; in other words, each term of the sequence is defined as a function of the preceding terms. For instance, the formula for the balance of an interest-bearing savings account after *t* years can be expressed recursively as follows.

$$A_t = A_{t-1}\left(1 + \frac{r}{n}\right)^n \text{ where } A_0 = P$$

RECURRENCE RELATION: an equation that defines a sequence recursively; in other words, each term of the sequence is defined as a function of the preceding terms

Here, *r* is the annual interest rate and *n* is the number of times the interest is compounded per year. Mortgage and annuity parameters can also be expressed in recursive form. Calculation of a past or future term by applying a recursive formula multiple times is called **ITERATION**.

ITERATION: the process of calculating a past or future term by applying a recursive formula multiple times

Sequences of numbers can be defined by iteratively applying a recursive pattern. For instance, the Fibonacci sequence is defined as follows.

$$F_i = F_{i-1} + F_{i-2} \quad \text{where } F_0 = 0 \text{ and } F_1 = 1$$

Applying this recursive formula gives the sequence $\{0, 1, 1, 2, 3, 5, 8, 13, 21, \ldots\}$.

It is sometimes difficult or impossible to write recursive relations in explicit or closed form. In such cases, especially when computer programming is involved, the recursive form can still be helpful. When the elements of a sequence of numbers or values depend on one or more previous values, then it is possible that a recursive formula could be used to summarize the sequence.

If a value or number from a later point in the sequence (that is, other than the beginning) is known and it is necessary to find previous terms, then the indices of the recursive relation can be adjusted to find previous values instead of later ones. Consider, for instance, the Fibonacci sequence.

$$F_i = F_{i-1} + F_{i-2}$$
$$F_{i+2} = F_{i+1} + F_i$$
$$F_i = F_{i+2} - F_{i+1}$$

Thus, if any two consecutive numbers in the Fibonacci sequence are known, then the previous numbers of the sequence can be found (in addition to the later numbers).

Example: Write a recursive formula for the following sequence: $\{2, 3, 5, 9, 17, 33, 65, \ldots\}$.

By inspection, it can be seen that each number in the sequence is equal to twice the previous number, less 1. If the numbers in the sequence are indexed such that, for the first number, $i = 1$, and so on, then the recursion relation is the following.

$$N_i = 2N_{i-1} - 1$$

Example: If a recursive relation is defined by $N_i = N_{i-1}^2$, and the fourth term is 65,536, what is the first term?

Adjust the indices of the recursion and then solve for N_i.

$$N_{i+1} = N_i^2$$
$$N_i = \sqrt{N_{i+1}}$$

Use this relationship to backtrack to the first term.

$$N_3 = \sqrt{N_4} = \sqrt{65{,}536} = 256$$
$$N_2 = \sqrt{N_3} = \sqrt{256} = 16$$
$$N_1 = \sqrt{N_2} = \sqrt{16} = 16$$

The first term of the sequence is 4.

Converting Between Recursive and Closed Forms

It helpful in some situations to convert between the recursive form and the closed form of a function. Given a closed-form representation of a function, the recursive form can be found by writing out the corresponding series or sequence and then determining a pattern or formula that accurately represents that series or sequence. Consider, for instance, the mortgage principal formula in recursive form:

$$A_i = A_{i-1}(1 + \tfrac{r}{n}) - M \qquad \text{where } A_0 = P.$$

Here, A_i is the remaining principal on the mortgage after the ith payment, r is the annual interest rate, which is compounded n times annually, and M is the monthly payment. The initial value P is the original loan amount for the mortgage. To obtain a closed-form expression for this recursive formula, first write out the terms of the corresponding sequence.

$$A_0 = P$$
$$A_1 = P(1 + \tfrac{r}{n}) - M$$
$$A_2 = A_1(1 + \tfrac{r}{n}) - M = P(1 + \tfrac{r}{n})^2 - M(1 + \tfrac{r}{n}) - M$$
$$A_3 = A_2(1 + \tfrac{r}{n}) - M = P(1 + \tfrac{r}{n})^3 - M(1 + \tfrac{r}{n})^2 - M(1 + \tfrac{r}{n}) - M$$

This pattern continues until $i = k$, where k is the total number of payments in the mortgage term. Note that the term A_k can be written as follows, where $z = 1 + \tfrac{r}{n}$:

$$A_k = Pz^k - M\{z^{k-1} + z^{k-2} + \ldots z^2 + z + 1\}.$$

But the expression in the curly brackets is simply a geometric series, which can be written in closed form as

$$z^{k-1} + z^{k-2} + \ldots z^2 + z + 1 = \frac{1 - z^k}{1 - z}.$$

Thus, the closed form expression for the principle remaining after k payments on the mortgage is

$$A_k = Pz^k - M\frac{1 - z^k}{1 - z} \qquad \text{where } z = 1 + \tfrac{r}{n}.$$

The process for converting from closed form to recursive form is similar (it is essentially the reverse of the process described above). Simply write out the terms, determine the pattern and then write the ith value in terms of the value of $(i - 1)$ or $(i + 1)$.

SKILL 4.3 **Applying properties of numbers and operations to algebraic expressions**

See Skill 2.3 for properties of number operations.

The following examples apply properties of numbers and operations to algebraic expressions:

Example: Prove that for every integer y, if y is an even number, then y² is even.

The definition of *even* implies that for each integer y there is at least one integer x such that $y = 2x$.

$$y = 2x$$
$$y^2 = 4x^2$$

Since $4x^2$ is always evenly divisible by two ($2x^2$ is an integer), y^2 is even for all values of y.

Example: If a, b, and c are positive real numbers, prove that c(a + b) = (b + a)c.

Use the properties of the set of real numbers.

$$c(a + b) = c(b + a) \qquad \text{Additive commutativity}$$
$$= cb + ca \qquad \text{Distributivity}$$
$$= bc + ac \qquad \text{Multiplicative commutativity}$$
$$= (b + a)c \qquad \text{Distributivity}$$

Example: Given real numbers a, b, c, and d, where ad = -bc, prove that (a + bi)(c + di) is real.

Expand the product of the complex numbers.

$$(a + bi)(c + di) = ac + bci + adi + bdi^2$$

Use the definition of i^2.

$$(a + bi)(c + di) = ac - bd + bci + adi$$

Apply the fact that $ad = -bc$.

$$(a + bi)(c + di) = ac - bd + bci - bci = ac - bd$$

Since a, b, c and d are all real, $ac - bd$ must also be real.

Example: Determine if the set of integers is closed under division.

For the set of integers to be closed under division, it must be the case that $\frac{a}{b}$ is an integer for any integers a and b. Consider $a = 2$ and $b = 3$.

$$\frac{a}{b} = \frac{2}{3}$$

This result is not an integer. Therefore, the set of integers is not closed under division.

Solving problems involving arithmetic and geometric sequences and series

Sequences and Series

> *A sequence is a set of numbers; a series is the sum of the terms of a sequence.*

Sequences and series can take on a vast range of different forms and patterns. Sequences and series are essentially two different representations of a set of numbers: a sequence is the set of numbers, and a series is the sum of the terms of the sequence. That is, a sequence such as

$$a_1, a_2, a_3, \ldots$$

has a corresponding series S such that

$$S = a_1 + a_2 + a_3 + \ldots.$$

Two of the most common forms of series are the arithmetic and geometric series, both of which are discussed below.

Arithmetic series

> **ARITHMETIC SERIES:** a finite series of numbers for which the difference between successive terms is constant

A finite series of numbers for which the difference between successive terms is constant is called an **ARITHMETIC SERIES**. An arithmetic series with n terms can be expressed as follows, where a and d are constants. (The constant a is the first term, and d is the difference between successive terms.)

$$a + (a + d) + (a + 2d) + (a + 3d) + \ldots (a + [n - 1]d)$$

To derive the general formula, examine the series sum for several small values of n.

n	Sum
1	a
2	$2a + d$
3	$3a + 3d$
4	$4a + 6d$
5	$5a + 10d$
6	$6a + 15d$
$\vdots$	$\vdots$
n	$na + d\sum\limits_{i=1}^{n-1} i$

The result in the table for n terms is found by examining the pattern of the previous series. All that is necessary, then, is to determine a closed expression for the summation.

By inspection, it can be seen that the product of n and $(n + 1)$, divided by 2, is the expression for the sum of $1 + 2 + 3 + 4 + 5 + \ldots + n$. Then:

$$\sum_{i=1}^{n} i = \tfrac{1}{2}n(n + 1).$$

A simple derivation of this relationship may be made as follows:

$S_n = 1 + 2 + 3 + \ldots\ldots\ldots + n.$

Writing the terms in reverse order:

$S_n = n + (n - 1) + (n - 2) + \ldots\ldots\ldots + 1.$

Adding the two expressions for S_n term by term, we get

$$2S_n = (1 + n) + (2 + n - 1) + (3 + n - 2) + \ldots\ldots (n + 1)$$
$$= (1 + n) + (1 + n) + (1 + n) + \ldots\ldots\ldots\ldots (n + 1)$$
$$= n(n + 1)$$

Therefore, $S_n = \dfrac{n(n + 1)}{2}$.

For the general case (with first term a and common difference d), therefore, the sum for a series with n terms is given by

$$na + d\sum_{i=1}^{n-1} i = na + d\frac{(n-1)(n)}{2} = \tfrac{1}{2}n(2a + d(n + 1)).$$

Often, closed formulas for series such as the arithmetic series must be found by inspection, as a more rigorous derivation is difficult. The result can be proven using mathematical induction, however.

Example: Calculate the sum of the series $1 + 5 + 9 + \ldots + 57$.

This is an arithmetic series, as the difference between successive terms, d, is constant ($d = 4$). Determine the total number of terms by subtracting the first term from the last term, dividing by d, and adding 1.

$$n = \frac{57 - 1}{4} + 1 = \frac{56}{4} + 1 = 14 + 1 = 15$$

That this approach works can be seen by testing simple examples. For instance, if the series is $1 + 5 + 9$, then

$$n = \frac{9 - 1}{4} + 1 = \frac{8}{4} + 1 = 2 + 1 = 3.$$

There are indeed three terms in this simple series. Next, apply the formula, noting that $a = 1$.

$$\tfrac{1}{2}n[2a + d(n - 1)] = \tfrac{1}{2}(15)[2(1) + (4)(15 - 1)]$$
$$= \tfrac{15}{2}[2 + 4(14)] = \tfrac{15}{2}(58) = 435$$

Thus, the answer is 435.

Geometric series

GEOMETRIC SERIES:
a series whose succes-
sive terms are related by a
common factor

A **GEOMETRIC SERIES** is a series whose successive terms are related by a common factor (rather than the common difference of the arithmetic series). Assuming that a is the first term of the series and r is the common factor, the general n-term geometric series can be written as follows.

$$a + ar + ar^2 + ar^3 + \ldots + ar^{n-1}$$

The geometric series can also be written using sum notation.

$$a + ar + ar^2 + \ldots + ar^{n-1} = \sum_{i=0}^{n=1} ar^i$$

To derive the closed-form expression for this finite series, let the sum for n terms be defined as S_n. Multiply S_n by r.

$$S_n = a + ar + ar^2 + \ldots + ar^{n-1}$$
$$rS_n = ar + ar^2 + ar^3 + \ldots + ar^n$$

Note that if a is added to this new series, the result is the sum S_{n+1}, which has $n + 1$ terms.

$$a + rS_n = a + ar + ar^2 + ar^3 + \ldots + ar^n = S_{n+1}$$

But S_{n+1} is simply $S_n + ar^n$, so the above expression can be written solely in terms of S_n.

$$a + rS_n = S_{n+1} = S_n + ar^n$$

Rearrange the result to obtain a simple formula for the geometric series.

$$a + rS_n = S_n + ar^n$$
$$a - ar^n = S_n - rS_n$$
$$a(1 - r^n) = S_n(1 - r)$$
$$S_n = a\frac{1 - r^n}{1 - r}$$

Infinite geometric series

The infinite geometric series is the limit of S_n as n approaches infinity.

$$a + ar + ar^2 + \ldots = \lim_{n \to \infty} a\frac{1 - r^n}{1 - r}$$

Three cases are of interest: $r \geq 1$, $r \leq -1$, and $-1 < r < 1$. To determine the limit in each case, first apply L'Hopital's rule.

$$\lim_{n \to \infty} a\frac{1 - r^n}{1 - r} = a\frac{\lim_{n \to \infty} \frac{d}{dr}(1 - r^n)/\frac{d}{dr}(1 - r)}{} = a\lim_{n \to \infty} \frac{-nr^{n-1}}{-1}$$

$$\lim_{n \to \infty} a\frac{1 - r^n}{1 - r} = a\lim_{n \to \infty} nr^{n-1}$$

Thus, it can be seen that if r is either 1 or -1, the limit goes to infinity due to the factor n. The same reasoning applies if r is greater than 1 or less than -1. For $-1 < r < 1$, rearrange the original form of the limit.

$$\lim_{n \to \infty} a\frac{1 - r^n}{1 - r} = a\frac{1 - r^\infty}{1 - r}$$

Since the magnitude of r is less than 1, r^∞ must be zero. This yields a closed form for the infinite geometric series, which converges only if $-1 < r < 1$.

$$a + ar + ar^2 + \ldots = \frac{a}{1 - r}$$

Example: Evaluate the following series: $1 + \frac{1}{2} + \frac{1}{4} + \frac{1}{8} + \ldots$.
Note that this series is an infinite geometric series with $a = 1$ and $r = \frac{1}{2}$ (or 0.5).

Use the formula to evaluate the series.

$$1 + \frac{1}{2} + \frac{1}{4} + \frac{1}{8} + \ldots = \frac{a}{1 - r} = \frac{1}{1 - 0.5} = \frac{1}{0.5} = 2$$

The answer is 2.

COMPETENCY 5
UNDERSTAND THE PROPERTIES AND REPRESENTATIONS OF FUNCTIONS

SKILL 5.1 Identifying the characteristics of functions

A RELATION is any set of ordered pairs. The DOMAIN OF A RELATION is the set containing all the first coordinates of the ordered pairs, and the RANGE OF A RELATION is the set containing all the second coordinates of the ordered pairs.

A FUNCTION is a relation in which each value in the domain corresponds to only one value in the range. It is notable, however, that a value in the range may correspond to any number of values in the domain. Thus, although a function is necessarily a relation, not all relations are functions, since a relation is not bound by this rule.

RELATION: any set of ordered pairs

DOMAIN OF A RELATION: the set containing all the first coordinates of the ordered pairs

RANGE OF A RELATION: the set containing all the second coordinates of the ordered pairs

FUNCTION: a relation in which each value in the domain corresponds to only one value in the range

Example: Which set illustrates a function?

A. { (0, 1)   (0, 2)   (0, 3)   (0, 4) }

B. { (3, 9)   (−3, 9)   (4, 16)   (−4, 16) }

C. { (1, 2)   (2, 3)   (3, 4)   (1, 4) }

D. { (2, 4)   (3, 6)   (4, 8)   (4, 16) }

For a relation to be a function, each number in the domain can be matched with only one number in the range. Choice A is not a function because 0 is mapped to 4 different numbers in the range. In choice C, 1 is mapped to two different numbers. In choice D, 4 is also mapped to two different numbers. So the answer is choice B.

A relation can also be described algebraically. An equation such as $y = 3x + 5$ describes a relation between the independent variable x and the dependent variable y. Thus, y is written as $f(x)$ or a "function of x."

On a graph, use the vertical line test to check whether a relation is a function. If any vertical line intersects the graph of a relation in more than one point, then the relation is not a function.

Example: Determine whether the following graph depicts a function.

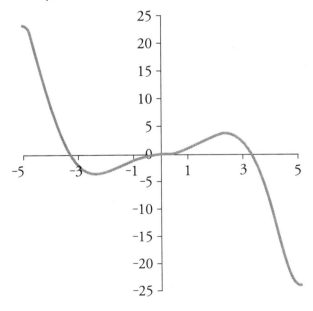

Use the vertical line test on the graph, as shown below. Every vertical line crosses the plotted curve only once. Therefore, the graph depicts a function.

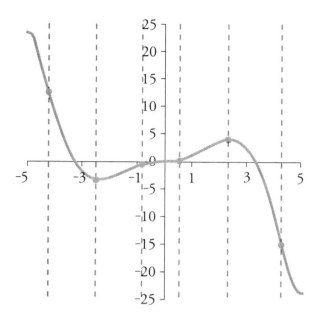

A mapping is essentially the same as a function. Mappings (or maps) can be depicted using diagrams with arrows drawn from each element of the domain to the corresponding element (or elements) of the range. If two arrows originate from any single element in the domain, then the mapping is not a function. Likewise, for a function, if each arrow is drawn to a unique value in the range (that is, there are no cases where more than one arrow is drawn to a given value in the range), then the relation is one-to-one.

Example: Are the mappings shown below true functions?

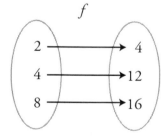
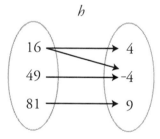

The mapping *f* is a function, but *h* is not.

The domain and the range of a function may be determined by inspecting the graph of the function or by analyzing the algebraic formula for the function.

> A mapping is essentially the same as a function. Mappings (or maps) can be depicted using diagrams with arrows drawn from each element of the domain to the corresponding element (or elements) of the range.

Example: Determine the domain and the range of the following graph:

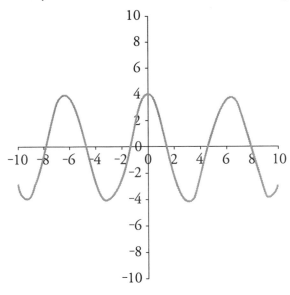

The domain of the function shown in the graph is infinite in both directions. Since the function is periodic and the y values vary between +4 and -4, the range of the function is -4 to +4.

Example: Determine the domain of the function depicted in the following graph.

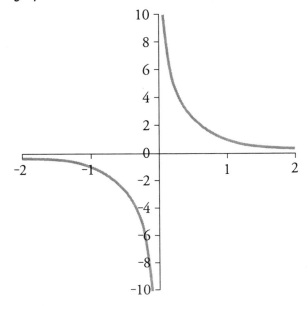

Note that this function is not continuous. It has two asymptotes: one for $y = 0$ and one for $x = 0$. It is apparent that the function is not defined for $x = 0$, but that it has finite values everywhere else. Thus, the domain of the function is all real numbers except 0.

The function plotted here is $y = \frac{1}{x}$; thus, by way of the function, it is clear that the range includes all real values except 0, for which the function goes to either positive or negative infinity in the limit (depending on the direction).

Example: Give the domain for the function over the set of real numbers:
$$y = \frac{3x + 2}{2x^2 - 3}$$

Find the values of x for which the denominator is 0. These values are excluded from the domain.

$$2x^2 - 3 = 0$$
$$2x^2 = 3$$
$$x^2 = \frac{3}{2}$$
$$x = \pm \sqrt{\frac{3}{2}} = \pm \sqrt{\frac{3}{2}} \times \sqrt{\frac{2}{2}} = \pm \frac{\sqrt{6}}{2}$$

Example: Determine the domain and the range of this mapping.

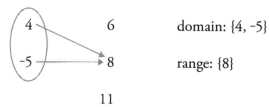

4 → 6	domain: {4, -5}
-5 → 8	range: {8}
11	

SKILL 5.2 Identifying equivalent forms of algebraic expressions

One can translate between equivalent forms of algebraic expressions in various ways. One common transformation of algebraic expressions involves expressing a polynomial function as a product of factor functions.

To factor a polynomial, follow these steps:

1. Factor out any GCF (greatest common factor).

2. For a binomial (2 terms), check to see if the problem is the difference of perfect squares. If both factors are perfect squares, then it factors as:

$$a^2 - b^2 = (a - b)(a + b)$$

** The sum of a perfect square does NOT factor.

PATTERNS, RELATIONS, AND FUNCTIONS

Example: Factor completely:

$16yx^4 - 64y^3$

$= 16y(x^4 - 4y^2)$ ← GCF

$= 16y((x^2)^2 - (2y)^2)$

$= 16y(x^2 + 2y)(x^2 - 2y)$ ← *apply formula*

3. If the problem is not the difference of perfect squares, check to see if the problem is either the sum or difference of perfect cubes.

$a^3 - b^3 = (a - b)(a^2 + ab + b^2)$ ← difference

$a^3 + b^3 = (a + b)(a^2 - ab + b^2)$ ← sum

Example: Factor completely:

$16x^3 + 54y^3$

$= 2(8x^3 + 27y^3)$ ← GCF

$= 2((2x)^3 + (3y)^3)$

$= 2(2x + 3y)(4x^2 - 6xy + 9y^2)$ ← *apply formula*

4. Trinomials can be factored into 2 binomials (unFOILing). Break up the middle term of the trinomial into two parts using the factors of the product of the coefficients of the first and last term. Factor by grouping the terms in twos.

Example: Factor completely:

$2x^2 + x - 6$

$= 2x^2 + 4x - 3x - 6$ ← *The middle term is broken up into two terms using 3 and 4, ... factors of $6 \times 2 = 12$*

$= 2x(x + 2) - 3(x + 2)$ ← *group terms by twos*

$= (x + 2)(2x - 3)$

Equivalent algebraic expressions may also be related through the properties of logarithms and exponentials.

Exponentials and logarithms are complementary. The general relationship for logarithmic and exponential functions is

$y = \log_b x$ if and only if $x = b^y$.

For the exponential base e and the natural logarithm (ln) the relationship is

$y = \ln x$ if and only if $e^y = x$.

When changing common logarithms to exponential form,

$y = \log_b x$ if and only if $x = b^y$.

Natural logarithms can be changed to exponential form by using
$\log_e x = \ln x$, or $\ln x = y$ can be written as $e^y = x$.

Logarithms

Example: Express in exponential form.

$\log_3 81 = 4$

$x = 81 \qquad b = 3 \qquad y = 4 \qquad$ Identify values.

$81 = 3^4 \qquad\qquad\qquad\qquad\qquad$ Rewrite in exponential form.

Example: Solve by writing in exponential form.

$\log_x 125 = 3$

$\qquad x^3 = 125 \qquad\qquad\qquad$ Write in exponential form.

$\qquad x^3 = 5^3 \qquad\qquad\qquad$ Write 125 in exponential form.

$\qquad x = 5 \qquad\qquad\qquad$ Bases must be equal if exponents are equal.

Use a scientific calculator to solve.

Example: Find ln 72.

$\ln 72 = 4.2767$

Use the "$\ln x$" key to find natural logs.

Example: Find ln x = 4.2767

Write in exponential form to find x.

$\qquad e^{4.2767} = x \qquad\qquad$ Use the "e^x" key (or "2nd" "$\ln x$").

$\qquad x = 72.002439 \qquad$ The small difference is due to rounding.

The following properties of logarithms are helpful in solving equations.

PROPERTIES OF LOGARITHMS	
Multiplication Property	$\log_b mn = \log_b m + \log_b n$
Quotient Property	$\log_b \frac{m}{n} = \log_b m - \log_b n$
Powers Property	$\log_b n^r = r \log_b n$
Equality Property	$\log_b n = \log_b m$ if and only if $n = m$
Change of Base Formula	$\log_b n = \frac{\log n}{\log b}$
	$\log_b b^x = x$ and $b^{\log_b x} = x$

Exponentials

The following properties can be used to simplify expressions involving exponents.

KEY EXPONENT RULES: FOR 'a' NONZERO AND 'm' AND 'n' REAL NUMBERS		
Product Rule	$a^m \times a^n = a^{(m+n)}$ $a^m \times b^m = (ab)^m$ $(a^m)^n = a^{mn}$	$(3^4)(3^5) = 3^9$ $(4^2)(5^2) = 20^2$ $(2^3)^2 = 2^6$
Quotient Rule	$\dfrac{a^m}{a^n} = a^{(m-n)}$	$2^5 \div 2^3 = 2^2$
Rule of Negative Exponents	$a^{-m} = \dfrac{1}{a^m}$	$2^{-2} = \dfrac{1}{2^2}$

Example: Simplify $\dfrac{3^5(3^{-2} + 3^{-3})}{9}$.

$$\frac{3^5(3^{-2} + 3^{-3})}{9} = \frac{3^5(3^{-2} + 3^{-3})}{3^2} = 3^3(3^{-2} + 3^{-3})$$

$$= 3^3 3^{-2} + 3^3 3^{-3} = 3^{3-2} + 3^{3-3} = 3 + 1 = 4$$

Example: Simplify $\dfrac{3^2 \times 5^{-2} \times 2^5}{6^2 \times 5}$.

$$\frac{3^2 \times 5^{-2} \times 2^5}{6^2 \times 5} = \frac{3^2 \times 5^{-2} \times 2^5}{3^2 \times 2^2 \times 5} = 5^{-2-1} \times 2^{5-2} = \frac{2^3}{5^3} = \frac{8}{125}$$

Unless the negative sign is inside the parentheses and the exponent is outside the parentheses, the sign is not affected by the exponent.

Example:

$$(-2)^4 = (-2) \times (-2) \times (-2) \times (-2) = 16$$

In this case, -2 is multiplied by itself 4 times.

$$-2^4 = -(2 \times 2 \times 2 \times 2) = -16$$

In this case, 2 is multiplied by itself 4 times and the answer is negated.

A radical may also be expressed using a rational exponent.

$$\sqrt[n]{a} = a^{\frac{1}{n}}$$

Example:

$$\sqrt{5} = 5^{\frac{1}{2}}; \quad \sqrt[5]{7} = 7^{\frac{1}{5}}$$

All the exponent laws discussed above also apply to rational exponents.

Example:

$$(\sqrt[5]{6})^3 = (6^{\frac{1}{5}})^3 = 6^{(\frac{1}{5}) \times 3} = 6^{\frac{3}{5}}$$

Example: Simplify $(-32)^{\frac{3}{5}} + 16^{\frac{3}{4}}$.

$$(-32)^{\frac{3}{5}} + 16^{\frac{3}{4}} = (\sqrt[5]{-32})^3 + (\sqrt[4]{16})^3 = (-2)^3 + 2^3 = -8 + 8 = 0$$

SKILL 5.3 Translating among different representations *(e.g., tables, equations, graphs)* of functions

A relationship between two quantities can be represented in a variety of ways, including as a symbolic expression (for instance, $f(x) = 3x^2 + \sin x$), a graph, a table of values, and a common-language expression (for example, "The speed of the car increases linearly from zero to 100 miles per hour in twelve seconds"). In the following example, the rule $y = 9x$ describes the relationship between the total amount earned, y, and the total number of $9 sunglasses sold, x. In a relationship of this type, one of the quantities (e.g., total amount earned) is dependent on the other (e.g., number of glasses sold). They are known as the dependent and independent variables, respectively.

A table using these data would appear as:

Number of Sunglasses Sold	1	5	10	15
Total Dollars Earned	9	45	90	135

Each (x, y) relationship between a pair of values is called the COORDINATE PAIR that can be plotted on a graph. The coordinate pairs (1, 9), (5, 45), (10, 90), and (15, 135) are plotted on the graph below.

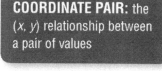

COORDINATE PAIR: the (x, y) relationship between a pair of values

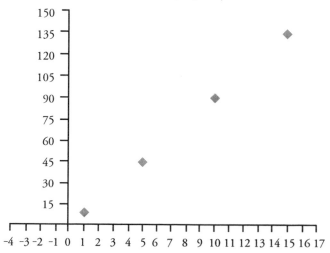

This graph shows a linear relationship. A linear relationship is one in which two quantities are proportional to each other. Doubling x also doubles y. On a graph, a straight line depicts a linear relationship.

The function or relationship between two quantities may be analyzed to determine how one quantity depends on the other.

For example, the function above shows a relationship between y and x:

$y = 2x + 1$.

The relationship between two or more variables can be analyzed using a table, graph, written description, or symbolic rule. The function $y = 2x + 1$ is written as a symbolic rule. The same relationship is also shown in the table below:

x	0	2	3	6	9
y	1	5	7	13	19

This relationship could be written in words by saying that the value of y is equal to two times the value of x, plus one. This relationship could be shown on a graph by plotting given points such as the ones shown in the table above.

The ability to convert among various representations of a function depends on how much information is provided. For instance, although a graph of a function can provide some clues as to its symbolic representation, it is often difficult or impossible to obtain an exact symbolic form based only on a graph. The same difficulty applies to tables.

Converting from a symbolic form to a graph or table, however, is relatively simple, especially if a computer is available. The symbolic expression need simply be evaluated for a representative set of points that can be used to produce a sufficiently detailed graph or table.

It is important to note that the particular symbols used in function notation are not important, as long as they are used consistently. Thus, the following are all the same function with different symbols used to represent the erstwhile x and y notation.

$f(\alpha) = \alpha^2$

$\beta(r) = r^2$

$\pi(W) = W^2$

The fundamental principle for this function notation is to represent that for each x (or other variable) value, the function (be it f, β, or any other symbol) has only one value.

SKILL 5.4 Demonstrating knowledge of the use of technology (e.g., spreadsheets) to represent and solve problems

Computers have made it possible to greatly expand the scope and extent of mathematical modeling. A computer model, particularly a dynamic one, is often known as a simulation. Simulations in various disciplines are now so accurate that, in many cases, for example in building cars or airplanes, they can be used to replace expensive prototype building or experimentation.

Spreadsheets are particularly useful tools for teaching modeling in the clasroom. Spreadsheet software is easy to learn and relatively simple to handle, and can be surprisingly effective in modeling simple systems. Most spreadsheet programs can also display graphs and statistics related to the model, making them fairly complete modeling tools. Spreadsheets are particularly useful tools for teaching modeling in the classroom.

Graphing calculators are the most common form of technology used in the classroom to solve ordinary math problems. The general procedure for solving a quadratic equation using a graphing calculator is outlined below. Specific commands are not given since they will be different for different calculators.

Very large, detailed, and extremely accurate models of systems can be created using the computing power available to us now. Dynamic behavior of a system over time can also be displayed visually or graphically using different kinds of software.

1. First express the equation as $ax^2 + bx + c = 0$ if it is not already given in that form.

2. Enter the function in the calculator, e.g., $y = x^2 + x + 1$.

3. Press the "Graph" button to display the graph. You can see the points where the graph intersects the x-axis. These are the roots of the equation since $y = 0$ at these values of x.

4. The graph shows you the approximate position of a root. To find the exact value you need to use the "root" function. In many calculators it is CALC-ROOT or CALC-ZERO.

5. When you select the "root" function, you are typically asked to enter upper and lower bounds for the root. You can move a marker on the graph to a point just right of the intersection of the graph and the x-axis and another marker just left of the intersection.

6. The calculator uses the information you have provided to return a root value between the bounds.

7. Repeat the process of setting bounds to identify other roots.

Notes:

A. The calculator may not give you an exact value since it uses numerical methods to approximate an answer. You will soon start to recognize that a number such as 0.9999987 is equal to 1.

B. In cases where a quadratic function has complex roots, the graph will not intersect the x-axis. These roots cannot be found using a graphing calculator.

SKILL 5.5 **Recognizing an algebraic expression that represents mathematical and real-world problems**

For examples of algebraic representations of mathematical and real-world problems, see Skills 6.1, 6.3, and 7.3.

SKILL 5.6 **Analyzing problems involving direct and indirect variation**

Direct and Inverse Variation

If two parameters vary directly, then as one gets larger, the other also gets larger. If one gets smaller, then the other gets smaller as well. If x and y vary directly, there should be a constant, c, such that $y = cx$. The parameters are not necessarily limited to linear values such as x and y, but can include such expressions as x^2, $\ln x$ and $\sin x$. For instance, the statement "y varies directly with the natural logarithm of x" leads to the equation $y = c\ln x$, where c is an unspecified multiplicative constant that determines the magnitude of variation.

If two parameters vary inversely, then as one gets larger, the other gets smaller instead. If x and y vary inversely, there should be a constant, c, such that $xy = c$ or $y = \frac{c}{x}$. As with direct variation, inverse variation can involve any number of expressions involving x or y.

Example: If $30 were paid for 5 hours work, how much would be paid for 19 hours work?
This is direct variation and $30 = 5c$, so the constant is 6 ($6/hour). So $y = 6(19)$ or $y = 114.

This could also be done as a proportion:

$$\frac{\$30}{5} = \frac{y}{19}$$
$$5y = 570$$
$$y = 114$$

Example: On a 546-mile trip from Miami to Charlotte, one car drove 65 mph while another car drove 70 mph. How does this affect the driving time for the trip?

This is an inverse variation, since increasing your speed should decrease your driving time. Use the equation $t = \frac{d}{r}$ where t = driving time, r = speed and d = distance traveled.

When $r = 65$ mph and $d = 546$ miles, $t = 8.4$ hours (slower speed = more time). When $r = 70$ mph and $d = 546$ miles, $t = 7.8$ hours (faster speed = less time).

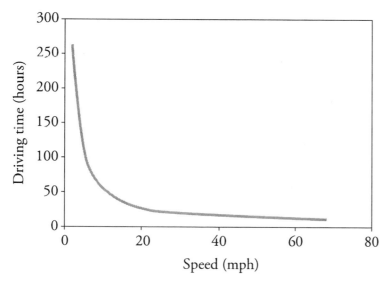

A quantity may also vary with different exponents of another quantity as shown in the examples below.

Example: A varies inversely as the square of R. When A = 2, R = 4. Find A if R = 10.

Since A varies inversely as the square of R,

$A = \frac{k}{R^2}$ (equation 1), k is a constant.

Use equation 1 to find k when $A = 2$ and $R = 4$.

$$2 = \frac{k}{4^2} \rightarrow 2 = \frac{k}{16} \rightarrow k = 32$$

Substituting $k = 32$ into equation 1 with $R = 10$, we get

$$A = \frac{32}{10^2} \rightarrow A = \frac{32}{100} \rightarrow A = 0.32.$$

COMPETENCY 6
ANALYZE LINEAR FUNCTIONS AND INEQUALITIES AND THEIR APPLICATIONS

SKILL Analyzing linear equations and inequalities based on their
6.1 characteristics *(e.g., points, slope, intercepts)*

LINEAR FUNCTION: a function defined by the equation $f(x) = mx + b$ where m is the slope of the line representing the function and b is the y-intercept, or the y-coordinate where the line crosses the y-axis

A **LINEAR FUNCTION** is a function defined by the equation $f(x) = mx + b$ where m is the slope of the line representing the function and b is the y-intercept, or the y-coordinate where the line crosses the y-axis. In a linear function, the rate of change is constant.

Many real-world situations involve linear relationships. One example is the relationship between the elapsed time and the distance traveled when a car is moving at a constant speed. The relationship between the price and the quantity of a bulk item bought at a store is also linear, assuming that the unit price remains constant. These relationships can be expressed using the equation of a straight line and the slope is often used to describe a constant or average rate of change expressed in miles per hour or dollars per year, for instance. Where the line intercepts an axis indicates a starting point or a point at which values change from positive to negative or negative to positive.

Many real-world situations involve linear relationships. One example is the relationship between the elapsed time and the distance traveled when a car is moving at a constant speed. The relationship between the price and the quantity of a bulk item bought at a store is also linear, assuming that the unit price remains constant.

Example: A man drives a car at a speed of 30 mph along a straight road. Express the distance d *traveled as a function of the time* t *assuming the man's initial position is* d_0.

The equation relating d and t in this case is

$d = 30t + d_0$.

Notice that this equation is in the familiar slope-intercept form $y = mx + b$. In this case, time t (in hours) is the independent variable, the distance d (in miles) is the dependent variable. The slope is the rate of change of distance in relation to time, i.e., the speed (in mph). The y-intercept, or intercept on the distance axis d_0, represents the initial position of the car at the start time $t = 0$.

The above equation is plotted below with $d_0 = 15$ miles (the point on the graph where the line crosses the y-axis).

$d = 30t + d_0$

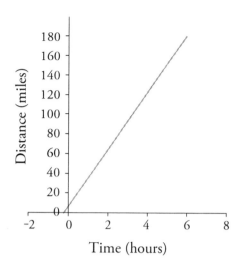

The x-intercept, or intercept on the time axis, represents the time at which the car would have been at $d = 0$ assuming it was traveling with the same speed before $t = 0$. This value can be found by setting d equal to 0 in the equation.

$$0 = 30t + 15$$
$$30t = -15$$
$$t = \frac{-15}{30} = -\frac{1}{2} \, \text{hr}$$

This simply means that if the car was at $d = 15$ miles when we started measuring the time ($t = 0$), it was at $d = 0$ miles half an hour before that.

A model for the distance traveled by a migrating monarch butterfly is $f(t) = 80t$, where t represents time in days. We interpret this to mean that the average speed of the butterfly is 80 miles per day and distance traveled may be computed by substituting the number of days traveled for t.

Example: The town of Verdant Slopes has been experiencing a boom in population growth. By the year 2000, the population had grown to 45,000, and by 2005, the population had reached 60,000.

Using the formula for slope as a model, find the average rate of change in population growth, expressing your answer in people per year. Then using the average rate of change determined, predict the population of Verdant Slopes in the year 2010.

Let t represent the time and p represent population growth. The two observances are represented by (t_1, p_1) and (t_2, p_2).

1st observance $= (t_1, p_1) = (2000, 45000)$
2nd observance $= (t_2, p_2) = (2005, 60000)$

Use the formula for slope to find the average rate of change.

$$\text{Rate of change} = \frac{P_2 - P_1}{t_2 - t_1}$$
$$= \frac{60000 - 45000}{2005 - 2000}$$
$$= \frac{15000}{5} = 3000 \text{ people/year}$$

The average rate of change in population growth for Verdant Slopes between the years 2000 and 2005 was 3,000 people per year. The population of Verdant Slopes can be predicted using the following:

3,000 people per year × 5 years = 15,000 people,
60,000 people + 15,000 people = 75,000 people.

At a continuing average rate of growth of 3000 people per year, the population of Verdant Slopes could be expected to reach 75,000 by the year 2010.

For a discussion of linear inequalities, see Skill 6.2.

SKILL 6.2 **Translating between different representations of linear functions and inequalities**

For different representations of linear functions see Skills 5.3 and 6.1.

The connection between algebraic and graphical representations of linear inequalities is discussed below.

Graphing Linear Inequalities

INEQUALITY: a mathematical expression containing the symbol $>$, $<$, $\geq$, or $\leq$

To graph an INEQUALITY, solve the inequality for y. This gets the inequality in SLOPE INTERCEPT FORM—for example: $y < mx + b$. The point $(0, b)$ is the y-intercept and m is the line's slope.

- If the inequality solves to $x >$, $\geq$, $<$, or $\leq$ any number, then the graph includes a *vertical line.*

- If the inequality solves to $y >$, $\geq$, $<$, or $\leq$ any number, then the graph includes a *horizontal line.*

SLOPE INTERCEPT FORM: $y = mx + b$, where m is the slope of the line and $(0, b)$ is the y-intercept

When graphing a linear inequality, the line will be dotted if the inequality sign is $<$ or $>$. If the inequality sign is either $\geq$ or $\leq$, the line on the graph will be a solid line. Shade above the line when the inequality sign is $\geq$ or $>$. Shade below the line when the inequality sign is $\leq$ or $<$. For inequalities of the forms $x >$ number, $x \leq$ number, $x <$ number, or $x \geq$ number, draw a vertical line (solid or dotted). Shade to the right for $>$ or $\geq$. Shade to the left for $<$ or $\leq$.

Remember: Dividing or multiplying by a negative number will reverse the direction of the inequality sign.

Use these rules to graph and shade each inequality. The solution to a system of linear inequalities consists of the part of the graph where the shaded areas for all the inequalities in the system overlap. For instance, if the graph of one inequality was shaded with red, and the graph of another inequality was shaded with blue, then the overlapping area would be shaded with purple. The points in the purple area would be the solution set of this system.

Example: Solve by graphing:

$$x + y \leq 6$$
$$x - 2y \leq 6$$

Solving the inequalities for y, we find that they become:

$$y \leq -x + 6 \text{ (}y\text{-intercept of 6 and slope} = -1)$$
$$y \geq \frac{1}{2x - 3} \text{ (}y\text{-intercept of -3 and slope} = \tfrac{1}{2})$$

A graph with shading is shown below:

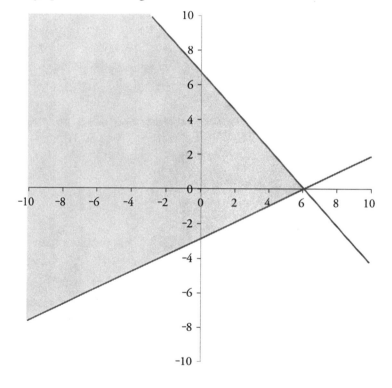

$$x + y \leq 6$$
$$x - 2y \leq 6$$

Linear Models

For some examples of situations modeled using linear equations, see the beginning of this competency.

Many word problems may be modeled and solved using systems of linear equations and inequalities. Some examples are given below.

> *Many word problems may be modeled and solved using systems of linear equations and inequalities.*

Example: Farmer Greenjeans bought 4 cows and 6 sheep for $1,700. Mr. Ziffel bought 3 cows and 12 sheep for $2,400. If all the cows were the same price and all the sheep were another fixed price, find the price charged for a cow and the price charged for a sheep.

Let x = price of a cow

Let y = price of a sheep

Then Farmer Greenjeans's equation would be: $\quad 4x + 6y = 1700$

Mr. Ziffel's equation would be: $\quad 3x + 12y = 2400$

To solve by addition-subtraction:

Multiply the first equation by -2: $\quad -2(4x + 6y = 1700)$

Keep the other equation the same: $\quad (3x + 12y = 2400)$

Now the equations can be added to each other to eliminate one variable, and you can solve for the other variable.

$-8x - 12y = -3400$

$\underline{3x + 12y = 2400} \qquad$ Add these equations.

$-5x \qquad\quad = -1000$

$x = 200 \leftarrow$ the price of a cow was $200.

Solving for y, $y = 150 \leftarrow$ the price of a sheep was $150. (This problem can also be solved by substitution or determinants.)

Example: Mrs. Allison bought 1 pound of potato chips, a 2-pound beef roast, and 3 pounds of apples for a total of $8.19. Mr. Bromberg bought a 3-pound beef roast and 2 pounds of apples for $9.05. Kathleen Kaufman bought 2 pounds of potato chips, a 3-pound beef roast, and 5 pounds of apples for $13.25. Find the per pound price of each item.

To solve by substitution:

Let x = price of a pound of potato chips.

Let y = price of a pound of roast beef.

Let z = price of a pound of apples.

Mrs. Allison's equation is	$1x + 2y + 3z = 8.19$.
Mr. Bromberg's equation is	$3y + 2z = 9.05$.
K. Kaufman's equation is	$2x + 3y + 5z = 13.25$.

Solve the first equation for x. (This equation was chosen because x is the easiest variable to isolate in this set of equations.) This equation becomes

$x = 8.19 - 2y - 3z$.

Substitute this expression into the other equations in place of x.

Equation 2: $3y + 2z = 9.05$
Equation 3: $2(8.19 - 2y - 3z) + 3y + 5z = 13.25$

Simplify the equation by combining like terms.

Equation 2: $3y + 2z = 9.05$
Equation 3: $-1y - 1z = -3.13$

Solve equation 3 for either y or z.

$y = 3.13 - z$ (*)

Substitute this into equation 2 for y.

Equation 2: $3(3.13 - z) + 2z = 9.05$
Equation 3: $-1y - 1z = -3.13$

Combine like terms in equation 2.

$9.39 - 3z + 2z = 9.05$
$z = \$0.34$ per pound (price of apples)

Substitute .34 for z in the above equation marked with an asterisk (*) and solve for y.

$y = 3.13 - z$
$y = 3.13 - .34$
$y = \$2.79 =$ per pound price of roast beef

Substitute .34 for z and 2.79 for y in one of the original equations and solve for x.

$1x + 2y + 3z = 8.19$
$1x + 2(2.79) + 3(.34) = 8.19$
$x + 5.58 + 1.02 = 8.19$
$x + 6.60 = 8.19$
$x = \$1.59 =$ per pound of potato chips
$(x, y, z) = (\$1.59, \$2.79, \$0.37)$

Example: Aardvark Taxi charges $4.00 initially, plus $1.00 for every mile traveled. Baboon Taxi charges $6.00 initially, plus $.75 for every mile traveled. Determine when it is cheaper to ride with Aardvark Taxi and when it is cheaper to ride with Baboon Taxi.

Aardvark Taxi's equation:	$y = 1x + 4$
Baboon Taxi's equation:	$y = .75x + 6$
Using substitution:	$.75y + 6 = 1x + 4$
Multiplying by 4:	$3y + 24 = 4x + 16$
Solving for x:	$8 = x$

This tells you that at eight miles, the total charge for the two companies is the same. If you compare the charge for one mile, Aardvark charges $5.00 and Baboon charges $6.75. Therefore, Aardvark is cheaper for distances up to eight miles, but Baboon Taxi is cheaper for distances greater than eight miles.

This problem can also be solved by graphing the two equations.

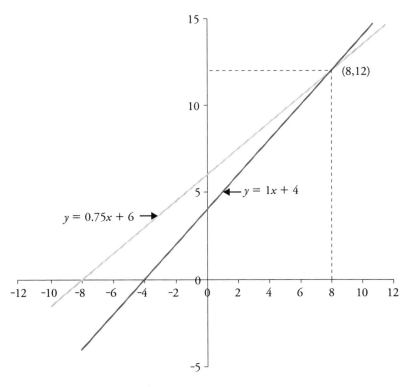

The lines intersect at (8,12); therefore, at eight miles, both companies charge $12.00. At values of less than eight miles, Aardvark Taxi charges less (the graph is below Baboon). At values greater than eight miles, Aardvark charges more (the graph is above Baboon).

LINEAR PROGRAMMING is the optimization of a linear quantity that is subject to constraints expressed as linear equations or inequalities. It is often used in various industries, ecological sciences, and governmental organizations to determine or

LINEAR PROGRAMMING: the optimization of a linear quantity that is subject to constraints expressed as linear equations or inequalities

project production costs, the amount of pollutants dispersed into the air, etc. The key to most linear programming problems is to organize the information in the word problem into a chart or graph of some type.

Example: The YMCA wants to sell raffle tickets to raise at least $32,000. If they must pay $7,250 in expenses and prizes out of the money collected from the tickets, how many $25 tickets must they sell?

Since they want to raise *at least* $32,000, that means they would be happy to get 32,000 *or more*. This requires an inequality.

    Let x = number of tickets sold.

    Then $25x$ = total amount of money collected for x tickets.

The total amount of money minus expenses is greater than $32,000.

    $25x - 7{,}250 \geq 32{,}000$

    $25x \geq 39{,}250$

    $x \geq 1{,}570$

If they sell 1,570 tickets or more, they will raise at least $32,000.

Example: A printing manufacturer makes two types of printers, a Printmaster and a Speedmaster. The Printmaster requires 10 cubic feet of space and weighs 5,000 pounds; the Speedmaster takes up 5 cubic feet of space and weighs 600 pounds. The total available space for storage before shipping is 2,000 cubic feet and the weight limit for the space is 300,000 pounds. The profit on the Printmaster is $125,000 and the profit on the Speedmaster is $30,000. How many of each machine should be stored to maximize profitability and what is the maximum possible profit?

Let x represent the number of Printmaster units sold and let y represent the number of Speedmaster units sold. The equation for the space required to store the units is

    $10x + 5y \leq 2000$

    $2x + y \leq 400.$

Since the number of units for both models cannot be less than 0, also impose the restrictions that $x \geq 0$ and $y \geq 0$. The restriction on the total weight can be expressed as

    $5000x + 600y \leq 300000$

    $25x + 3y \leq 1500.$

The expression for the profit P from sales of the printer units is

    $P = \$125{,}000x + \$30{,}000y$

The solution to this problem is found by maximizing P subject to the constraints given in the preceding inequalities, along with the constraints that $x \geq 0$ and $y \geq 0$. The equations are grouped below for clarity.

$$x \geq 0$$
$$y \geq 0$$
$$2x + y \leq 400$$
$$25x + 3y \leq 1500$$
$$P = \$125{,}000x + \$30{,}000y$$

The two inequalities in two variables are plotted in the graph below. The shaded region represents the set of solutions that obey both inequalities. (Note that the shaded region in fact includes only points where both x and y are whole numbers.)

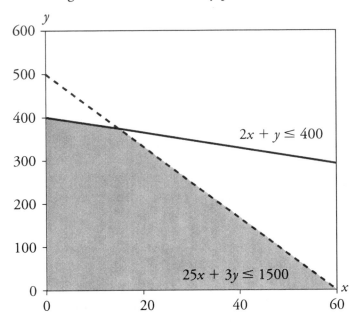

Note that the border of the shaded region that is formed by the two inequalities includes the solutions that constitute the maximum value of y for a given value of x. Note also that x cannot exceed 60 (since it would violate the second inequality). The solution to the problem must lie on the border of the shaded region since the border spans all the possible solutions that maximize the use of space and weight for a given number x.

To visualize the solution, plot the profit as a function of the solutions to the inequalities that lie along the border of the shaded area.

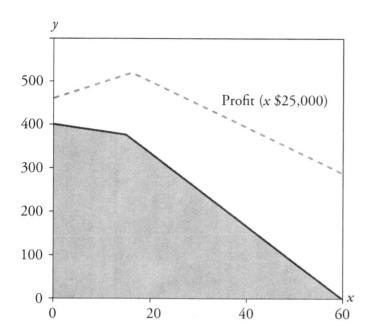

The profit curve shows a maximum at about $x = 16$. Verify this result by using a table to test several values.

x	y	P (x$25,000)
15	370	519
16	366	519.2
17	358	514.6

Also double check to be sure that the result obeys the two inequalities.

$2(16) + (366) = 398 \leq 400$

$25(16) + 3(366) = 1498 \leq 1500$

The optimum result is storage of 16 Printmaster and 366 Speedmaster printer units.

Example: Sharon's Bike Shoppe can assemble a 3-speed bike in 30 minutes and a 10-speed bike in 60 minutes. The profit on each bike sold is $60 for a 3 speed or $75 for a 10-speed bike. How many of each type of bike should be assembled during an 8-hour day (480 minutes) to maximize the possible profit? Total daily profit must be at least $300.

Let x be the number of 3-speed bikes and y be the number of 10-speed bikes. Since there are only 480 minutes to use each day, the first inequality is

$30x + 60y \leq 480$

$x + 2y \leq 16$.

Since the total daily profit must be at least $300, the second inequality can be written as follows, where P is the profit for the day:

$$P = \$60x + \$75y \geq \$300$$
$$4x + 5y \geq 20.$$

To visualize the problem, plot the two inequalities and show the potential solutions as a shaded region.

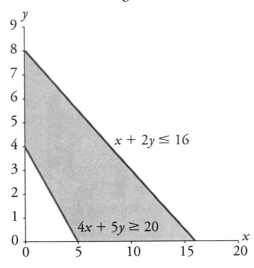

The solution to the problem is the ordered pair of whole numbers in the shaded area that maximizes the daily profit. The profit curve is added as shown below.

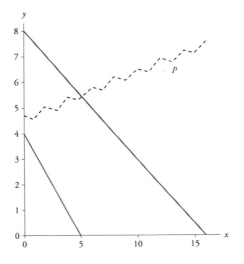

Based on the above plot, it is clear that the profit is maximized for the case where only 3-speed bikes (corresponding to x) are manufactured. Thus, the correct solution can be found by solving the first inequality for x when $y = 0$.

$$x + 2(0) \leq 16$$
$$x \leq 16$$

The manufacture of sixteen 3-speed bikes (and no 10-speed bikes) maximizes profit to $960 per day.

SKILL Solving problems using linear equations and inequalities and
6.4 systems of linear equations and inequalities

See Skill 6.3

COMPETENCY 7

ANALYZE NONLINEAR FUNCTIONS AND THEIR APPLICATIONS AND THE CONCEPT OF THE DERIVATIVE

SKILL Analyzing nonlinear equations *(e.g., quadratic, polynomial, exponential)*
7.1 based on their characteristics

Graphing

The general technique for graphing quadratics is the same as that for graphing linear equations. Graphing a quadratic equation, however, results in a parabola instead of a straight line.

The general form of a quadratic function is $y = ax^2 + bx + c$. Once a function is identified as quadratic, it is helpful to recognize several features that can indicate the form of the graph. The parabola has an axis of symmetry along $x = -\frac{b}{2a}$ which is the x-coordinate of the vertex (turning point) of the graph.

> *The general technique for graphing quadratics is the same as that for graphing linear equations. Graphing a quadratic equation, however, results in a parabola instead of a straight line.*

This can be understood more clearly if we consider an alternate form of a quadratic equation, the standard form for a parabola

$$y = a(x - h)^2 + k,$$

where point (h, k) denotes the coordinates of the vertex of the parabola.

By transforming the general form $y = ax^2 + bx + c$ into the above form, we get

$$y = a\left(x^2 + \frac{b}{a}x\right) + c$$
$$y = a\left(x^2 + 2\frac{b}{2a}x + \left(\frac{b}{2a}\right)^2\right) - \frac{b^2}{4a} + c$$
$$y = a\left(x + \frac{b}{2a}\right)^2 - \frac{b^2}{4a} + c$$

The coordinates of the vertex are given as $\left(-\frac{b}{2a}, -\frac{b^2}{4a} + c\right)$.

Example: Graph y = 3x² + x − 2.

Expressing this function in standard form we get

$$y = 3\left(x + \tfrac{1}{6}\right)^2 - \tfrac{25}{12}.$$

The graph is a parabola with an axis of symmetry $x = -\tfrac{1}{6}$,

and the vertex is located at the point $\left(-\tfrac{1}{6}, -\tfrac{25}{12}\right)$.

x	y = 3x² + x − 2
-2	8
-1	0
0	-2
1	2
2	12

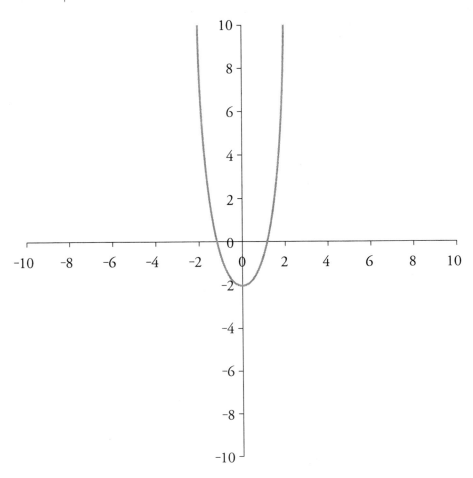

If the quadratic term is positive, the parabola is concave up; if the quadratic term is negative, the parabola is concave down. The function $-x^2 - 2x - 3$ is one such example and is shown below.

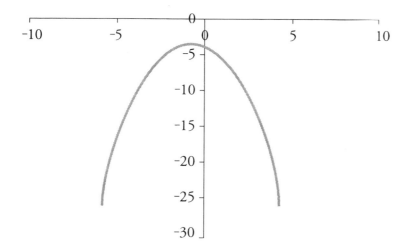

A quadratic function with two real roots (see example problems above) will have two crossings of the x-axis. A quadratic function with one real root will graph as a parabola that is tangent to the x-axis. An example of such a quadratic function is shown in the example below for the function $x^2 + 2x + 1$. The function has a single real root at $x = -1$.

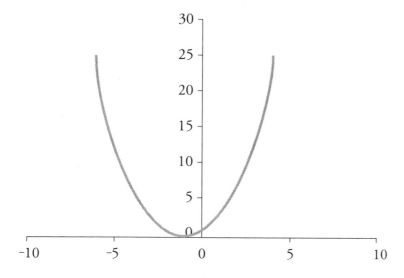

A quadratic function with no real roots will not cross the x-axis at any point. An example is the function $x^2 + 2x + 2$, which is plotted below.

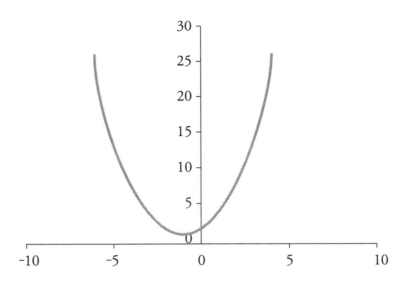

Example: Solve by graphing: $x^2 - 8x + 15 = 0$.

The roots of the polynomial $x^2 - 8x + 15$ are the x values for which the graph intersects the x-axis.

x	$y = x^2 - 8x + 15$
-2	35
-1	24
0	15
1	8
2	3

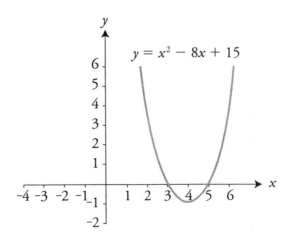

From the above graph, the *x*-intercepts, or zeros, are 3 and 5. So the solutions of the given quadratic equation are 3 and 5.

To graph a quadratic inequality, graph the quadratic as if it were an equation; however, if the inequality sign is $>$ or $<$, the curved line is dotted; if the inequality sign is $\geq$ or $\leq$, the curved line is solid. Shade above the curve for $>$ or $\geq$. Shade below the curve for $<$ or $\leq$.

Example: Graph the inequality $y < -x^2 + x - 2$.
The quadratic function $-x^2 + x - 2$ is plotted with a dotted line since the inequality sign is $<$ and not $\leq$. Since *y* is "less than" this function, the shading is done below the curve.

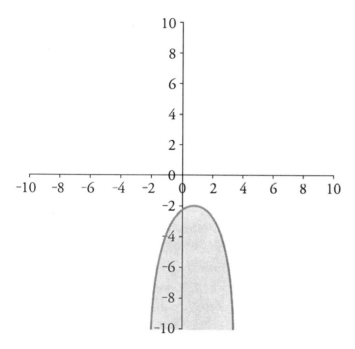

Example: Graph the inequality $y \geq x^2 - 2x - 9$.
The quadratic function $x^2 - 2x - 9$ is plotted with a solid line since the inequality sign is $\geq$. Since *y* is "greater than or equal to" this function, the shading is done above the curve.

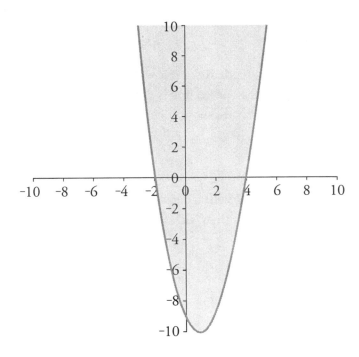

Polynomial Functions

A polynomial is a sum of terms where each term is a constant multiplied by a variable raised to a positive integer power. The general form of a polynomial $P(x)$ is

$$P(x) = a_n x^n + a_{n-1} x^{n-1} + \ldots + a_2 x^2 + a_1 x + a_0$$

Polynomials written in standard form have the terms written in decreasing exponent value, as shown above. The DEGREE OF A POLYNOMIAL FUNCTION IN ONE VARIABLE is the value of the largest exponent to which the variable is raised. The above expression is a polynomial of degree n (assuming that $a_n \neq 0$). Any function that represents a line is a polynomial function of degree one. Quadratic functions are polynomials of degree two. For instance, $5x^2 - 4x - 6$ is a second degree polynomial, whereas $2x^3 - 5x^2 + x$ is a polynomial of degree three. If a term has more than one variable (e.g., $2xy$) it is necessary to add the exponents of the variables within the term to get the degree of the polynomial. Since $1 + 1 = 2$, $2xy$ is a polynomial of the second degree.

A polynomial may also be represented in tabular or graphical form, as shown in the example below.

> **DEGREE OF A POLYNOMIAL FUNCTION IN ONE VARIABLE:** the value of the largest exponent to which the variable is raised

Any function that represents a line is a polynomial function of degree one. Quadratic functions are polynomials of degree two. For instance, $5x^2 - 4x - 6$ is a second degree polynomial, whereas $2x^3 - 5x^2 + x$ is a polynomial of degree three.

Example: Express the polynomial $x^3 - 6x + 4$ in tabular and graphical form.

x	y
-3	-5
-2	8
-1	9
0	4
1	-1
2	0
3	13

Note the change in sign of the y value between $x = -3$ and $x = -2$. This indicates there is a zero between $x = -3$ and $x = -2$. Since there is another change in sign of the y value between $x = 0$ and $x = -1$, there is a second root there. When $x = 2$, $y = 0$ so $x = 2$ is an exact root of this polynomial.

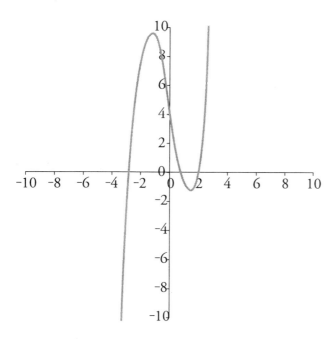

Rational functions

A rational function can be written as the ratio of two polynomial expressions. A rational function is given in the form $f(x) = \frac{p(x)}{q(x)}$. In the equation, $p(x)$ and $q(x)$ both represent polynomial functions ($q(x)$ does not equal zero).

Examples of rational functions are $r(x) = \frac{x^2 + 2x + 4}{x - 3}$ and $r(x) = \frac{x}{x - 3}$, which both are ratios of two polynomials.

The branches of rational functions approach asymptotes. Setting the denominator equal to zero and solving will give the value(s) of the vertical asymptotes since the function will be undefined at this point. If the value of $f(x)$ approaches b as $|x|$ increases, the equation $y = b$ is a horizontal asymptote. To find the horizontal asymptote, it is necessary to make a table of values for x that are to the right and left of the vertical asymptotes. The pattern for the horizontal asymptotes will become apparent as $|x|$ increases.

If there is more than one vertical asymptote, remember to choose numbers to the right and left of each one in order to find the horizontal asymptotes and have sufficient points to graph the function.

Example: Graph $f(x) = \dfrac{3x + 1}{x - 2}$.

$x - 2 = 0$ 1. Set the denominator equal to 0 to find the vertical
$x = 2$ asymptote.

x	f(x)
3	10
10	3.875
100	3.07
1000	3.007
1	-4
-10	2.417
-100	2.93
-1000	2.99

2. Make a table choosing numbers to the right and left of the vertical asymptote

3. The pattern shows that as $|x|$ increases, $f(x)$ approaches the value 3 therefore asymptote exists at $y = 3$

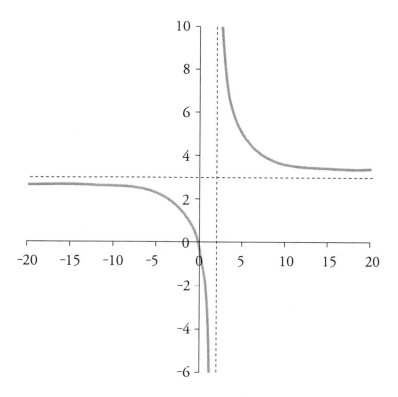

Note that $x = 2$ is excluded from the domain of the function and $y = 3$ is excluded from the range.

In some cases, the restriction on a rational function owing to the denominator being zero will not be a vertical asymptote but simply a hole in the graph. This happens when the value of x that reduces the denominator to zero is also a zero of the numerator.

Example: Plot the function $\frac{x - 2}{x^2 - 4}$.

Factoring the denominator, we see that the denominator goes to zero at $x = -2$ and $x = 2$.

$$\frac{x - 2}{x^2 - 4} = \frac{x - 2}{(x + 2)(x - 2)}$$

There is a vertical asymptote at $x = h - 2$. Since the function can be simplified to the form $\frac{1}{(x + 2)}$ by canceling $(x - 2)$ from the numerator and denominator, there is no asymptote at $x = 2$. The point $x = 2$, however, must be excluded from the function. Hence, there is a hole in the graph at $x = 2$.

Studying the function, we see that for large values of x the function goes to zero. Thus there is a horizontal asymptote at $y = 0$.

x	y	
-6	$-\frac{1}{4}$	
-4	$-\frac{1}{2}$	
-3	-1	
-2.5	-2	
-1.5	2	
-1	1	
0	$\frac{1}{2}$	
1	$\frac{1}{3}$	
2	$\frac{1}{4}$	(location of hole)
3	$\frac{1}{5}$	

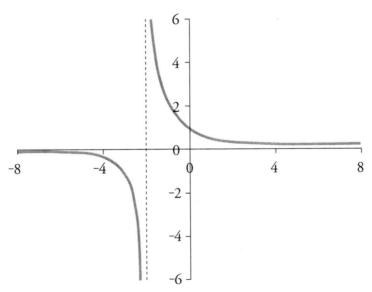

Absolute Value Functions

The absolute value function for a first-degree equation is $y = m|x - h| + k$. Its graph is V-shaped. The point (h, k) is the location of the maximum/minimum point on the graph. The slopes of the two sides of the V are "$\pm m$." The graph opens up if m is positive and down if m is negative.

Following are examples of graphs of absolute value functions.

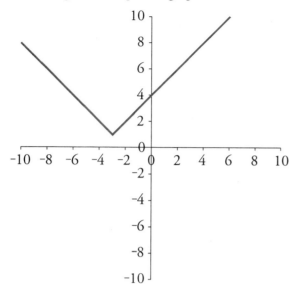

$$y = |x + 3| + 1$$

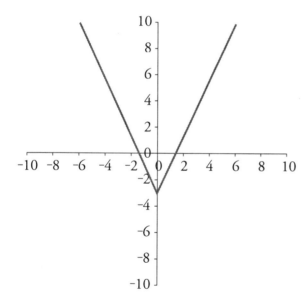

$$y = 2|x| - 3$$

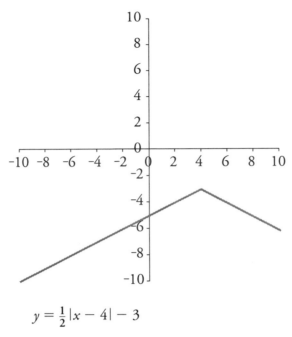

$$y = \tfrac{1}{2}|x - 4| - 3$$

Note that on the first graph, the graph opens up since m is $+1$. Its minimum point is (-3, 1). The slopes of the two upward rays are ± 1. The second graph also opens up since m is positive. Its minimum point is (0, -3). The slopes of the two upward rays are ± 2. The third graph opens downward because m is $-\tfrac{1}{2}$. The maximum point on the graph is (4, -3). The slopes of the two downward rays are $\pm \tfrac{1}{2}$.

Radical Functions

Radical functions are those that depend on a root of the independent variable x, typically the square root. Some examples are $3\sqrt{x} + 5$, $\sqrt{7 - x}$ and $2\sqrt{x + 3} - 5$.

Plotting a radical function follows a process similar to that of plotting virtually any other function. A set of representative points is needed, and prior knowledge of the domain of the function is helpful (for instance, if only real numbers are considered, the expression under the square root sign must always be positive). Typically, a calculator is needed to find the values of the function for specific variable values.

Plotting a radical function follows a process similar to that of plotting virtually any other function. A set of representative points is needed, and prior knowledge of the domain of the function is helpful (for instance, if only real numbers are considered, the expression under the square root sign must always be positive).

Example: Tabulate and plot the function $3\sqrt{x} + 5$.

x	y
0	5
1	8
4	11
9	14
16	17
25	20

Note that *x* must always be positive. Hence, the domain of the function is $x > 0$.

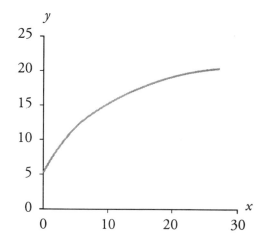

Piecewise Functions

Functions defined by two or more formulas are PIECEWISE FUNCTIONS. The formula used to evaluate piecewise functions varies depending on the value of *x*. The graphs of piecewise functions consist of two or more pieces, or intervals, and are often discontinuous.

PIECEWISE FUNC-TIONS: functions defined by two or more formulas

Example 1

$f(x) = x + 1$ if $x > 2$

       $x - 2$ if $x < 2$

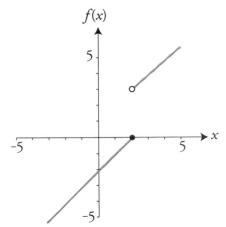

Example 2

$f(x) = x$ if $x > 1$

       x^2 if $x < 1$

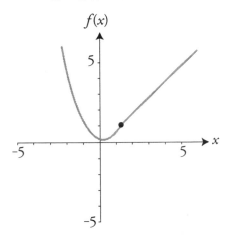

When graphing or interpreting the graph of piecewise functions, it is important to note the points at the beginning and end of each interval because the graph must clearly indicate what happens at the end of each interval. Note that in the graph of Example 1, point $(2, 3)$ is not part of the graph and is represented by an empty circle. On the other hand, point $(2, 0)$ is part of the graph and is represented as a solid circle. Note also that the graph of Example 2 is continuous despite representing a piecewise function.

Exponential Functions

An exponential function is defined by the equation $y = ab^x$, where a is the starting value, b is the growth factor, and x is the exponent of the growth factor. For exponential functions, the ratio between successive ys, or outputs, are constant. In other words, each y, or output, is a constant multiple of the previous y.

If $a > 0$ and b is between 0 and 1 the graph of the exponential function will be decreasing or decaying.

If $a > 0$ and b is greater than 1, the graph will be increasing or growing.

> *An exponential function is defined by the equation $y = ab^x$, where a is the starting value, b is the growth factor, and x is the exponent of the growth factor. For exponential functions, the ratio between successive ys or outputs are constant. In other words, each y or output, is a constant multiple of the previous y.*

Example: Identify the pattern represented by y = 100(0.5)ˣ

x	y	Ratio of change is a constant 50% increase indicated by multiplying by 1.5:
0	100	
1	150	1.5(100) = 150
2	225	1.5(150) = 225
3	337.5	1.5(225) = 337.5
4	506.25	1.5(337.51) = 506.25

Logarithmic functions of base a are of the basic form
$$f(x) = \log_a x, \text{ where } a > 0 \text{ and not equal to } 1.$$

Expressed verbally, the logarithm $f(x)$ of a number x is the exponent or power to which the base must be raised to equal x. For example, 10 raised to the power 3 is 1000. Therefore, the base 10 logarithm of 1000 is 3.

The logarithmic function essentially transforms a geometrical progression into an arithmetic one. This is clear if one considers that the base 10 logarithm of 10, 10^2, 10^3, ... is 1, 2, 3, and so on.

Graphing exponential and logarithmic functions involves finding a set of representative points, plotting these points on a graph, and then connecting the points with appropriate curves. The domain of an exponential function includes all real numbers; the domain of a logarithmic function includes only the positive real numbers. The basic shapes of the exponential and logarithmic functions are illustrated below.

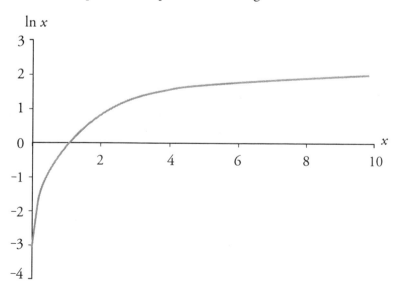

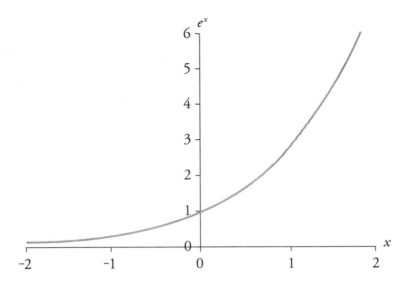

Note that the function e^x has an asymptote at $y = 0$ (the limit of the exponential function as x goes to negative infinity is zero), and the function $\ln x$ has an asymptote at $x = 0$. (The limit of the natural logarithmic function as x goes to zero from the right is negative infinity.) The x-intercept of the logarithmic function, irrespective of base, is always $(1, 0)$ since any number raised to the power of 0 is equal to one. The y-intercept of e^x is $(0, 1)$ because any base raised to the power of 0 equals 1.

SKILL 7.2 **Translating between different representations of a nonlinear function**

See Skill 7.1

SKILL 7.3 **Solving problems using nonlinear equations**

Quadratic Models

Certain word problems may be modeled using quadratic equations or inequalities. Examples of this type of problem follow.

Example: A family is planning to add a new room to their house. They would like the room to have a length that is 10 feet more than the width and a total area of 375 square feet. Find the length and width of the room.

Let x be the width of the room. The length of the room is then $x + 10$. The quadratic equation is

$$x(x + 10) = 375$$
$$x^2 + 10x - 375 = 0.$$

Factor the quadratic expression to solve the equation.

$$x^2 + 25x - 15x - 375 = 0 \quad \text{Break up the middle}$$
$$x(x + 25) - 15(x + 25) = 0 \quad \text{term using factors of 375}$$
$$(x + 25)(x - 15) = 0$$
$$x = -25 \text{ or } x = 15$$

Since the dimensions of a room cannot be negative, we choose the positive solution, $x = 15$. The width of the room is 15 feet and the length of the room is 25 feet.

Example: The formula for the maximum height of a projectile fired upward at a velocity of v meters per second from an original height of h meters is y = h + vx − 4.9x². If a rocket is fired from an original height of 250 meters with an original velocity of 4800 meters per second, find the approximate time the rocket would drop to sea level (a height of 0).

Substituting the height and velocity into the equation yields $y = 250 + 4800x - 4.9x^2$. If the height at sea level is 0, then $y = 0$, so $0 = 250 + 4800x - 4.9x^2$. Use the quadratic formula to solve for x.

$$x = \frac{-4800 \pm \sqrt{4800^2 - 4(-4.9)(250)}}{2(-4.9)}$$
$$x \approx 979.53 \text{ or } x \approx -0.05 \text{ seconds}$$

Since the time has to be positive, it will be approximately 980 seconds until the rocket reaches sea level.

Example: A family wants to enclose 3 sides of a rectangular garden, at least 4800 square feet in area, with 200 feet of fence. A wall borders the fourth side of the garden. How long can the garden be?

In order to have a garden with an area of at least 4800 square feet, find the dimensions the garden should have.

Solution:

Let x = distance from the wall

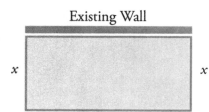

Then amount of fence needed for these 2 sides is $2x$ feet. The side opposite the existing wall would use the remainder of the 200 feet of fence, that is, $200 - 2x$ feet of fence. Therefore the width (w) of the garden is x feet and the length (l) is $(200 - 2x)$ feet.

The area is calculated using the formula $A = lw = x(200 - 2x) = 200x - 2x^2$, and the area needs to be greater than or equal to 4800 square feet. The expression for this inequality is $4800 \leq 200x - 2x^2$. Subtract 4800 from each side and the inequality becomes

$$2(-x^2 + 100x - 2400) \geq 0$$
$$-x^2 + 100x - 2400 \geq 0$$
$$(-x + 60)(x - 40) \geq 0$$
$$-x + 60 \geq 0$$
$$-x \geq -60$$
$$x \leq 60$$
$$x - 40 \geq 0$$
$$x \geq 40.$$

The area will be at least 4800 square feet if the width of the garden is from 40 up to 60 feet. (The length of the rectangle would vary from 120 feet to 80 feet depending on the width of the garden.)

Polynomial Equations

Some situations require higher-order polynomials. Other problems can be modeled using rational or radical functions. The rational and radical equations can usually be simplified to yield a polynomial equation. Some examples are given below.

Example: A cubic container is modified so that its length is increased by 4 inches and its width is shortened by 2 inches. The height of the container remains unchanged. If the volume of the container is 16 cubic inches, what is it height?

Let the side of the original cube be x inches.
The volume of the modified container is given by
$$x(x + 4)(x - 2) = 16.$$

Distributing and rearranging we get
$$x(x^2 + 2x - 8) = 16$$
$$\rightarrow x^3 + 2x^2 - 8x - 16 = 0.$$

The third order polynomial equation above can be grouped and factored as follows:

$$x^2(x + 2) - 8(x + 2) = 0$$
$$\rightarrow (x + 2)(x^2 - 8) = 0.$$

The solutions to the equation are, therefore, $x = -2$ and $\pm 2\sqrt{2}$.

Since the height of the box must be a positive number, we choose the positive solution. The height is $2\sqrt{2}$ inches.

Example: Elly Mae can feed the animals in 15 minutes. Jethro can feed them in 10 minutes. How long will it take them to feed the animals if they work together?

If Elly Mae can feed the animals in 15 minutes, then she could feed $\frac{1}{15}$ of them in 1 minute, $\frac{2}{15}$ of them in 2 minutes, and $\frac{x}{15}$ of them in x minutes. In the same fashion, Jethro could feed $\frac{x}{10}$ of them in x minutes. Together they complete 1 job. The equation is:

$$\frac{x}{15} + \frac{x}{10} = 1$$

Multiply each term by the LCD (least common denominator) of 30:

$$2x + 3x = 30$$
$$x = 6 \text{ minutes}$$

Example: A salesman drove 480 miles from Pittsburgh to Hartford. The next day he returned the same distance to Pittsburgh in half an hour less time than his original trip took because he increased his average speed by 4 mph. Find his original speed.

Since distance = rate $\times$ time, then time = $\frac{\text{distance}}{\text{rate}}$.

The form of the equation is original time $- \frac{1}{2}$ hour = shorter return time.

$$\frac{480}{x} - \frac{1}{2} = \frac{480}{x + 4}$$

Multiplying by the LCD of $2x(x + 4)$, the equation becomes:

$$480[2(x + 4)] - 1[x(x + 4)] = 480(2x)$$
$$960x + 3840 - x^2 - 4x = 960x$$
$$x^2 + 4x - 3840 = 0$$
$$(x + 64)(x - 60) = 0 \qquad \text{Either } (x - 60 = 0) \text{ or } (x + 64 = 0) \text{ or both} = 0$$
$$x = 60 \qquad\qquad\qquad 60 \text{ mph is the original speed.}$$

This is the solution since the time cannot be negative. Check your answer.

$$x + 4 = 64$$
$$\frac{480}{60} - \frac{1}{2} = \frac{480}{64}$$
$$8 - \frac{1}{2} = 7\frac{1}{2}$$
$$7\frac{1}{2} = 7\frac{1}{2}$$

Example: For a cone of height h and radius r, the slant height is given by the formula $s = \sqrt{r^2 + h^2}$. The lateral surface area is represented by πrs and the area of the base by πr^2.

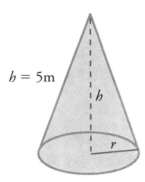

$h = 5m$

If the lateral surface area of a cone is twice that of its base and the height of the cone is 5m, find the radius.

The problem given may be modeled using the following radical equation:
$$\pi r \sqrt{25 + r^2} = 2\pi r^2.$$

Canceling the common factor πr from both sides and squaring both sides we get
$$25 + r^2 = 4r^2$$
$$\rightarrow 3r^2 = 25$$
$$\rightarrow r = \sqrt{\tfrac{25}{3}} = 2.9$$

Thus, the radius of the cone is 2.9m.

Exponential Growth

> *A quantity which grows by a fixed percent at regular intervals (i.e., in proportion to the existing amount) demonstrates exponential growth.*

A quantity which grows by a fixed percent at regular intervals (i.e., in proportion to the existing amount) demonstrates exponential growth. If a population has a constant birth rate through the years and is not affected by famine or disease, it has exponential growth. The birth rate alone controls how fast the population grows exponentially.

Example: A population of a city is 20,000 and it increases at an annual rate of 20%. What will be the population of the city after 10 years?

The formula for the growth is $y = a(1 + r)^t$, where a is the initial amount, r is the growth rate, and t is the number of time intervals.

In this case,
$$a = 20000$$
$$r = 20\% = 0.2$$
$$t = 10$$

Substituting the values,

$$population\ growth = y = 20000(1 + 0.2)^{10}$$
$$= 20000(1 + 0.2)^{10}$$
$$= 20000(1.2)^{10}$$
$$= 20000(6.19)$$
$$= 123800.$$

The population of the city after 10 years is 123,800.

What will be the population of the city after 50 years?

In 50 years,

$$population = 20000(1 + 0.2)^{50}$$
$$= 20000(1 + 0.2)^{50}$$
$$= 20000(1.2)^{50}$$
$$= 20000(9100.44)$$
$$= 182008800$$

The population after 50 years will be 182,008,800.

Exponential Decay

Exponential decay is decrease by a fixed percent at regular intervals of time. Radioactive decay is an example of this.

Example: If 40 grams of radioactive iodine has reduced to 20 grams in 6 days, what is the rate of decay?

The formula for exponential decay is $Q = ae^{rt}$, where Q is the amount of material at time t, a is the initial amount, r is the decay rate and t is the time period in days.

$$Q = ae^{rt}$$
$$20 = 40e^{r(6)} \qquad \text{Isolate } e$$
$$0.5 = e^{6r} \qquad \text{Take ln of both sides}$$
$$\ln 0.5 = 6r \qquad \text{Solve for } r$$
$$\frac{\ln 0.5}{6} = r$$
$$r = -0.1155$$

Note: r is negative because it is decay.
The rate of decay is 0.1155, or 11.55%.

Example: A 10-gram sample of Einsteinium-254 decays radioactively with a half-life of about 276 days. What is the remaining mass of Einsteinium-254 after 5 years (assume each year is 365 days).

Use the exponential decay formula derived above, where $m(t)$ is the mass (m) of Einsteinium in the sample at time t.

$$m(t) = Ce^{kt}$$

The initial mass of Einsteinium-254 is 10 grams. Use this to find the value of C.

$$m(0) = 10\text{g} = Ce^{k(0)} = C$$

Thus, C is 10 grams. To find k, note that, after 276 days, the amount of remaining Einsteinium-254 must be half the initial amount.

$$m(276\text{d}) = (10\text{g})e^{k(276\text{d})} = 5\text{g}$$
$$e^{k(276\text{d})} = \frac{1}{2}$$

Solve for k. Note that, to make the argument of the exponential dimensionless, the units of k should be inverse days.

$$\ln[e^{k(276\text{d})}] = \ln\frac{1}{2}$$
$$(276\text{d})k = \ln\frac{1}{2}$$
$$k = \frac{1}{276\text{d}}\ln\frac{1}{2}$$
$$k \approx -0.00251\frac{1}{2}$$

The complete expression for m is the following, where t is in days:

$$m(t) \approx (10\text{g})e^{-0.00251t}$$

Finally, calculate the amount of Einsteinium remaining after 5 years (1,825 days).

$$m(1825) \approx (10\text{g})e^{-0.00251(1825)}$$
$$m(1825) \approx 0.102\text{g}$$

After 5 years, only about 0.102 grams of the initial sample remain.

SKILL 7.4 Applying the concept of the derivative to problems involving rates of change

The rate of change of a function is equivalent to its slope (change in the vertical direction for a given change in the horizontal direction). For nonlinear functions, the slope is continuously changing over the domain. The rate of change of a function can be found as an average rate of change over some portion of the domain (a difference quotient), or it can be found at a particular domain value (derivative).

Difference Quotient

The **DIFFERENCE QUOTIENT** is the average rate of change over an interval. For a function f, the difference quotient is represented by the formula

$$\frac{f(x + h) - f(x)}{h}.$$

This formula computes the slope of the secant line through two points on the graph of f. These are the points with x-axis coordinates x and $x + h$.

Example: Find the difference quotient for the function $f(x) = 2x^2 + 3x - 5$.

Use the difference quotient formula and simplify the results.

$$\frac{f(x + h) - f(x)}{h} = \frac{2(x + h)^2 + 3(x + h) - 5 - (2x^2 + 3x - 5)}{h}$$

$$= \frac{2(x^2 + 2hx + h^2) + 3x + 3h - 5 - 2x^2 - 3x + 5}{h}$$

$$= \frac{2x^2 + 4hx + 2h^2 + 3x + 3h - 5 - 2x^2 - 3x + 5}{h}$$

$$= \frac{4hx + 2h^2 + 3h}{h}$$

$$= 4x + 2h + 3$$

> **DIFFERENCE QUOTIENT:** the average rate of change over an interval

Derivative

The **DERIVATIVE** is the slope of a line tangent to a graph $f(x)$ at x, and is usually denoted $f'(x)$. This is also referred to as the instantaneous rate of change. The derivative of $f(x)$ at $x = a$ is found by taking the limit of the average rates of change (computed by the difference quotient) as h approaches zero.

$$f'(a) = \lim_{h \to 0} \frac{f(a + h) - f(a)}{h}$$

> **DERIVATIVE:** the slope of a line tangent to a graph $f(x)$ at x, usually denoted $f'(x)$

Pick a point (for instance, $x = -3$) on the graph of a function and draw a tangent line at that point. Find the derivative of the function and substitute the value $x = -3$. This result will be the slope of the tangent line.

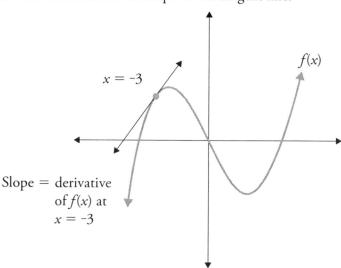

$x = -3$

$f(x)$

Slope = derivative
of $f(x)$ at
$x = -3$

Example: Suppose a company's annual profit (in millions of dollars) is represented by the above function, f(x) = 2x² + 3x − 5, and x represents the number of years in the interval. Compute the rate at which the annual profit was changing over a period of 2 years.

$$f'(a) = \lim_{h \to 0} \frac{f(a + h) - f(a)}{h}$$
$$= f'(2) = \lim_{h \to 0} \frac{f(2 + h) - f(2)}{h}$$

Using the difference quotient we computed previously, $4x + 2h + 3$, yields

$$f'(2) = \lim_{h \to 0} (4(2) + 2h + 3)$$
$$= 8 + 3$$
$$= 11.$$

The annual profit for the company has increased at the average rate of $11 million per year over the two-year period.

Rules of Differentiation

The following properties of the derivative allow for differentiation of a wide range of functions (although the process of differentiation may be more or less difficult, depending on the complexity of the function). For illustration, consider two arbitrary functions, $f(x)$ and $g(x)$, and an arbitrary constant, c.

DIFFERENTIATION RULES	
Rule for Multiplicative Constants	$\frac{d}{dx}(cf) = cf'$
Sum and Difference Rules	$\frac{d}{dx}(f + g) = f' + g'$ $\frac{d}{dx}(f - g) = f' - g'$
Product Rule	$\frac{d}{dx}(fg) = fg' + gf'$
Quotient Rule	$\frac{d}{dx}\left(\frac{f}{g}\right) = \frac{gf' - fg'}{g^2}$
Chain Rule	$\frac{df}{dx} = \frac{df}{du}\frac{du}{dx}$

The chain rule, as expressed above, allows for differentiation of composite functions. The variable u can be an independent variable or it can be a function (of x). Note that the differential elements du in the numerator of the first factor and in the denominator of the second factor can otherwise cancel, making the right side of the equation identical to the left side.

Derivation of Differentiation Rules

As mentioned previously, the formal definition of the derivative can be used to determine the general form of the derivative for certain families of functions. The formal definition of the derivative is expressed in terms of the limit of a difference quotient, as given below.

$$f'(x) = \lim_{\Delta x \to 0} \frac{f(x + \Delta x) - f(x)}{\Delta x}$$

Using this definition, the derivatives of algebraic functions (including, for instance, polynomial, trigonometric, and logarithmic functions) can be derived. In addition, the general differentiation rules above can also be derived by applying in each case the properties of limits to the definition given above.

The use of the formal definition in deriving a general rule of differentiation for a family of functions is best illustrated by way of an example. Consider polynomial functions, as mentioned previously. Note that the sum and difference rules for differentiation, along with the multiplicative constant rule, allow polynomials to be differentiated on a term-by-term basis. Thus, it suffices to simply derive the rule for differentiating the generic term x^n, where n is a constant and x is the variable of the function. Use the formal definition of the derivative given above and substitute this algebraic term for $f(x) =$ (that is, use $f(x) = x^n$).

$$f'(x) = \lim_{\Delta x \to 0} \frac{(x + \Delta x)^n - (x)^n}{\Delta x}$$

Simplify the expression and apply the binomial expansion to the result.

$$f'(x) = \lim_{\Delta x \to 0} \frac{1}{\Delta x}[(x + \Delta x)^n - x^n]$$

$$f'(x) = \lim_{\Delta x \to 0} [\tbinom{n}{0}x^n + \tbinom{n}{1}x^{n-1} \Delta x + \tbinom{n}{2}x^{n-2} (\Delta x)^2 + ... + \tbinom{n}{n}(\Delta x)^n - x^n]$$

In the above expression, the combinatorial form $\tbinom{n}{k}$ represents the number of combinations of n objects taken k at a time, or $\frac{n!}{k!(n-k)!}$.

$$f'(x) = \lim_{\Delta x \to 0} \frac{1}{\Delta x}[x^n + nx^{n-1}\Delta x + \tbinom{n}{2}x^{n-2} (\Delta x)^2 + ... + (\Delta x)^n - x^n]$$

$$f'(x) = \lim_{\Delta x \to 0} \frac{1}{\Delta x}[nx^{n-1}\Delta x + \tbinom{n}{2}x^{n-2} (\Delta x)^2 + ... + (\Delta x)^n]$$

$$f'(x) = \lim_{\Delta x \to 0} [nx^{n-1} + \tbinom{n}{2}x^{n-2} \Delta x + ... + (\Delta x)^{n-1}]$$

Note that, with the exception of the first term, all the terms in the brackets have a factor Δx. Thus, when the limit is applied, these terms all become zero, leaving the result of the differentiation.

$$f'(x) = nx^{n-1}$$

This is the well-known rule for differentiating polynomial terms with exponent n.

Example: Find the first derivative of the function y = 5x⁴.

$$\frac{dy}{dx} = (5)(4)x^{4-1}$$

$$\frac{dy}{dx} = 20x^3$$

Example: Find y' where y = $\frac{1}{4x^3}$.

First, rewrite the function using a negative exponent, then apply the differentiation rule.

$$y' = \frac{1}{4}x^{-3}$$

$$y' = \frac{1}{4}(-3)x^{-3-1}$$

$$y' = -\frac{3}{4}x^{-4} = -\frac{3}{4x^4}$$

Example: Find the first derivative of y = 3$\sqrt{x^5}$.

Rewrite using $\sqrt[z]{x^n} = x^{\frac{n}{z}}$, then take the derivative.

$$y = 3x^{\frac{5}{2}}$$

$$\frac{dy}{dx} = (3)(\tfrac{5}{2})x^{\frac{5}{2}-1}$$

$$\frac{dy}{dx} = (\tfrac{15}{2})x^{\frac{3}{2}}$$

$$\frac{dy}{dx} = 7.5\sqrt{x^3} = 7.5x\sqrt{x}$$

The derivatives of other families of functions can be found in a similar manner. Below is a summary of the rules of differentiation for various transcendental (including trigonometric, logarithmic, and exponential) functions.

SUMMARY OF DIFFERENTIATION RULES FOR TRANSCENDENTAL FUNCTIONS	
$\frac{d}{dx}\sin x = \cos x$	$\frac{d}{dx}\csc x = -\csc x \cot x$
$\frac{d}{dx}\cos x = -\sin x$	$\frac{d}{dx}\sec x = \sec x \tan x$
$\frac{d}{dx}\tan x = \sec^2 x$	$\frac{d}{dx}\cot x = -\csc^2 x$
$\frac{d}{dx}\arcsin x = \dfrac{1}{\sqrt{1-x^2}}$	$\frac{d}{dx}\text{arc csc } x = -\dfrac{1}{|x|\sqrt{x^2-1}}$
$\frac{d}{dx}\text{arccos } x = -\dfrac{1}{\sqrt{1-x^2}}$	$\frac{d}{dx}\text{arc sec } x = \dfrac{1}{|x|\sqrt{x^2-1}}$
$\frac{d}{dx}\arctan x = \dfrac{1}{1+x^2}$	$\frac{d}{dx}\text{arc cot } x = -\dfrac{1}{1+x^2}$
$\frac{d}{dx}\ln x = \frac{1}{x}$	$\frac{d}{dx}e^x = e^x$

Example: Find the derivative of the function $y = 4e^{x^2} \sin x$.

Apply the appropriate rules (product and chain rules) to the function.

$$\frac{dy}{dx} = 4(\sin x \frac{d}{dx}e^{x^2} + e^{x^2}\frac{d}{dx}\sin x)$$

$$\frac{dy}{dx} = 4(\sin x[2xe^{x^2}] + e^{x^2}\cos x)$$

$$\frac{dy}{dx} = 8xe^{x^2} \sin x + 4e^{x^2} \cos x$$

Example: Find the derivative of the function $y = \frac{5}{e^{\sin x}}$.

Rewrite the function with a negative exponent and use the chain rule.

$$y = 5e^{-\sin x}$$

$$\frac{dy}{dx} = 5\frac{d}{dx}e^{-\sin x}$$

$$\frac{dy}{dx} = 5e^{-\sin x}[-\cos x]$$

$$\frac{dy}{dx} = 5e^{-\sin x}\cos x = -\frac{5\cos x}{e^{\sin x}}$$

Finding Slope of a Tangent Line at a Point

Using these properties of derivatives, the slopes (and therefore equations) of tangent lines can be found for a wide range of functions. The procedure simply involves finding the slope of the function at the given point using the derivative then determining the equation of the line using point-slope form.

Example: Find the slope of the tangent line for the given function at the given point: $y = \frac{1}{x-2}$ at (3, 1).

Find the derivative of the function.

$$y' = \frac{d}{dx}(x-2)^{-1}$$

$$y' = (-1)(x-2)^{-2}(1) = -\frac{1}{(x-2)^2}$$

Evaluate the derivative at $x = 3$:

$$y' = -\frac{1}{(3-2)^2} = -1$$

Thus, the slope of the function at the point is -1.

Example: Find the points at which the tangent to the curve $f(x) = 2x^2 + 3x$ is parallel to the line $y = 11x - 5$.

For the tangent line to be parallel to the given line, the only condition is that the slopes are equal. Thus, find the derivative of f, set the result equal to 11, and solve for x.

$$f'(x) = 4x + 3 = 11$$

$$4x = 8$$

$$x = 2$$

To find the y value of the point, simply substitute 2 into f.
$$f(2) = 2(2)^2 + 3(2) = 8 + 6 = 14$$

Thus, the tangent to f is parallel to $y = 11x - 5$ at the point (2, 14) only.

Example: Find the equation of the tangent line to $f(x) = 2e^{x^2}$ at $x = -1$.
To find the tangent line, a point and a slope are needed. The x value of the point is given; the y value can be found by substituting $x = -1$ into f.
$$f(-1) = 2e^{(-1)^2} = 2e$$

Thus, the point is $(-1, 2e)$. The slope is found by substituting -1 into the derivative of f.
$$f'(x) = 2e^{x^2}(2x) = 4xe^{x^2}$$
$$f'(-1) = 4(-1)e^{(-1)^2} = -4e$$

Use the point-slope form of the line to determine the correct equation.
$$y - 2e = -4e(x - [-1])$$
$$y = 2e - 4ex - 4e = -4ex - 2e$$

Thus, the equation of the line tangent to f at $x = -1$ is $y = -4ex - 2e$.

Problems Involving Rectilinear Motion

If a particle (such as a car, bullet, or other object) is moving along a line, then the position of the particle can be expressed as a function of time.

The first derivative of the position function yields the velocity function.

The rate of change of position with respect to time is the velocity of the object; thus, the first derivative of the position function yields the velocity function for the particle. Substituting a value for time into this expression provides the instantaneous velocity of the particle at that time. The absolute value of the derivative is the speed (magnitude of the velocity) of the particle. A positive value for the velocity indicates that the particle is moving forward (that is, in the positive x direction); a negative value indicates the particle is moving backward (that is, in the negative x direction).

The second derivative of the position function (which is also the first derivative of the velocity function) yields the acceleration function.

The acceleration of the particle is the rate of change of the velocity. The second derivative of the position function (which is also the first derivative of the velocity function) yields the acceleration function. If a value for time produces a positive acceleration, the particle's velocity is increasing; if it produces a negative value, the particle's velocity is decreasing. If the acceleration is zero, the particle is moving at a constant speed.

*Example: A particle moves along a line according to the equation s(t) =
20 + 3t − 5t², where s is in meters and t is in seconds. Find the position,
velocity, and acceleration of the particle at t = 2 seconds.*

To find the position, simply use $t = 2$ in the given position function. Note that
the initial position of the particle is $s(0) = 20$ meters.

$$s(2) = 20 + 3(2) − 5(2)^2$$
$$s(2) = 20 + 6 − 20 = 6m$$

To find the velocity of the particle, calculate the first derivative of $s(t)$ and then
evaluate the result for $t = 2$ seconds.

$$s'(t) = v(t) = 3 − 10t$$
$$v(2) = 3 − 10(2) = 3 − 20 − \text{-17m/s}$$

Finally, for the acceleration of the particle, calculate the second derivative of $s(t)$
(also equal to the first derivative of $v(t)$) and evaluate for $t = 2$ seconds.

$$s''(t) = v'(t) = a(t) = \text{-10m/s}^2$$

Since the acceleration function $a(t)$ is a constant, the acceleration is always -10m/
s² (the velocity of the particle decreases every second by 10 meters per second).

Related Rate Problems

Some rate problems may involve functions with different parameters that are
each dependent on time. In such a case, implicit differentiation may be required.
Often, related rate problems give certain rates in the description, thus eliminating the need to have specific functions of time for every parameter. Related rate
problems are otherwise solved in the same manner as other similar problems.

*Example: A spherical balloon is inflated such that its radius is increasing at a
constant rate of 1 inch per second. What is the rate of increase of the volume
of the balloon when the radius is 10 inches?*

First, write the equation for the volume of a sphere in terms of the radius, r.

$$V(r) = \tfrac{4}{3}\pi r^3$$

Differentiate the function implicitly with respect to time, t, by using the
chain rule.

$$\frac{dV(r)}{dt} = \tfrac{4}{3}\pi \frac{d}{dt}(r^3)$$

$$\frac{dV(r)}{dt} = \tfrac{4}{3}\pi (3r^2)\frac{dr}{dt} = 4\pi r^2 \frac{dr}{dt}$$

To find the solution to the problem, use the radius value $r = 10$ inches and the rate of increase of the radius $\frac{dr}{dt} = 1\text{in/sec}$. Calculate the resulting rate of increase of the volume, $\frac{dV(r)}{dt}$.

$$\frac{dV(10)}{dt} = 4\pi(10\text{in})^2 \, 1\text{in/sec} = 400\pi\text{in}^3/\text{sec} \approx 1257 \text{ in}^3/\text{sec}$$

The problem is thus solved.

DOMAIN III
SHAPE AND SPACE

PERSONALIZED STUDY PLAN

✗ **KNOWN MATERIAL/ SKIP IT**

PAGE	COMPETENCY AND SKILL	
93	**8: Apply principles of measurement and geometry to solve problems**	☐
	8.1: Solving problems involving conversions within and between different systems of measurement, including dimensional analysis	☐
	8.2: Solving mathematical and real-world problems involving measurable attributes of simple or composite figures and shapes	☐
	8.3: Solving mathematical and real-world problems involving indirect measurement	☐
	8.4: Solving problems involving the effects of changing the dimensions of a figure or shape on its area and volume	☐
109	**9: Analyze figures and shapes in two and three dimensions**	☐
	9.1: Demonstrating knowledge of the axioms of Euclidean geometry	☐
	9.2: Applying the properties of polygons and circles to solve mathematical and real-world problems	☐
	9.3: Applying the properties of two- and three-dimensional shapes to solve mathematical and real-world problems	☐
	9.4: Evaluating formal and informal arguments and proofs	☐
139	**10: Analyze figures and shapes using coordinate and transformational geometry**	☐
	10.1: Analyzing two- and three-dimensional figures and shapes in the coordinate plane	☐
	10.2: Applying geometric properties and the concepts of distance, midpoint, and slope in coordinate systems to solve mathematical and real-world problems	☐
	10.3: Applying transformations to figures in the coordinate plane	☐
	10.4: Analyzing the use of the techniques of coordinate geometry in geometric proofs	☐

COMPETENCY 8
APPLY PRINCIPLES OF MEASUREMENT AND GEOMETRY TO SOLVE PROBLEMS

> **SKILL Solving problems involving conversions within and between**
> **8.1 different systems of measurement, including dimensional analysis**

In ancient times, baskets, jars, and bowls were used to measure capacity. An inch originated as the length of three barley grains placed end to end. The word "carat," used for measuring the weight of precious gems, was derived from carob seeds. Even now, nonstandard units are sometimes used when standard instruments might not be available. For example, students might measure the length of a room by their arm spans. Seeds or stones might be used for measuring weight.

Systems of Units

The Customary (Imperial) System

CUSTOMARY, OR IMPERIAL, UNITS are the familiar everyday units used in the United States.

Customary System units

Inch, foot, yard, and mile are commonly used units of length.

1 yard	=	3 feet	=	36 inches
1 mile	=	1,760 yards		

Rod, furlong, and acre (a unit of area) are less familiar units defined in terms of yards:

1 rod	=	$5\frac{1}{2}$ yards		
1 furlong	=	220 yards		
1 acre	=	4,840 sq. yards	=	160 sq. rods

> "When you can measure what you are speaking about and express it in numbers, you know something about it; but when you cannot measure it, when you cannot express it in numbers, your knowledge is of a meager and unsatisfactory kind."
>
> —Lord Kelvin

> **CUSTOMARY, OR IMPERIAL, UNITS:** the familiar everyday units used in the United States

The basic unit of weight is pound (lb).

1 pound	=	16 ounces (oz)	
1 ounce	=	16 drams	
Short ton (U.S.)	=	2,000 lb	
Long ton (British)	=	2,240 lb	

The basic unit of liquid measure, or liquid capacity, is the gallon.

1 gallon	=	4 quarts	=	8 pints	=	16 cups	=	128 ounces

The basic unit of dry measure, or dry capacity, is the bushel.

1 bushel	=	4 pecks	=	32 dry quarts	=	64 dry pints	=	2,150.42 cubic inches
1 barrel	=	105 dry quarts						

The metric (SI) system

The metric, or SI, system is used in most countries around the world for making everyday measurements. It is also the standard system used for scientific measurements. The metric system is convenient to use because units at different scales are related by multiples of ten.

The basic metric unit for length is the meter (m). The basic metric unit for weight or mass is the gram (g). The basic metric unit for volume is the liter (L).

The following table shows the most commonly used units.

COMMON METRIC UNITS		
1 cm	=	10 mm
1 m	=	1000 mm
1 m	=	100 cm
1 km	=	1000 m
1 L	=	1000 mL
1 kL	=	1000 L
1 g	=	1000 mg
1 kg	=	1000 g

Appropriate units and equivalents

Different units within the same system of measurement are selected based on the scale at which the measurement is being made. For example, the height of a person is measured in feet whereas the distances between cities are measured in miles. To estimate measurements of familiar objects, it is necessary to first determine the units to be used.

Examples of appropriate units:

LENGTH	
The coastline of Florida	miles or kilometers
The width of a ribbon	inches or millimeters
The thickness of a book	inches or centimeters
The length of a football field	yards or meters
The depth of water in a pool	feet or meters

WEIGHT OR MASS	
A bag of sugar	pounds or grams
A school bus	tons or kilograms
A dime	ounces or grams

CAPACITY	
Bucket of paint for bedroom	gallons or liters
Glass of milk	cups or liters
Bottle of soda	quarts or liters
Medicine for child	ounces or milliliters

To estimate measurements, it is helpful to have a familiar reference with a known measurement. For instance, you can use the knowledge that a dollar bill is about 6 inches long or that a nickel weighs about 5 grams to make estimates of length and weight without actually measuring with a ruler or a balance.

APPROXIMATE MEASUREMENTS OF COMMON ITEMS		
ITEM APPROXIMATELY EQUAL TO	METRIC	IMPERIAL
carton of milk	1 liter	1 quart
yardstick	1 meter	1 yard
distance between highway markers	1 kilometer	1 mile
man's foot	30 centimeters	1 foot
math textbook	1 kilogram	2 pounds
average-sized man	75 kilograms	170 pounds
large paper clip	1 gram	1 ounce
thickness of a dime	2 millimeters	0.1 inch
1 football field	6400 sq. yd.	
boiling point of water	100°C	212°F
freezing point of water	0°C	32°F
1 cup of liquid	240 ml	8 fl. oz.
1 teaspoon	5 ml	

Estimate the measurement of the following items:

The length of an adult cow = _____ meters

The thickness of a compact disc = _____ millimeters

Your height = _____ meters

length of your nose = _____ centimeters

weight of your math textbook = _____ kilograms

weight of an automobile = _____ kilograms

weight of an aspirin = _____ grams

Conversions: unit analysis

There are many methods for converting measurements to other units within a system or between systems. One method is multiplication of the given measurement by a conversion factor. This conversion factor is the following ratio, which is always equal to unity.

$$\frac{\text{new units}}{\text{old units}} \quad \text{OR} \quad \frac{\text{what you want}}{\text{what you have}}$$

The fundamental feature of *unit analysis* or *dimensional analysis* is that conversion factors may be multiplied together and units cancelled in the same way as numerators and denominators of numerical fractions. The following examples help clarify this point.

Example: Convert 3 miles to yards.

Multiply the initial measurement by the conversion factor, cancel the mile units, and solve:

$$\frac{3 \text{ miles}}{1} \times \frac{1760 \text{ yards}}{1 \text{ mile}} = 5280 \text{ yards}$$

Example: It takes Cynthia 45 minutes to get ready each morning. How many hours does she spend getting ready each week?

Multiply the initial measurement by the conversion factors from minutes to hours and from days to weeks, cancel the minute and day units and solve:

$$\frac{45 \text{ min}}{\text{day}} \times \frac{1 \text{ hour}}{60 \text{ min.}} \times \frac{7 \text{ days}}{\text{week}} = \frac{5.25 \text{ hours}}{\text{week}}$$

Conversion factors for different types of units are listed below.

Conversion factors

MEASUREMENTS OF LENGTH (ENGLISH SYSTEM)		
12 inches (in)	=	1 foot (ft)
3 feet (ft)	=	1 yard (yd)
1760 yards (yd)	=	1 mile (mi)

MEASUREMENTS OF LENGTH (METRIC SYSTEM)		
Kilometer (km)	=	1000 meters (m)
Hectometer (hm)	=	100 meters (m)
Decameter (dam)	=	10 meters (m)
Meter (m)	=	1 meter (m)

Continued on next page

Decimeter (dm)	=	$\frac{1}{10}$ meter (m)
Centimeter (cm)	=	$\frac{1}{100}$ meter (m)
Millimeter (mm)	=	$\frac{1}{1000}$ meter (m)

CONVERSION OF WEIGHT FROM METRIC TO ENGLISH		
28.35 grams (g)	=	1 ounce (oz)
16 ounces (oz)	=	1 pound (lb)
2000 pounds (lb)	=	1 ton (t) (short ton)
1 metric ton (t)	=	1.1 ton (t)

MEASUREMENTS OF WEIGHT (METRIC SYSTEM)		
kilogram (kg)	=	1000 grams (g)
gram (g)	=	1 gram (g)
milligram (mg)	=	1/1000 gram (g)

CONVERSION OF VOLUME FROM ENGLISH TO METRIC		
1 teaspoon (tsp)	≈	5 milliliters
1 fluid ounce	≈	15 milliliters
1 cup	≈	0.24 liters
1 pint	≈	0.47 liters

CONVERSION OF WEIGHT FROM ENGLISH TO METRIC		
1 ounce	≈	28.35 grams
1 pound	≈	0.454 kilogram
1.1 ton	=	1 metric ton

MEASUREMENT OF VOLUME (ENGLISH SYSTEM)		
8 fluid ounces (oz)	=	1 cup (c)
2 cups (c)	=	1 pint (pt)
2 pints (pt)	=	1 quart (qt)
4 quarts (qt)	=	1 gallon (gal)

MEASUREMENT OF VOLUME (METRIC SYSTEM)		
Kiloliter (kl)	=	1000 liters (l)
Liter (l)	=	1 liter (l)
Milliliter (ml)	=	$\frac{1}{1000}$ liter (ml)

CONVERSION OF VOLUME FROM ENGLISH TO METRIC		
1 teaspoon (tsp)	≈	5 milliliters
1 fluid ounce	≈	29.57 milliliters
1 cup	≈	0.24 liters
1 pint	≈	0.47 liters
1 quart	≈	0.95 liters
1 gallon	≈	3.8 liters

Note: (') represents feet and (") represents inches.

Example: Convert 8,750 meters to kilometers.

$$\frac{8,750 \text{ meters}}{1} \times \frac{1 \text{ kilometer}}{1000 \text{ meters}} = \underline{\hspace{2cm}} \text{ km}$$
$$= 8.75 \text{ kilometers}$$

Example: 4 mi. = _____ *yd.*

1760 yd. = 1 mi.

$$4 \text{ mi.} \times 1760 \frac{\text{yd.}}{\text{mi.}} = 7040 \text{ yd.}$$

Square units can be derived with knowledge of basic units of length by squaring the equivalent measurements.

> 1 square foot (sq. ft. or ft^2) = 144 sq. in.
> 1 sq. yd. = 9 sq. ft.
> 1 sq. yd. = 1296 sq. in.

Example: 14 sq. yd. = _____ sq. ft.

> 1 sq. yd. = 9 sq. ft.
>
> 14 sq. yd. $\times$ 9 $\frac{\text{sq. ft.}}{\text{sq. yd.}}$ = 126 sq. ft.

Example: A car skidded 170 yards on an icy road before coming to a stop. How long is the skid distance in kilometers?

Since 1 yard $\approx$ 0.9 meters, multiply 170 yards by 0.9 meters/1 yard.

> 170 yd. $\times \frac{0.9 \text{ m}}{1 \text{ yd.}}$ = 153 m

Since 1000 meters = 1 kilometer, multiply 153 meters by 1 kilometer/1000 meters.

> 153 m $\times \frac{1 \text{ km}}{1000 \text{ m}}$ = 0.153 km

Example: The distance around a race course is exactly 1 mile, 17 feet, and $9\frac{1}{4}$ inches. Approximate this distance to the nearest tenth of a foot.

Convert the distance to feet.

> 1 mile = 1760 yards = 1760 $\times$ 3 feet = 5280 feet.
>
> $9\frac{1}{4}$ in. = $\frac{37}{4}$ in. $\times \frac{1 \text{ ft.}}{12 \text{ in.}}$ = $\frac{37}{48}$ ft. = 0.77083 ft.

So 1 mile, 17 ft. and $9\frac{1}{4}$ in. = 5280 ft. + 17 ft. + 0.77083 ft.

> = 5297.$\underline{7}$7083ft.

Now we need to round to the nearest tenth. The underlined 7 is in the tenths place. The digit in the hundredths place, also a 7, is greater than 5. Therefore, the 7 in the tenths place needs to be rounded up to 8 to get a final answer of 5297.8 feet.

Example: If the temperature is 90° F, what is it expressed in Celsius units?

To convert between Celsius (C) and Fahrenheit (F), use the following formula.

> $\frac{C}{5} = \frac{F - 32}{9}$

If F = 90, then C = $5\frac{(90 - 32)}{9} = \frac{5 \times 58}{9}$ = 32.2.

Example: A map shows a scale of 1 inch = 2 miles. Convert this scale to a numerical ratio so that any unit system (such as metric) can be used to measure distances.

The scale is a ratio—1 inch:2 miles. If either value is converted so that the two values have the same units, then this scale can be converted to a purely numerical ratio. To avoid fractions, convert miles to inches.

$$2 \text{ mi} = 2 \text{ mi} \times \frac{5{,}280 \text{ ft}}{1 \text{ mi}} \times \frac{12 \text{ in.}}{1 \text{ ft.}} = 126{,}720 \text{ in.}$$

The ratio is 1:126,720.

SKILL 8.2 Solving mathematical and real-world problems involving measurable attributes of simple or composite figures and shapes (e.g., length, capacity, angle measure)

Area Problems

Some problems involve computing the area that remains when sections are cut out of a given figure composed of triangles, squares, rectangles, parallelograms, trapezoids, or circles. The strategy for solving problems of this nature should be to identify the given shapes and choose the correct formulas. Subtract the smaller cut-out shape from the larger shape.

Example: Find the area of one side of the metal in the circular flat washer shown below:

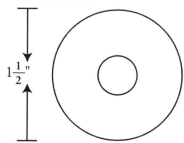

1. The shapes are both circles.

2. Use the formula $A = \pi r^2$ for both.
   (Inside diameter is $\frac{3}{8}$")

Area of larger circle
$A = \pi r^2$
$A = \pi(.75^2)$
$A = 1.76625 \text{ in}^2$

Area of smaller circle
$A = \pi r^2$
$A = \pi(.1875^2)$
$A = .1103906 \text{ in}^2$

Area of metal washer = larger area − smaller area
$\qquad = 1.76625 \text{ in}^2 - .1103906 \text{ in}^2$
$\qquad = 1.65585944 \text{ in}^2$

Example: You have decided to fertilize your lawn. The shapes and dimensions of your lot, house, pool, and garden are given in the diagram below. The shaded area will not be fertilized. If each bag of fertilizer costs $7.95 and covers 4,500 square feet, find the total number of bags needed and the total cost of the fertilizer.

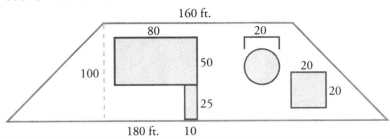

Area of Lot	Area of House	Area of Driveway	Area of Garden	Area of Pool
$A = \frac{1}{2}h(b_1 + b_2)$	$A = LW$	$A = LW$	$A = s^2$	$A = \pi r^2$
$A = \frac{1}{2}(100)(180 + 160)$	$A = (80)(50)$	$A = (10)(25)$	$A = (20)^2$	$A = \pi(10)^2$
A = 17,000 sq ft	A = 4,000 sq ft	A = 250 sq ft	A = 400 sq ft	A = 314.159 sq ft

Total area to fertilize = Lot area − (House + Driveway + Pool + Garden)
$$= 17,000 - (4,000 + 250 + 314.159 + 400)$$
$$= 12,035.841 \text{ sq ft}$$

Number of bags needed = Total area to fertilize/4,500 sq. ft. bag
$$= 12,035.841/4,500$$
$$= 2.67 \text{ bags}$$

Since we cannot purchase 2.67 bags we must purchase 3 full bags.

Total cost = Number of bags × $7.95
$$= 3 \times \$7.95$$
$$= \$23.85$$

Examining the change in area or volume of a given figure requires first finding the existing area given the original dimensions and then finding the new area given the increased dimensions.

Example: Given the rectangle below, determine the change in area if the length is increased by 5 and the width is increased by 7.

7

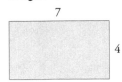

4

Draw and label a sketch of the new rectangle.

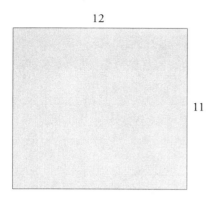

12

11

Find the areas.

Area of original $= LW$ Area of enlarged shape $= LW$

$= (7)(4)$ $= (12)(11)$

$= 28$ units^2 $= 132$ units^2

The change in area is $132 - 28 = 104$ units^2.

To find the area of a compound shape, cut the compound shape into smaller, more familiar shapes, and then compute the total area by adding the areas of the smaller parts.

Example: Find the area of the given shape.

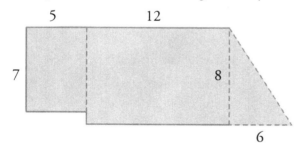

5   12

7   8

6

1. Using a dotted line, we have cut the shape into smaller parts that are familiar

2. Use the appropriate formula for each shape and find the sum of all areas

Area 1 $= LW$ Area 2 $= LW$ Area 3 $= \frac{1}{2}bh$

$= (5)(7)$ $= (12)(8)$ $= \frac{1}{2}(6)(8)$

$= 35$ units^2 $= 96$ units^2 $= 24$ units^2

Total area $=$ Area 1 $+$ Area 2 $+$ Area 3

$= 35 + 96 + 24$

$= 155$ units^2

Volume and Surface Area Problems

Use the following formulas to find volume and surface area.

FIGURE	VOLUME	TOTAL SURFACE AREA
Right Cylinder	$\pi r^2 h$	$2\pi rh + 2\pi r^2$
Right Cone	$\dfrac{\pi r^2 h}{3}$	$\pi r \sqrt{r^2 + h^2} + \pi r^2$
Sphere	$\dfrac{4}{3}\pi r^3$	$4\pi r^2$
Rectangular Solid	LWH	$2LW + 2WH + 2LH$

Note: $\sqrt{r^2 + h^2}$ is equal to the slant height of the cone.

Example: Given the figure below, find the volume and the surface area.

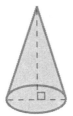

$r = 5$ in
$h = 6.2$ in

Volume $= \dfrac{\pi r^2 h}{3}$ First write the formula.

$= \dfrac{1}{3}\pi(5^2)(6.2)$ Then substitute.

$= 162.23333$ cubic inches   Compute.

Surface area $= \pi r \sqrt{r^2 + h^2} + \pi r^2$ First write the formula.

$= \pi 5 \sqrt{5^2 + 6.2^2} + \pi 5^2$ Then substitute.

$= 203.549$ square inches   Compute.

Note: *Volume is always given in cubic units, and area is always given in square units.*

Area and Perimeter Problems

FIGURE	AREA FORMULA	PERIMETER FORMULA
Rectangle	LW	$2(L + W)$
Triangle	$\dfrac{1}{2}bh$	$a + b + c$
Parallelogram	bh	sum of lengths of sides
Trapezoid	$\dfrac{1}{2}bh(a + b)$	sum of lengths of sides

Example: Find the area and perimeter of a rectangle if its length is 12 inches and its diagonal is 15 inches.

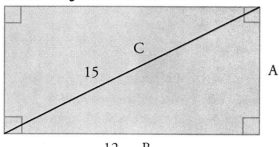

1. Draw and label sketch.
2. Since the height is still needed, use the Pythagorean formula to find missing leg of the triangle.

$A^2 + B^2 = C^2$

$A^2 + 12^2 = 15^2$

$A^2 = 15^2 - 12^2$

$A^2 = 81$

$A = 9$

Now use this information to find the area and perimeter.

$A = LW$	$P = 2(L + W)$	1. Write formula.
$A = (12)(9)$	$P = 2(12 + 9)$	2. Substitute.
$A = 108 \text{ in}^2$	$P = 42$ inches	3. Solve.

Circles

Given a circular figure, the formulas are as follows:

$$A = \pi r^2 \quad C = \pi d \text{ or } 2\pi r$$

Example:

If the area of a circle is 50 cm², find the circumference.

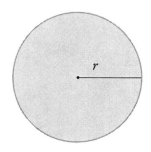

1. Draw a sketch.

$A = 50 \text{ cm}^2$

2. Determine what is still needed.

Use the area formula to find the radius.

$A = \pi r^2$	1. Write the formula.
$50 = \pi r^2$	2. Substitute.
$\frac{50}{\pi} = r^2$	3. Divide by π.
$15.924 = r^2$	4. Substitute.
$\sqrt{15.924} = \sqrt{r^2}$	5. Take the square root of both sides.
$3.99 \approx r$	6. Compute.

Use the approximate answer (due to rounding) to find the circumference.

$A = 2\pi r$	1. Write the formula.
$C = 2\pi(3.99)$	2. Substitute.
$C \approx 25.057$	3. Compute.

When using formulas to solve a geometry problem, it is helpful to use the same strategies used for general problem solving. First, draw and label a sketch if needed. Second, write down the formula and then substitute in the known values. This will assist in identifying what is still needed (the unknown). Finally, solve the resulting equation.

Being consistent in the strategic approach to problem solving is paramount to teaching the concept as well as solving it.

Example: Use the appropriate problem-solving strategies to find the solution.

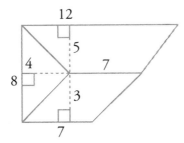

1. Find the area of the given figure.
2. Cut the figure into familiar shapes.
3. Identify what types of figures are given and write the appropriate formulas.

AREA OF FIGURE 1 (TRIANGLE)	AREA OF FIGURE 2 (PARALLELOGRAM)	AREA OF FIGURE 3 (TRAPEZOID)
$A = \frac{1}{2}bh$	$A = bh$	$A = \frac{1}{2}h(a + b)$
$A = \frac{1}{2}(8)(4)$	$A = (7)(3)$	$A = \frac{1}{2}(5)(12 + 7)$
$A = 16$ sq. ft.	$A = 21$ sq. ft.	$A = 47.5$ sq. ft.

Now find the total area by adding the area of all figures:

Total area $= 16 + 21 + 47.5$
$= 84.5$ sq. ft

Example: Given the figure below, find the area by dividing the polygon into smaller shapes.

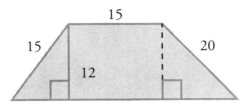

1. Divide the figure into two triangles and a rectangle.
2. Find the missing lengths.
3. Find the area of each part.
4. Find the sum of all of the areas.

Find the base of both right triangles using the Pythagorean formula:

$$a^2 + b^2 = c^2 \qquad\qquad a^2 + b^2 = c^2$$
$$a^2 + 12^2 = 15^2 \qquad\qquad a^2 + 12^2 = 20^2$$
$$a^2 = 225 - 144 \qquad\qquad a^2 = 400 - 144$$
$$a^2 = 81 \qquad\qquad\qquad a^2 = 256$$
$$a = 9 \qquad\qquad\qquad\quad a = 16$$

AREA OF TRIANGLE 1	AREA OF TRIANGLE 2	AREA OF RECTANGLE
$A = \frac{1}{2}bh$	$A = \frac{1}{2}bh$	$A = LW$
$A = \frac{1}{2}(9)(12)$	$A = \frac{1}{2}(16)(12)$	$A = (15)(12)$
$A = 54$ sq. units	$A = 96$ sq. units	$A = 180$ sq. units

Find the sum of all three figures:

$54 + 96 + 180 = 330$ square units

Surface Area and Volume of Geometric Solids

To compute the surface area and volume of right prisms, cones, cylinders, spheres, and solids that are combinations of these figures, use the following formulas:

FIGURE	LATERAL AREA	TOTAL AREA	VOLUME
Right Prism	Ph	$2B + Ph$	Bh
Regular Pyramid	$\frac{1}{2}Pl$	$\frac{1}{2}Pl + B$	$\frac{1}{3}Bh$

P = Perimeter; h = height; B = Area of Base; l = slant height

Example: Find the total area of the given figure.

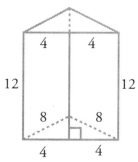

1. Since this is a triangular prism, first find the area of the bases.
2. Find the area of each rectangular lateral face.
3. Add the areas together.

$A = \frac{1}{2}bh$ $A = LW$ 1. Write the formula.

$8^2 = 4^2 + h^2$ 2. Find the height of the base triangle.

                        $A = (8)(12)$ 3. Substitute the known values.

$A = 27.713$ sq. units $A = 96$ sq. units   4. Compute.

Total Area $= 2(27.713) + 3(96)$

              $= 343.426$ sq. units

FIGURE	VOLUME	TOTAL SURFACE AREA	LATERAL AREA
Right Cylinder	$\pi r^2 h$	$2\pi rh + 2\pi r^2$	$2\pi rh$
Right Cone	$\frac{\pi r^2 h}{3}$	$\pi r\sqrt{r^2 + h^2} + \pi r^2$	$\pi r\sqrt{r^2 + h^2}$

Note: $\sqrt{r^2 + h^2}$ is equal to the slant height of the cone.

Example: A water company is trying to decide whether to use traditional cylindrical paper cups or to offer conical paper cups; they both cost the same. The traditional cups are 8 cm wide and 14 cm high. The conical cups are 12 cm wide and 19 cm high. The company will use the cup that holds more water.

Draw and label a sketch of each cup.

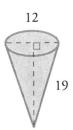

$V = \pi r^2 h$ $V = \frac{\pi r^2 h}{3}$ 1. Write a formula.

$V = \pi(4)^2(14)$ $V = \frac{1}{3}\pi(6)^2(19)$ 2. Substitute.

$V = 703.36$ cm^3 $V = 715.92$ cm^3 3. Solve.

The choice should be the conical cup, since its volume is greater.

FIGURE	VOLUME	TOTAL SURFACE AREA
Sphere	$\frac{4}{3}\pi r^3$	$4\pi r^2$

Example: How much material is needed to make a basketball that has a diameter of 15 inches? How much air is needed to fill the basketball?

Draw and label a sketch:

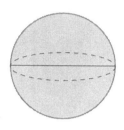

$D = 15$ inches

Total surface area	Volume	
$\text{TSA} = 4\pi r^2$	$V = \frac{4}{3}\pi r^3$	1. Write a formula.
$= 4\pi(7.5)^2$	$= \frac{4}{3}\pi(7.5)^3$	2. Substitute.
$= 706.5 \text{ in}^2$	$= 1766.25 \text{ in}^3$	3. Solve.

SKILL 8.3 Solving mathematical and real-world problems involving indirect measurement *(e.g., proportional reasoning, Pythagorean theorem, trigonometric ratios)*

Pythagorean Theorem

A RIGHT TRIANGLE is a triangle with one right angle. The side opposite the right angle is called the hypotenuse. The other two sides are the legs.

The Pythagorean Theorem states that, for any right triangle, the square of the length of the hypotenuse is equal to the sum of the squares of the lengths of the legs. Symbolically, this is stated as $c^2 = a^2 + b^2$.

Example: Given the right triangle below, find the missing side.

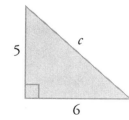

$c^2 = a^2 + b^2$	1. Write a formula.
$c^2 = 5^2 + 6^2$	2. Substitute known values.
$c^2 = 61$	3. Simplify.
$c = \sqrt{61}$ or 7.81	4. Take square root.

The Converse of the Pythagorean Theorem states that if the square of the longest side of a triangle is equal to the sum of the squares of the other two sides, the triangle is a right triangle.

> **RIGHT TRIANGLE:** a triangle with one right angle

> *The Pythagorean Theorem states that, for any right triangle, the square of the length of the hypotenuse is equal to the sum of the squares of the lengths of the legs.*

The Converse of the Pythagorean Theorem states that if the square of the longest side of a triangle is equal to the sum of the squares of the other two sides, the triangle is a right triangle.

Example: Given $\triangle XYZ$, with sides measuring 12, 16, and 20 cm, is this a right triangle?

$$c^2 = a^2 + b^2$$
$$20^2 \underset{?}{=} 12^2 + 16^2$$
$$400 \underset{?}{=} 144 + 256$$
$$400 = 400$$

Yes, the triangle is a right triangle.

This theorem can be expanded to determine if triangles are obtuse or acute.

If the square of the longest side of a triangle is greater than the sum of the squares of the other two sides, the triangle is an obtuse triangle. If the square of the longest side of a triangle is less than the sum of the squares of the other two sides, the triangle is an acute triangle.

Example: Given $\triangle LMN$ with sides measuring 7, 12, and 14 inches, is the triangle right, acute, or obtuse?

$$14^2 \underset{?}{=} 7^2 + 12^2$$
$$196 \underset{?}{=} 49 + 144$$
$$196 > 193$$

The triangle is obtuse.

When an altitude is drawn to the hypotenuse of a right triangle, the two triangles formed are similar to the original triangle and to each other.

When an altitude is drawn to the hypotenuse of a right triangle, the two triangles formed are similar to the original triangle and to each other.

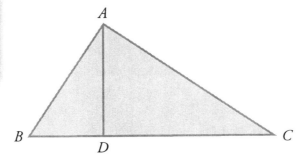

Given right triangle ABC with right angle at A, altitude AD drawn to hypotenuse BC at D, $\triangle ABC \sim \triangle ABD \sim \triangle ACD$.

GEOMETRIC MEAN: if a, b, and c are positive numbers such that $\frac{a}{b} = \frac{b}{c}$, then b is called the geometric mean of a and c

If a, b, and c are positive numbers such that $\frac{a}{b} = \frac{b}{c}$, b is called the **GEOMETRIC MEAN** of a and c.

The geometric mean is significant when the altitude is drawn to the hypotenuse of a right triangle.

The length of the altitude is the geometric mean between each segment of the hypotenuse. Also, each leg is the geometric mean between the hypotenuse and the segment of the hypotenuse that is adjacent to the leg.

Example:

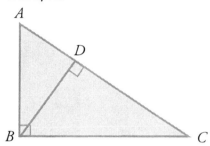

ΔABC is a right triangle and $\angle ABC$ is a right angle. $AB = 6$ and $AC - 12$. Find AD, CD, BD, and BC.

$$\frac{12}{6} = \frac{6}{AD} \qquad \frac{3}{BD} = \frac{BD}{9} \qquad \frac{12}{BC} = \frac{BC}{9}$$

$$12(AD) = 36 \qquad (BD)^2 = 27 \qquad (BC)^2 = 108$$

$$AD = 3$$

$$BD = \sqrt{27} = \sqrt{9 \times 3} = 3\sqrt{3}$$

$$BC = 6\sqrt{3}$$

$$CD = 12 - 3 = 9$$

Trigonometic Ratios

Trigonometric functions can be related to right triangles: each trigonometric function corresponds to a ratio of certain sides of the triangle with respect to a particular angle. Thus, given the generic right triangle diagram below, the following functions can be specified.

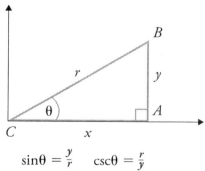

$$\sin\theta = \frac{y}{r} \qquad \csc\theta = \frac{r}{y}$$
$$\cos\theta = \frac{x}{r} \qquad \sec\theta = \frac{r}{x}$$
$$\tan\theta = \frac{y}{x} \qquad \cot\theta = \frac{x}{y}$$

Based on these definitions, the unknown characteristics of a particular right triangle can be calculated based on certain known characteristics. For instance, if the hypotenuse and one of the adjacent angles are both known, the lengths of the other two sides of the triangle can be calculated.

Trigonometry can also be understood in terms of a unit circle on the *x-y* plane. A unit circle has a radius of 1.

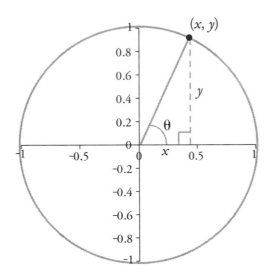

Notice that any given radius forms a right triangle with legs having lengths equal to the position of the point on the circle (*x*, *y*). Since the radius is equal to 1, the values of *x* and *y* are the following:

$$x = \cos\theta$$
$$y = \sin\theta$$

All the properties of trigonometric relationships for right triangles apply in this case as well.

The argument of a trigonometric function is an angle that is typically expressed in either degrees or radians. A DEGREE constitutes an angle corresponding to a sector that is $\frac{1}{360}$ of a circle. Therefore, a circle has 360 degrees. A RADIAN, on the other hand, is the angle corresponding to a sector of a circle where the arc length of the sector is equal to the radius of the circle. In the case of the unit circle (a circle of radius 1), the circumference is 2π. Thus, there are 2π radians in a circle. Conversion between degrees and radians is a simple matter of using the ratio between the total degrees in a circle and the total radians in a circle.

$$\text{(degrees)} = \frac{180}{\pi} \times \text{(radians)}$$
$$\text{(radians)} = \frac{\pi}{180} \times \text{(degrees)}$$

DEGREE: an angle corresponding to a sector that is $\frac{1}{360}$ of a circle

RADIAN: the angle corresponding to a sector of a circle where the arc length of the sector is equal to the radius of the circle

Trigonometric ratios can be used to solve problems involving distances and angles as in the examples below.

Example: Find the length of side x in the triangle below.

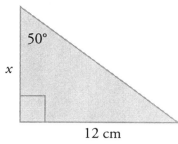

$$\tan 50 = \frac{\text{opposite}}{\text{adjacent}} = \frac{12}{x}$$
$$1.192 = \frac{12}{x}$$
$$x(1.192) = 12$$
$$x = 10.07 \text{ cm}$$

Trigonometric functions can also be applied to nonright triangles by way of the law of sines and the law of cosines. Consider the arbitrary triangle shown below with angles A, B, and C and corresponding opposite sides a, b, and c.

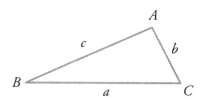

The law of sines is a proportional relationship between the lengths of the sides of the triangle and the opposite angles. The law of sines is given below:
$$\frac{a}{\sin A} = \frac{b}{\sin B} = \frac{c}{\sin C}$$

The law of cosines permits determination of the length of a side of an arbitrary triangle as long as the lengths of the other two sides, along with the angle opposite the unknown side, are known. The law of cosines is given below:
$$c^2 = a^2 + b^2 - 2ab \cos C$$

Example: An inlet is 140 feet wide. The lines of sight from each bank to an approaching ship are 79 degrees and 58 degrees. What are the distances from each bank to the ship?

First, draw an appropriate sketch of the situation with the appropriate labels for the parameters.

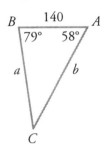

Since the sum of the angles in a triangle is 180°, angle C must be 43°. Use the law of sines to calculate the lengths of sides a and b.

For side b:
$$\frac{b}{\sin 79°} = \frac{140 \text{ feet}}{\sin 43°}$$
$$b = \frac{\sin 79°}{\sin 43°} 140 \text{ feet} \approx 201.5 \text{ feet}$$

And for side a:
$$\frac{a}{\sin 58°} = \frac{140 \text{ feet}}{\sin 43°}$$
$$a = \frac{\sin 58°}{\sin 43°} 140 \text{ feet} \approx 174.1 \text{ feet}$$

Example: Find side b in the triangle below if angle B = 87.5°, a = 12.3, and c = 23.2. (Compute to the nearest tenth).

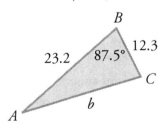

$$b^2 = a^2 + c^2 - (2ac)\cos B$$
$$b^2 = (12.3)^2 + (23.2)^2 - 2(12.3)(23.2)(\cos 87.5)$$
$$b^2 = 664.636$$
$$b = 25.8$$

Proportional Reasoning

Similar solids share the same shape but are not necessarily the same size. The ratio of any two corresponding measurements of similar solids is the scale factor.

For example, the scale factor for two square pyramids, one with a side measuring 2 inches and the other with a side measuring 4 inches, is 2:4.

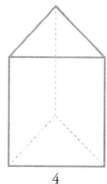

2   4

The base perimeter, the surface area, and the volume of similar solids are directly related to the scale factor. If the scale factor of two similar solids is $a{:}b$, then

- ratio of base perimeters $= a{:}b$

- ratio of areas $= a^2{:}b^2$

- ratio of volumes $= a^3{:}b^3$

Thus, for the above example,

- ratio of base perimeters $= 2{:}4$

- ratio of areas $= 2^2{:}4^2 = 4{:}16$

- ratio of volumes $= 2^3{:}4^3 = 8{:}64$

Example: What happens to the volume of a square pyramid when the lengths of the sides of the base are doubled?

scale factor $= a{:}b = 1{:}2$
ratio of volume $= 1^3{:}2^3 = 1{:}8$

The volume is increased 8 times.

Example: Given the following measurements for two similar cylinders with a scale factor of 2:5 (cylinder A to cylinder B), determine the height, radius, and volume of each cylinder.

cylinder A:$r = 2$
cylinder B:$h = 10$

For cylinder A,
$$\frac{h_a}{10} = \frac{2}{5}$$
$$5h_a = 20 \quad \text{Solve for } h_a$$
$$h_a = 4$$
Volume of cylinder A $= \pi r^2 h = \pi(2)^2 4 = 16\pi$

For cylinder B,

$$\frac{2}{r_b} = \frac{2}{5}$$

$$2r_b = 10 \quad \text{Solve for } r_b$$

$$r_b = 5$$

Volume of cylinder B $= \pi r^2 h = \pi(5)^2 10 = 250\pi$

SKILL 8.4 **Solving problems involving the effects of changing the dimensions of a figure or shape on its area and volume**

For examples of the effects of changing dimensions, see Skills 8.2 and 8.3.

COMPETENCY 9
ANALYZE FIGURES AND SHAPES IN TWO AND THREE DIMENSIONS

SKILL 9.1 **Demonstrating knowledge of the axioms of Euclidean geometry** *(e.g., points, lines, planes, angles)*

POINT: a dimensionless location that has no length, width, or height

LINE: connects a series of points and continues "straight" infinitely in two directions

LINE SEGMENT: a portion of a line; it has two endpoints

Euclidean geometry is the study of the properties of two-dimensional (planar) and three-dimensional (solid) figures. It is based on the undefined concepts of point, line, and plane and a set of self-evident statements or axioms. Starting from these building blocks, deductive reasoning is used to prove a set of propositions or theorems about the properties of different geometric figures. The axioms and theorems and the process of formal proof provide a consistent logical framework that can be used to derive further results.

A POINT is a dimensionless location and has no length, width, or height.

A LINE connects a series of points and continues "straight" infinitely in two directions. Lines extend in one dimension. A line is defined by any two points that fall on the line; therefore, a line may have multiple names.

A LINE SEGMENT is a portion of a line. A line segment is the shortest distance between two endpoints and is named using those endpoints. Line segments therefore have exactly two names (e.g., $\overline{AB}$ or $\overline{BA}$). Because line segments have two endpoints, they have a defined length or distance.

A RAY is a portion of a line that has only one endpoint and continues infinitely in one direction. Rays are named using the endpoint as the first point and any other point on the ray as the second.

Note that the symbol for a line includes two arrows (indicating infinite extent in both directions), the symbol for a ray includes only one arrow (indicating that it has one endpoint), and the symbol for a line segment has no arrows (indicating two endpoints).

Example: Use the diagram below, calculate the length of $\overline{AB}$ given that $\overline{AC}$ is 6 cm and $\overline{BC}$ is twice as long as $\overline{AB}$.

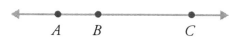

$\overline{AB} + \overline{BC} = \overline{AC}$
Let $x = \overline{AB}$
$x + 2x = 6$ cm
$3x = 6$ cm
$x - 2$ cm

A PLANE is a flat surface defined by three points. Planes extend indefinitely in two dimensions. A common example of a plane is the *x-y* plane used in the Cartesian coordinate system.

In geometry, the point, the line, and the plane are key concepts and can be discussed in relation to each other.

Collinear points
are all on the same line.

Noncollinear points
are not on the same line.

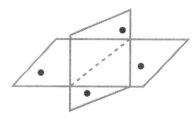

Coplanar points
are on the same plane.

Noncoplanar points
are not on the same plane.

Problems throughout this competency illustrate the use of these various geometric elements in the solution of problems.

> **SKILL 9.2** **Applying the properties of polygons and circles to solve mathematical and real-world problems**

Polygons

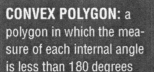

POLYGON: a simple closed figure composed of line segments

CONVEX POLYGON: a polygon in which the measure of each internal angle is less than 180 degrees

REGULAR POLYGON: a polygon for which all sides are the same length and all interior angles are the same measure

A **POLYGON** is a simple closed figure composed of line segments. Here we will consider only **CONVEX POLYGONS**, i.e., polygons for which the measure of each internal angle is less than 180°. Of the two polygons shown below, the one on the left is a convex polygon.

A **REGULAR POLYGON** is one for which all sides are the same length and all interior angles are the same measure.

The sum of the measures of the interior angles of a polygon can be determined using the following formula, where n represents the number of angles in the polygon.

$$\text{Sum of } \angle s = 180(n - 2)$$

The measure of each angle of a regular polygon can be found by dividing the sum of the measures by the number of angles.

$$\text{Measure of } \angle = \frac{180(n - 2)}{n}$$

Example: Find the measure of each angle of a regular octagon. Since an octagon has eight sides, each angle equals

$$\frac{180(8 - 2)}{8} = \frac{180(6)}{8} = 135°.$$

The sum of the measures of the *exterior angles* of a polygon, taken one angle at each vertex, equals 360°.

The measure of each exterior angle of a regular polygon can be determined using the following formula, where n represents the number of angles in the polygon.

Measure of exterior $\angle$ of regular polygon

$$\angle = 180 - \frac{180(n - 2)}{n} = \frac{360}{n}$$

Example: Find the measure of the interior and exterior angles of a regular pentagon.

Since a pentagon has five sides, each exterior angle measures:

$\frac{360}{5} = 72°$

Since each exterior angle is supplementary to its interior angle, the interior angle measures $180 - 72$, or $108°$.

Properties of Quadrilaterals

A QUADRILATERAL is a polygon with four sides. The sum of the measures of the angles of a convex quadrilateral is 360°.

A TRAPEZOID is a quadrilateral with exactly one pair of parallel sides.

The two parallel sides of a trapezoid are called the bases, and the two nonparallel sides are called the legs. If the two legs are the same length, then the trapezoid is called an ISOSCELES TRAPEZOID.

The segment connecting the midpoints of the legs is called the median. The median has the following two properties:

1. The median is parallel to the two bases.

2. The length of the median is equal to one-half the sum of the length of the two bases.

In an isosceles trapezoid, the nonparallel sides are congruent.

An isosceles trapezoid has the following properties:

1. The diagonals of an isosceles trapezoid are congruent.

2. The base angles of an isosceles trapezoid are congruent.

> **QUADRILATERAL:** a polygon with four sides
>
> **TRAPEZOID:** a quadrilateral with exactly one pair of parallel sides
>
> **ISOSCELES TRAPEZOID:** a trapezoid with two legs of equal length

Example: An isosceles trapezoid has a diagonal of 10 and a base angle measuring 30°. Find the measure of the other three angles.

Based on the properties of trapezoids, the measure of the other base angle is 30° and the measure of the other diagonal is 10. The other two angles have a measure of:

$$360 = 30(2) + 2x$$
$$x = 150°$$

The other two angles measure 150° each.

PARALLELOGRAM: a quadrilateral with two pairs of parallel sides

A **PARALLELOGRAM** is a quadrilateral with two pairs of parallel sides. A parallelogram has the following properties:

1. The diagonals bisect each other.

2. Each diagonal divides the parallelogram into two congruent triangles.

3. Both pairs of opposite sides are congruent.

4. Both pairs of opposite angles are congruent.

5. Two adjacent angles are supplementary.

Example: Find the measures of the other three angles of a parallelogram if one angle measures 38°.

Since opposite angles are equal, there are two angles measuring 38°. Since adjacent angles are supplementary, $180 - 38 = 142$. Hence, the other two angles measure 142° each.

Example: The measures of two adjacent angles of a parallelogram are 3x + 40 and x + 70. Find the measure of each angle.

$$2(3x + 40) + 2(x + 70) = 360$$
$$6x + 80 + 2x + 140 = 360$$
$$8x + 220 = 360$$
$$8x = 140$$
$$x = 17.5$$
$$3x + 40 = 92.5$$
$$x + 70 = 87.5$$

Thus the angles measure 92.5°, 92.5°, 87.5°, and 87.5°.

RECTANGLE: a parallelogram with a right angle

A **RECTANGLE** is a parallelogram with a right angle. Since a rectangle is a special type of parallelogram, it exhibits all the properties of a parallelogram. All the angles of a rectangle are right angles because of congruent opposite angles. Additionally, the diagonals of a rectangle are congruent.

A RHOMBUS is a parallelogram with all sides equal in length. A rhombus has all the properties of a parallelogram. Additionally, its diagonals are perpendicular to each other, and they bisect its angles.

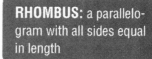

RHOMBUS: a parallelogram with all sides equal in length

A SQUARE is a rectangle with all sides equal in length. A square has all the properties of a rectangle and of a rhombus.

SQUARE: a rectangle with all sides equal in length

TRUE OR FALSE?	
All squares are rhombuses	True
All parallelograms are rectangles	False—*Some* parallelograms are rectangles
All rectangles are parallelograms	True
Some rhombuses are squares	True
Some rectangles are trapezoids	False—Trapezoids have only one pair of parallel sides
All quadrilaterals are parallelograms	False—*Some* quadrilaterals are parallelograms
Some squares are rectangles	False—*All* squares are rectangles
Some parallelograms are rhombuses	True

Example: In rhombus ABCD, side AB = 3x − 7 and side CD = x + 15. Find the length of each side.

Since all the sides are the same length,

$$3x - 7 = x + 15$$
$$2x = 22$$
$$x = 11$$

Since $3(11) - 7 = 25$ and $11 + 15 = 25$, each side measures 25 units.

Circles

The distance around a circle is called the CIRCUMFERENCE. The ratio of the circumference to the diameter is represented by the Greek letter pi (π), where $\pi \approx 3.14$. The circumference of a circle is given by the formula $C = 2\pi r$ or $C = \pi d$, where r is the radius of the circle and d is the diameter. The area of a circle is given by the formula $A = \pi r^2$.

> **CIRCUMFERENCE:** the distance around a circle

We can extend the area formula of a regular polygon to obtain the area of a circle by considering the fact that a circle is essentially a regular polygon with an infinite number of sides. The radius of a circle is equivalent to the apothem of a regular polygon. Thus, applying the area formula for a regular polygon to a circle, we get $\frac{1}{2} \times perimeter \times apothem = \frac{1}{2} \times 2\pi r \times r = \pi r^2$.

If two circles have radii that are in a ratio of $a{:}b$, then the following ratios also apply to the circles:

1. The diameters are in the ratio $a{:}b$

2. The circumferences are in the ratio $a{:}b$

3. The areas are in the ratio $a^2{:}b^2$, or the ratio of the areas is the square of the ratio of the radii.

> **CENTRAL ANGLE:** the angle formed by two radii that intersect in the center of a circle

If you draw two radii in a circle, the angle they form with the center as the vertex is a CENTRAL ANGLE. The piece of the circle "inside" the angle is an arc. Just like a central angle, an arc can have any degree measure from 0 to 360. The measure of an arc is equal to the measure of the central angle that forms the arc. Since a diameter forms a semicircle and the measure of a straight angle like a diameter is 180°, the measure of a semicircle is also 180°.

> **MINOR ARC:** an arc with measure less than 180°

Given two points on a circle, the two points form two different arcs. Except in the case of semicircles, one of the two arcs will always be greater than 180°, and the other will be less than 180°. The arc less than 180° is a MINOR ARC and the arc greater than 180° is a MAJOR ARC.

> **MAJOR ARC:** an arc with measure greater than 180°

Examples:

1.

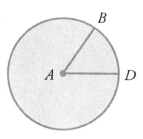

$m\sphericalangle BAD = 45°$

What is the measure of the major arc *BD*?

minor arc $BD = m\sphericalangle BAD = 45°$

$360 - 45 = $ major arc *BD*

Thus, major arc $BD = 315°$.

A major and minor arc always add up to 360°.

2.

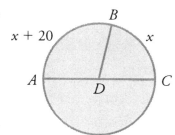

$\overline{AC}$ is a diameter of circle *D*.

What is the measure of $\sphericalangle BDC$?

$m\sphericalangle ADB + m\sphericalangle BDC = 180°$

$x + 20 + x = 180$

$2x + 20 = 180$

$2x = 160$

$x = 80$

A diameter forms a semicircle that has a measure of 180°.

minor arc $BC = 80°$

$m\sphericalangle BDC = 80°$

A central angle has the same measure as the arc it forms.

Although an arc has a measure associated to the degree measure of a central angle, it also has a length that is a fraction of the circumference of the circle. For each central angle and its associated arc, there is a sector of the circle that resembles a pie piece. The area of such a sector is a fraction of the area of the circle. The fractions used for the area of a sector and length of its associated arc are both equal to the ratio of the central angle to 360°.

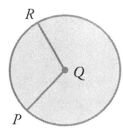

$$\frac{\angle PQR}{360°} = \frac{\text{length of arc } RP}{\text{circumference of circle}} = \frac{\text{area of sector } PQR}{\text{area of circle}}$$

Examples:

1.

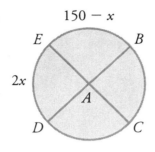

$$2x + 150 - x = 180$$
$$x + 150 = 180$$
$$x = 30$$

Arc $ED = 2(30) = 60°$

$$\frac{60}{360} = \frac{\text{arc length } ED}{2\pi 4}$$
$$\frac{1}{6} = \frac{\text{arc length}}{8\pi}$$
arc length $= \frac{8\pi}{6} = \frac{4\pi}{3}$

Circle A as a radius of 4 cm. What is the length of arc ED?

Arc BE and arc ED make a semicircle.

The ratio 60° to 360° is equal to the ratio of arc length ED to the circumference of circle A.

Cross-multiply and solve for the arc length.

2.

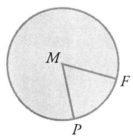

Circumference of circle $M = 2\pi(3) = 6\pi$

Area of circle $M = \pi \times 3^2 = 9\pi$

$$\frac{\text{area of } MPF}{9\pi} = \frac{2\pi}{6\pi}$$

$$\frac{\text{area of } MPF}{9\pi} = \frac{1}{3}$$
area of $MPF = \frac{9\pi}{3}$
area of $MPF = 3\pi$

The radius of circle M is 3 cm. The length of arc PF is 2π cm. What is the area of sector MPF?

Find the circumference and area of the circle.

The ratio of the sector area to the circle area is the same as that of the arc length to the circumference.

Solve for the area of the sector.

TANGENT LINE: a line that intersects or touches a circle in exactly one point

A **TANGENT LINE** to a circle intersects or touches the circle in exactly one point. If a radius is drawn to that point, the radius will be perpendicular to the tangent.

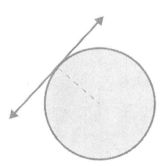

A SECANT LINE intersects a circle in two points and includes a CHORD, which is a line segment with endpoints on the circle. If a radius or diameter is perpendicular to a chord, the radius will cut the chord into two equal parts, and vice versa.

SECANT LINE: a line that intersects a circle in two points

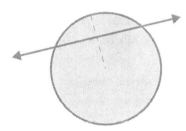

CHORD: a line segment with endpoints on a circle

If two chords in the same circle have the same length, the two chords will have arcs that are the same length, and the two chords will be equidistant from the center of the circle. Distance from the center to a chord is measured by finding the length of a segment from the center perpendicular to the chord.

Examples:

1.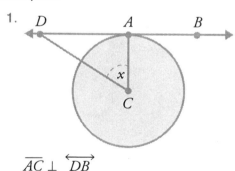

$\overleftrightarrow{DB}$ is tangent to circle C at A.
$m\angle ADC = 40°$. Find x.

$\overline{AC} \perp \overleftrightarrow{DB}$

A radius is $\perp$ to a tangent at the point of tangency.

$m\angle DAC = 90°$

Two segments that are $\perp$ form a 90° angle.

$40 + 90 + x = 180$

The sum of the angles of a triangle is 180°.

$x = 50°$

Solve for x.

2.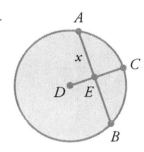

$\overline{CD}$ is a radius and
$\overline{CD} \perp$ chord $\overline{AB}$.

$\overline{AB} = 10$. Find x.

$x = \frac{1}{2}(10)$
$x = 5$

If a radius is $\perp$ to a chord, the
radius bisects the chord.

> **INSCRIBED ANGLE:** an angle whose vertex is on the circumference of a circle

An **INSCRIBED ANGLE** is an angle whose vertex is on the circumference of a circle. Such an angle could be formed by two chords, two diameters, two secants, or a secant and a tangent. An inscribed angle has one arc of the circle in its interior. The measure of the inscribed angle is one-half the measure of its intercepted arc. If two inscribed angles intercept the same arc, the two angles are congruent (i.e. their measures are equal). If an inscribed angle intercepts an entire semicircle, the angle is a right angle.

When two chords intersect inside a circle, two sets of vertical angles are formed in the interior of the circle. Each set of vertical angles intercepts two arcs that are across from each other. The measure of an angle formed by two chords in a circle is equal to one-half the sum of the arc intercepted by the angle and the arc intercepted by its vertical angle.

If an angle has its vertex outside of the circle and each side of the angle intersects the circle, then the angle contains two different arcs. The measure of the angle is equal to one-half the difference of the two arcs.

Examples:

1.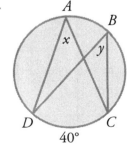
40°

Find x and y.

$m \angle DAC = \frac{1}{2}(40) = 20°$

$\angle DAC$ and $\angle DBC$ are both inscribed angles, so each one has a measure equal to one-half the measure of arc DC.

$m \angle DBC = \frac{1}{2}(40) = 20°$
$x = 20°$ and $y = 20°$

2.

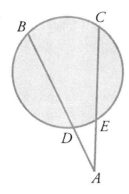

Find the measure of arc BC if the measure of arc DE is 30° and angle $BAC = 20$°.

$$m\angle BAC = \tfrac{1}{2}(mBC - mDE)$$
$$\rightarrow 2 \times m\angle BAC = mBC - mDE$$
$$\rightarrow mBC = 2 \times m\angle BAC + mDE = 2 \times 20° + 30° = 70°$$

If *two chords intersect inside a circle*, each chord is divided into two smaller segments. The product of the lengths of the two segments formed from one chord equals the product of the lengths of the two segments formed from the other chord.

If *two tangent segments intersect outside of a circle*, the two segments have the same length.

If *two secant segments intersect outside a circle*, a portion of each segment will lie inside the circle and a portion (called the exterior segment) will lie outside the circle. The product of the length of one secant segment and the length of its exterior segment equals the product of the length of the other secant segment and the length of its exterior segment.

If *a tangent segment and a secant segment intersect outside a circle*, the square of the length of the tangent segment equals the product of the length of the secant segment and its exterior segment.

Examples:

1.

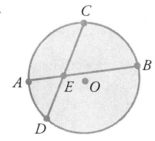

$\overline{AB}$ and $\overline{CD}$ are chords.

$CE = 10$, $ED = x$, $AE = 5$, $EB = 4$

$(AE)(EB) = (CE)(ED)$ Since the chords intersect in the circle, the products of the segment pieces are equal.

$5(4) = 10x$
$20 = 10x$
$x = 2$ Solve for x.

2.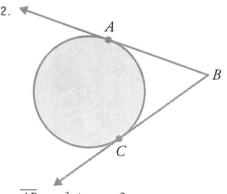

$\overline{AB}$ and $\overline{CD}$ are chords.

$\overline{AB} = x^2 + x - 2$

$\overline{CB} = 5 - 3x + x^2$

Find the length of $\overline{AB}$ and $\overline{BC}$

$\overline{AB} = x^2 + x - 2$
$\overline{BC} = x^2 - 3x + 5$

Given.

$\overline{AB} = \overline{BC}$

Intersecting tangents are equal.

$x^2 + x - 2 = x^2 - 3x + 5$

Set the expressions equal to each other and solve.

$4x = 7$
$x = 1.75$
$(1.75)^2 + 1.75 - 2 = \overline{AB}$
$\overline{AB} = \overline{BC} = 2.81$

Substitute and solve.

SKILL 9.3 **Applying the properties of two- and three-dimensional shapes to solve mathematical and real-world problems**

Congruence

CONGRUENT: having the same size and shape

CONGRUENT figures have the same size and shape; i.e., if one of the figures is superimposed on the other, the boundaries coincide exactly. Congruent line segments have the same length; congruent angles have equal measures. The symbol ≅ is used to indicate that two figures, line segments, or angles are congruent.

The reflexive, symmetric, and transitive properties described for algebraic equality relationships may also be applied to congruence. For instance, if $\angle A \cong \angle B$ and $\angle A \cong \angle D$, then $\angle B \cong \angle D$ (transitive property).

The polygons (pentagons) *ABCDE* and *VWXYZ* shown below are congruent since they are exactly the same size and shape.

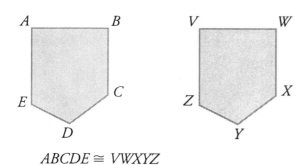

$ABCDE \cong VWXYZ$

Corresponding parts are congruent angles and congruent sides. For the polygons shown above:

corresponding angles   corresponding sides

$\angle A \leftrightarrow \angle V$ $AB \leftrightarrow VW$

$\angle B \leftrightarrow \angle W$ $BC \leftrightarrow WX$

$\angle C \leftrightarrow \angle X$ $CD \leftrightarrow XY$

$\angle D \leftrightarrow \angle Y$ $DE \leftrightarrow YZ$

$\angle E \leftrightarrow \angle Z$ $AE \leftrightarrow VZ$

Two triangles are congruent if each of the three angles and three sides of one triangle match up in a one-to-one fashion with the corresponding angles and sides of the second triangle. To see how the sides and angles match up, it is sometimes necessary to imagine rotating or reflecting one of the triangles so the two figures are oriented in the same position.

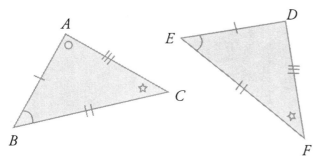

In the example above, the two triangles ABC and DEF are congruent if these 6 conditions are met:

1. $\angle A \cong \angle D$ 4. $\overline{AB} \cong \overline{DE}$

2. $\angle B \cong \angle E$ 5. $\overline{BC} \cong \overline{EF}$

3. $\angle C \cong \angle F$ 6. $\overline{AC} \cong \overline{DF}$

The congruent angles and segments "correspond" to each other.

It is not always necessary to demonstrate all of the above six conditions to prove that two triangles are congruent. There are several "shortcut" methods described below.

SAS POSTULATE: (also called side-angle-side) if two sides and the included angle of one triangle are congruent to two sides and the included angle of another triangle, then the two triangles are congruent

The **SAS POSTULATE** (side-angle-side) states that if two sides and the included angle of one triangle are congruent to two sides and the included angle of another triangle, then the two triangles are congruent.

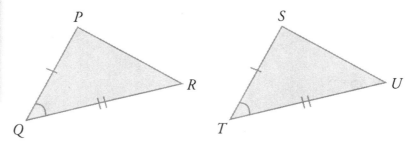

To see why this is true, imagine moving the triangle *PQR* (shown above) in such a way that the point *P* coincides with the point *S*, and line segment *PQ* coincides with line segment *ST*. Point *Q* will then coincide with *T*, since $PQ \cong ST$. Also, segment *QR* will coincide with *TU*, because $\angle Q \cong \angle T$. Point *R* will coincide with *U*, because $QR \cong TU$. Since *P* and *S* coincide and *R* and *U* coincide, *PR* will coincide with *SU* because two lines cannot enclose a space. Thus the two triangles match perfectly point for point and are congruent.

Example: Are the following triangles congruent?

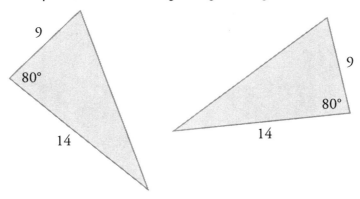

Each of the two triangles has a side that is 14 units and another that is 9 units. The angle included in the sides is 80° in both triangles. Therefore, the triangles are congruent by SAS.

SSS POSTULATE: (also called side-side-side) if three sides of one triangle are congruent to three sides of another triangle, then the two triangles are congruent

The **SSS POSTULATE** (side-side-side) states that if the three sides of one triangle are congruent to the three sides of another triangle, then the two triangles are congruent.

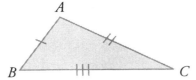

Since $AB \cong XY$, $BC \cong YZ$ and $AC \cong XZ$, then $\triangle ABC \cong \triangle XYZ$.

Example: Given isosceles triangle ABC with D being the midpoint of base AC, prove that triangles ABD and ADC are congruent.

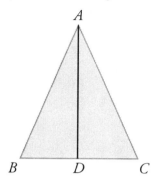

Proof:

1. Isosceles triangle *ABC*,
   D midpoint of base *AC*   Given

2. $AB \cong AC$ An isosceles triangle has two congruent sides

3. $BD \cong DC$ Midpoint divides a line into two equal parts

4. $AD \cong AD$ Reflexive property

5. $\triangle ABD \cong \triangle BCD$ SSS

The **ASA POSTULATE** (angle-side-angle) states that if two angles and the included side of one triangle are congruent to two angles and the included side of another triangle, the triangles are congruent.

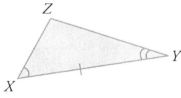

$\angle A \cong \angle X$, $\angle B \cong \angle Y$, $AB \cong XY$ then $\triangle ABC \cong \triangle XYZ$ by ASA

> **ASA POSTULATE:** (also called angle-side-angle) if two angles and the included side of one triangle are congruent to two angles and the included side of another triangle, the triangles are congruent

Example: Given two right triangles with one leg (AB and KL) of each measuring 6 cm and the adjacent angle 37°, prove the triangles are congruent.

Proof:

1. Right $\triangle ABC$ and $\triangle KLM$ Given
    $AB = KL = 6$ cm
    $\angle A = \angle K = 37°$

2. $AB \cong KL$; $\angle A \cong \angle K$ Figures with the same measure are congruent

3. $\angle B \cong \angle L$ All right angles are congruent

4. $\triangle ABC \cong \triangle KLM$ ASA

Example: What method could be used to prove that triangles ABC and ADE are congruent?

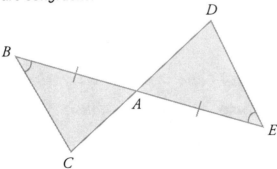

The sides AB and AE are given as congruent, as are $\angle BAC$ and $\angle DAE$. $\angle BAC$ and $\angle DAE$ are vertical angles and are therefore congruent. Thus triangles ABC and ADE are congruent by the ASA postulate.

The **HL THEOREM** (hypotenuse-leg) is a congruence shortcut that can only be used with right triangles. According to this theorem, if the hypotenuse and leg of one right triangle are congruent to the hypotenuse and leg of the other right triangle, then the two triangles are congruent.

> **HL THEOREM:** if the hypotenuse and leg of one right triangle are congruent to the hypotenuse and leg of another right triangle, then the two triangles are congruent

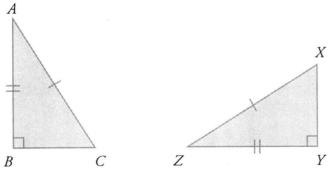

If $\angle B$ and $\angle Y$ are right angles and $AC \cong XZ$ (hypotenuse of each triangle), $AB \cong YZ$ (corresponding leg of each triangle), then $\triangle ABC \cong \triangle XYZ$ by HL.

Proof:

1. $\angle B \cong \angle Y$
   $AB \cong YZ$
   $AC \cong XZ$ Given

2. $BC = \sqrt{AC^2 - AB^2}$ Pythagorean theorem

3. $XY = \sqrt{XZ^2 - YZ^2}$ Pythagorean theorem

4. $XY = \sqrt{AC^2 - AB^2} = BC$ Substitution ($XZ \cong AC$, $YZ \cong AB$)

5. $\triangle ABC \cong \triangle XYZ$ SAS ($AB \cong YZ$, $\angle B \cong \angle Y$, $BC \cong XY$)

Similarity

Two figures that have the same shape are **SIMILAR**. To be the same shape, corresponding angles must be equal. Therefore, polygons are similar if and only if there is a one-to-one correspondence between their vertices such that the corresponding angles are congruent. For similar figures, the lengths of corresponding sides are proportional. The symbol ~ is used to indicate that two figures are similar.

> **SIMILAR:** having the same shape but not necessarily the same size

> *For similar figures, the lengths of corresponding sides are proportional.*

The polygons *ABCDE* and *VWXYZ* shown below are similar.

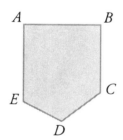 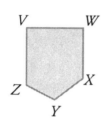

ABCDE ~ VWXYZ

Corresponding angles: $\angle A = \angle V$, $\angle B = \angle W$, $\angle C = \angle X$, $\angle D = \angle Y$, $\angle E = \angle Z$

Corresponding sides: $\frac{AB}{VW} = \frac{BC}{WX} = \frac{CD}{XY} = \frac{DE}{YZ} = \frac{AE}{VZ}$

Example: Given two similar quadrilaterals, find the lengths of sides x, y, and z.

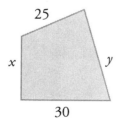 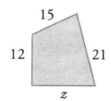

Since corresponding sides are proportional, $\frac{15}{25} = \frac{3}{5}$, so the scale factor is $\frac{3}{5}$.

$$\frac{12}{x} = \frac{3}{5} \qquad\qquad \frac{21}{y} = \frac{3}{5} \qquad\qquad \frac{z}{30} = \frac{3}{5}$$
$$3x = 60 \qquad\qquad 3y = 105 \qquad\qquad 5z = 90$$
$$x = 20 \qquad\qquad y = 35 \qquad\qquad z = 18$$

Just as for congruence, there are shortcut methods that can be used to prove similarity.

AA SIMILARITY POSTULATE: if two angles of one triangle are congruent to two angles of another triangle, then the triangles are similar

According to the **AA SIMILARITY POSTULATE**, if two angles of one triangle are congruent to two angles of another triangle, then the triangles are similar. It is obvious that if two of the corresponding angles are congruent, the third set of corresponding angles must be congruent as well. Hence, showing AA is sufficient to prove that two triangles are similar.

SAS SIMILARITY THEOREM: if an angle of one triangle is congruent to an angle of another triangle, and the sides adjacent to those angles are in proportion, then the triangles are similar

The **SAS SIMILARITY THEOREM** states that if an angle of one triangle is congruent to an angle of another triangle, and the sides adjacent to those angles are in proportion, then the triangles are similar.

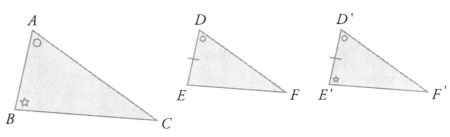

If $\angle A = \angle D$ and $\frac{AB}{DE} = \frac{AC}{DF}$, $\triangle ABC \sim \triangle DEF$.

Example: A graphic artist is designing a logo containing two triangles. The artist wants the triangles to be similar. Determine whether the artist has created similar triangles.

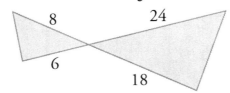

The sides are proportional ($\frac{8}{24} = \frac{6}{18} = \frac{1}{3}$) and vertical angles are congruent. The two triangles are therefore similar by the SAS similarity theorem.

SSS SIMILARITY THEOREM: if the sides of two triangles are in proportion, then the triangles are similar

According to the **SSS SIMILARITY THEOREM**, if the sides of two triangles are in proportion, then the triangles are similar.

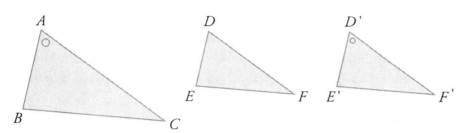

If $\frac{AB}{DE} = \frac{AC}{DF} = \frac{BC}{EF}$, $\triangle ABC \sim \triangle DEF$

Example: Tommy draws and cuts out 2 triangles for a school project. One of them has sides of 3, 6, and 9 inches. The other triangle has sides of 2, 4, and 6. Is there a relationship between the two triangles?

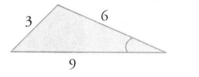 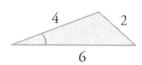

Determine the proportions of the corresponding sides.

$$\frac{2}{3} \qquad \frac{4}{6} = \frac{2}{3} \qquad \frac{6}{9} = \frac{2}{3}$$

The smaller triangle is $\frac{2}{3}$ the size of the large triangle, therefore they are similar triangles by the SSS similarity theorem.

See Skill 8.3 for a discussion of similar solids.

SKILL 9.4 Evaluating formal and informal arguments and proofs

A PROOF is an argument that demonstrates the truth (or falsity) of a proposition. Mathematical proofs begin with certain axioms or known propositions and, by some line of reasoning, deduce a particular conclusion. (For more on deduction and induction, see the next skill section.)

Because not all concepts in mathematics can be proven or otherwise defined (if this were the case, then either circular definitions/proofs would be required—but these are not informative—or an infinite regression of definitions/proofs would be required—but these are impossible), mathematical proofs necessarily start from certain unproven or undefined concepts. In geometry, for instance, the concept of a point is undefined.

Mathematical proofs attempt to reason in a consistent and orderly way from known premises (as long as they are either defined to be true or are proven to be

> **PROOF:** an argument that demonstrates the truth (or falsity) of a proposition

> *Mathematical proofs begin with certain axioms or known propositions and, by some line of reasoning, deduce a particular conclusion.*

true) to nontrivial conclusions. This process may involve positively demonstrating a proposition through direct proof, which involves showing that the proposition is true, or it may involve indirect proof, which involves showing that the negation (opposite) of the proposition is false. Both approaches are valid, but one or the other may be simpler.

Because some propositions can be shown to be false through a single counter-example, indirect proof is sometimes the simplest method of proof. Indirect proof may also involve using the opposite of the proposition being proved to demonstrate that a contradiction is reached. In such a case, assuming that all other premises are true, then the opposite of the proposition being proved must be false. Consider the following example.

Example: Prove that there are no even prime numbers other than the number 2.

A direct proof of this proposition may be possible, but an indirect proof is much simpler. Assume that the opposite is true: There is an even prime number other than 2. Let this number be called x (an integer). Since x is even, then the following must be true, where y is an integer.

$$\frac{x}{2} = y$$

But if x is evenly divisible by 2, it cannot be a prime number. Thus, a contradiction is reached with the originally assumed proposition that x is prime. This proves that there are no even prime numbers other than 2.

Inductive and Deductive Reasoning

The two forms of reasoning are inductive and deductive. INDUCTIVE REASONING involves making inferences from specific facts to general principles; DEDUCTIVE REASONING involves making inferences from general principles to specific facts. As such, inductive reasoning is generally weaker than deductive reasoning. (Inductive reasoning—or induction—should not be confused with mathematical induction, which is not an example of inductive reasoning, strictly speaking.)

INDUCTIVE REASON-ING: makes inferences from specific facts to general principles

DEDUCTIVE REASON-ING: makes inferences from general principles to specific facts

Inductive reasoning

Inductive reasoning generally involves finding a representative set of examples that support the general application of a broader principle. In a common context, an example of inductive reasoning would be inferring from the fact that only black crows have ever been spotted to the general statement that all crows are black. This inference has a foundation in numerous observations, and it thereby gains significant weight. Nevertheless, it is feasible that somewhere a white (or other-colored) crow does exist but hasn't yet been spotted. Thus, inductive inferences can never acquire 100% certainty, regardless of the amount of information in support of them.

Regardless of the uncertainty associated with induction, inductive inferences can be helpful for building a theory or for making a conjecture about some aspect of life, mathematics, or any other area. The physical sciences are a particular example where induction is commonly used to develop theories about the universe. Although these theories may be founded on a large body of empirical and mathematical evidence, a single counterexample could topple their status. Thus, inductive reasoning can be helpful, but it is much weaker than deductive reasoning.

> *Inductive inferences can be helpful for building a theory or for making a conjecture about some aspect of life, mathematics, or any other area.*

Inductive reasoning, because it is weaker than deduction, is also less rigorous in its application of specific rules for the process of arriving at conclusions. For instance, there is no rule concerning how much evidence constitutes a sufficient reason to inductively accept a particular hypothesis. (Thus, there is no minimum number of sightings of black crows that is required prior to making an inference that all crows are black.) The particular area in which inductive reasoning is applied and the amount of potential evidence that could reasonably be gathered are factors that help determine what constitutes an acceptable inductive inference.

In a mathematical context, induction can serve to make conjectures for which a proof (or a proof of the contrary) can then be sought. For instance, Fermat's Last Theorem states that there are no integer solutions x, y, and z to the expression $x^n + y^n = z^n$ for $n > 2$. Although this theorem was suspected to be true (largely by induction from numerous test cases) for hundreds of years, only recently was a deductive proof discovered. Thus, induction can serve as a less rigorous method of making tentative conclusions pending a formal proof.

Deductive reasoning

Deductive reasoning is a method of reasoning that is stronger and more rigorous than inductive reasoning. Deductive arguments reason from a set of premises to a conclusion and are classified as invalid, valid, or sound. An **INVALID ARGUMENT** is one in which the conclusion does not necessarily follow from the premises. A **VALID ARGUMENT** is one in which the conclusion necessarily follows from the premises. A **SOUND ARGUMENT** is a valid argument for which all the premises are true. Thus, the following argument is valid but not sound:

Premise 1:   All dogs are black.
Premise 2:   Rover is a dog.
Conclusion: Rover is black.

> **INVALID ARGUMENT:** one in which the conclusion does not necessarily follow from the premises

> **VALID ARGUMENT:** one in which the conclusion necessarily follows from the premises

> **SOUND ARGUMENT:** a valid argument for which all the premises are true

Were premises 1 and 2 both true, the conclusion would necessarily be true as well. Premise 1 is false, however, so the argument is valid but not sound. On the other hand, the following argument is both valid *and* sound.

Premise 1:   All integers are real numbers.

Premise 2:   1 is an integer.

Conclusion: 1 is a real number.

Both premises 1 and 2 are true, and the conclusion follows from the premises. Specific examples of deductive logical steps that can be taken in developing or evaluating an argument include *modus ponens* ("if A, then B" and "A is true" necessarily implies "B is true") and *modus tollens* ("if A, then B" and "B is false" necessarily implies "A is false").

Because deductive reasoning is more rigorous and the rules clearer, the process of arriving at an acceptable conclusion from a given set of premises (or the process of evaluating a deductive argument) is likewise clearer. Demonstrating the truth of the premises, however, may still be a complicated process. The premises may even require inductive reasoning to demonstrate their truth (at least tentatively). Thus, whether a deductive argument is sound can still be a matter that rests on the strength of a particular instance of inductive reasoning.

Formal Reasoning

Formal reasoning, which includes deductive reasoning, follows a structured and orderly approach according to various rules of inference. Informal reasoning, which includes inductive reasoning, is less structured and tends not to be as rigorous as formal reasoning. Both of these types of reasoning, however, can be used to justify mathematical ideas.

Formal reasoning is applied for rigorous proofs and deriving conclusions in a way that provides certainty of the results. Informal reasoning is applied to situations where it is necessary to lend evidence to a conjecture or to build a strong (but not necessarily conclusive) case for some conclusion. Because it is less rigorous, informal reasoning tends to provide less certainty, but informal reasoning can be very helpful for finding potential solutions or possible avenues of approach for otherwise intractable problems.

COMPETENCY 10

ANALYZE FIGURES AND SHAPES USING COORDINATE AND TRANSFORMATIONAL GEOMETRY

SKILL 10.1 Analyzing two- and three-dimensional figures and shapes in the coordinate plane

Any two-dimensional geometric figure can be represented in the CARTESIAN, or RECTANGULAR, COORDINATE SYSTEM. This system is formed by two perpendicular axes (coordinate axes): the x-axis and the y-axis. If the dimensions of a two-dimensional, or planar, figure are known, this coordinate system can be used to create a visual representation of the figure.

> **CARTESIAN, or RECT-ANGULAR, COORDI-NATE SYSTEM:** a system formed by two perpendicular axes: the x-axis and the y-axis

Example: Represent an isosceles triangle with two sides of length 4.
Draw the two sides along the x and y axes and connect the points (vertices).

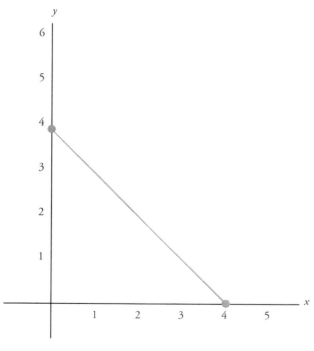

The vertices of the isosceles triangle are found at (0, 0), (4, 0) and (0, 4) with equal sides on the x and y axes.

If a polygon is shown in the coordinate plane and the coordinates of the vertices must be determined, then the characteristics of the polygon can be used to this end. Consider the following example.

Example: The rectangle shown in the graph below has sides of length 2 parallel to the y-axis and sides of length 4 parallel to the x-axis. Determine the coordinates of the vertices.

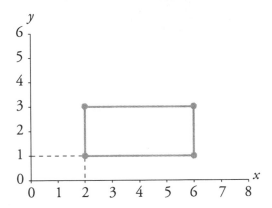

From the graph, it is clear that one of the vertices is located at (2, 1). Using the properties of rectangles (or by inspection of the graph in this case), the other vertices (going in a counterclockwise direction from the first vertex) are (6, 1), (6, 3) and (2, 3).

Examples that are more difficult may involve polygons with sides that are not parallel to either of the axes. In such cases, knowledge (either given or by inspection) of the location of at least one vertex is necessary, as is the type of polygon (regular or irregular). Calculation of the slopes of the line segments between vertices may be necessary in some cases to determine the location of unknown vertices. This approach is also helpful in cases where, as with the first example, the polygon must be drawn on the coordinate plane. When possible, it is helpful to draw one or more vertices (or entire sides) of a polygon on the axes. This usually simplifies calculation or representation of the remainder of the polygon.

A three-dimensional geometric figure can be plotted using a basic set of three-dimensional axes, as shown below.

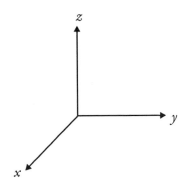

Points can be plotted by traversing the required distance parallel to each axis. Thus, the point (3, 3, 3) is plotted as shown below.

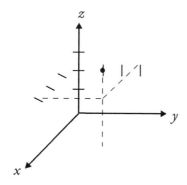

A cube with sides of length 2 can then be represented as shown below.

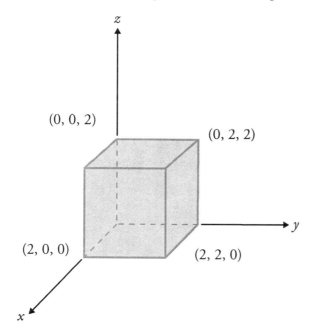

SKILL **Applying geometric properties and the concepts of distance,**
10.2 **midpoint, and slope in coordinate systems to solve mathematical**
and real-world problems

The Distance Formula

In order to accomplish the task of finding the distance from a given point to another given line, the perpendicular line that intersects the point and line must be drawn, and the equation of the other line must be written. From this information, the point of intersection can be found. This point and the original point are used in the distance formula given below:

$$D = \sqrt{(x_2 - x_1)^2 + (y_2 - y_1)^2}$$

Example: Given the point (-4, 3) and the line y = 4x + 2, find the distance from the point to the line.

$y = 4x + 2$	Find the slope of the given line by solving for y.
$y = 4x + 2$	The slope is $\frac{4}{1}$; the perpendicular line will have a slope of $-\frac{4}{1}$.
$y = (-\frac{1}{4})x + b$	Use the new slope and the given point to find the equation of the perpendicular line.
$3 = (-\frac{1}{4})(-4) + b$	Substitute (-4, 3) into the equation.
$3 = 1 + b$	Solve.
$2 = b$	Given the value for b, write the equation of the perpendicular line.
$y = (-\frac{1}{4})x + 2$	Write in standard form.
$x + 4y = 8$	Use both equations to solve by elimination to get the point of intersection.
$-4x + y = 2$	Multiply the bottom row by 4.
$\underline{x + 4y = 8}$	

$-4x + y = 2$	Solve.
$\underline{4x + 16y = 32}$	
$17y = 34$	
$y = 2$	
$y = 4x + 2$	Substitute to find the x value.
$2 = 4x + 2$	Solve.
$x = 0$	

(0, 2) is the point of intersection. Use this point on the original line and the original point to calculate the distance between them.

$D = \sqrt{(x_2 - x_1)^2 + (y_2 - y_1)^2}$, where points are (0, 2) and (-4, 3).

$D = \sqrt{(-4 - 0)^2 + (3 - 2)^2}$ 	Substitute.

$D = \sqrt{(16) + (1)}$ 	Simplify.

$D = \sqrt{17}$

The distance between two parallel lines, such as line AB and line CD as shown below, is the line segment RS, the perpendicular between the two parallels.

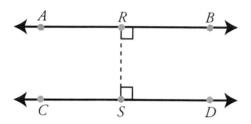

Example: Given the geometric figure below, find the distance between the two parallel sides AB and CD.

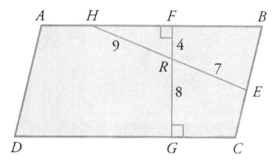

The distance FG is 12 units.

The key to applying the distance formula is to understand the problem before beginning.

$$D = \sqrt{(x_2 - x_1)^2 + (y_2 - y_1)^2},$$

Example: Find the perimeter of a figure with vertices at (4, 5), (-4, 6), and (-5, -8).

The figure being described is a triangle. Therefore, the distance for all three sides must be found. Carefully identify all three sides before beginning.

Side 1 = (4, 5) to (-4, 6)
Side 2 = (-4, 6) to (-5, -8)
Side 3 = (-5, -8) to (4, 5)

$$D_1 = \sqrt{(-4 - 4)^2 + (6 - 5)^2} = \sqrt{65}$$
$$D_2 = \sqrt{((-5 - (-4))^2 + (-8 - 6)^2} = \sqrt{197}$$
$$D_3 = \sqrt{((4 - (-5))^2 + (5 - (-8))^2} = \sqrt{250} \text{ or } 5\sqrt{10}$$

$$\text{Perimeter} = \sqrt{65} + \sqrt{197} + 5\sqrt{10}$$

The Midpoint Formula

If a line segment has endpoints of (x_1, y_1) and (x_2, y_2), then the midpoint can be found using

$$(\frac{x_1 + x_2}{2}, \frac{y_1 + y_2}{2})$$

Example: Find the center of a circle with a diameter whose endpoints are (3, 7) and (-4, -5).

Midpoint $= (\frac{3 + (-4)}{2}, \frac{7 + (-5)}{2})$

Midpoint $= (\frac{-1}{2}, 1)$

Example: Find the midpoint given the two points (5, 8 $\sqrt{6}$) and (9, -4 $\sqrt{6}$).

Midpoint $= (\frac{5 + 9}{2}, \frac{8\sqrt{6} + (-4\sqrt{6})}{2})$

Midpoint $= (7, 2\sqrt{6})$

SKILL 10.3 **Applying transformations** *(e.g., rotations, reflections, dilations)* **to figures in the coordinate plane**

Transformational Geometry

TRANSFORMATIONAL GEOMETRY: the study of the manipulation of objects through movement, rotation, and scaling

TRANSFORMATIONAL GEOMETRY is the study of the manipulation of objects through movement, rotation, and scaling. The transformation of an object is called its image. If the original object is labeled with letters, such as *ABCD*, the image can be labeled with the same letters followed by a prime symbol: *A'B'C'D'*. Transformations can be characterized in different ways.

Types of transformations

ISOMETRY: a linear transformation that maintains the dimensions of a geometric figure

An ISOMETRY is a linear transformation that maintains the dimensions of a geometric figure.

SYMMETRY is exact similarity between two parts or halves, as if one were a mirror image of the other.

SYMMETRY: the exact similarity between two parts or halves, as if one were a mirror image of the other

A TRANSLATION is a transformation that "slides" an object a fixed distance in a given direction. The original object and its translation have the same shape and size, and they face in the same direction.

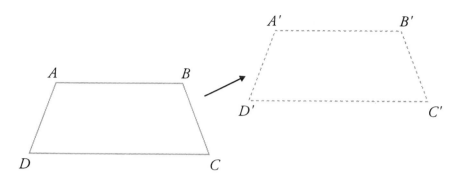

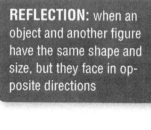

TRANSLATION: a transformation that "slides" an object a fixed distance in a given direction

A **ROTATION** is a transformation that turns a figure about a fixed point, which is called the center of rotation. An object and its rotation are the same shape and size, but the figures may be oriented in different directions. Rotations can occur in either a clockwise or a counterclockwise direction.

ROTATION: a transformation that turns a figure about a fixed point, called the center of rotation

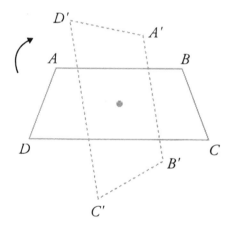

An object and its **REFLECTION** have the same shape and size, but the figures face in opposite directions. The line (where a hypothetical mirror may be placed) is called the line of reflection. The distance from a point to the line of reflection is the same as the distance from the point's image to the line of reflection.

REFLECTION: when an object and another figure have the same shape and size, but they face in opposite directions

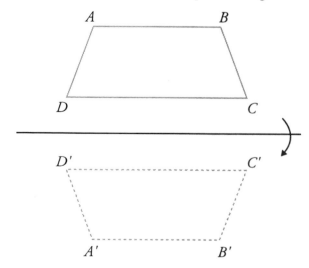

A **GLIDE REFLECTION** involves a combined translation along and a reflection across a single specified line. The characteristic that defines a glide reflection as opposed to a simple combination of an arbitrary translation and arbitrary reflection is that the direction of translation is parallel with the line of reflection. An example of a glide reflection is shown below.

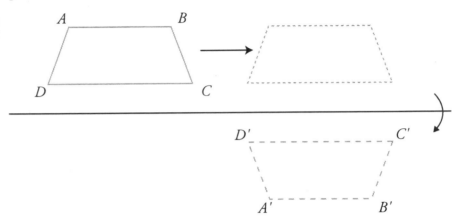

The examples of a translation, a rotation, and a reflection given above are for polygons, but the same principles apply to the simpler geometric elements of points and lines. In fact, a transformation performed on a polygon can be viewed equivalently as the same transformation performed on the set of points (vertices) and lines (sides) that compose the polygon. Thus, to perform complicated transformations on a figure, it is helpful to perform the transformations on all the points (or vertices) of the figure, then reconnect the points with lines as appropriate.

Dilation

DILATIONS involve an expansion of a figure and a translation of that figure while maintaining the figure's angles and relative proportions (the translation may be for a distance zero). These two transformations are obtained by first defining a center of dilation, C, which is some point that acts like an origin for the dilation. The distance from C to each point in a figure is then altered by a scale factor, s. If the magnitude of s is greater than zero, the size of the figure is increased; if the magnitude of s is less than zero, the size is decreased.

The expansion of a geometric figure is a result of the scale factor, s. For instance, if $s = 2$, the expanded figure will be twice the size of the original figure. The translation of a geometric figure is a result of the location of the center of dilation, C. If C is located at the center of the figure, for instance, the figure is dilated without any translation of its center.

Example: Dilate the figure shown by a scale factor of 2 using the origin of the coordinate system as the center of dilation.

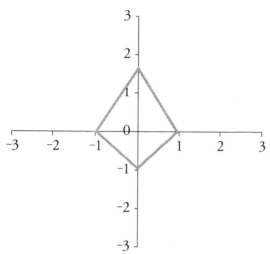

To perform this dilation, the distance between the origin and each point on the figure must be increased by a factor of 2. It is sufficient, however, to simply increase the distance of the vertices of the figure by a factor of 2 and then connect them to form the dilated figure.

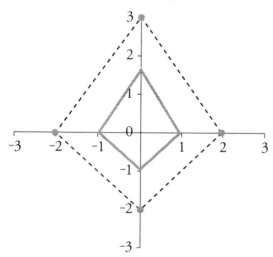

The resulting figure, represented by a dashed line, is the dilation of the original figure.

The points on a figure are dilated by increasing or decreasing their respective distances from a center of dilation, *C*. As a result, each point *P* on a figure is essentially translated along the line through *P* and *C*. To show that a dilation of this type preserves angles, consider some angle formed by two line segments, with a center of dilation at some arbitrary location. The dilation is for some scale factor *s*.

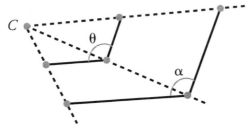

To show that the angles θ and α are equal, it is sufficient to show that the two pairs of overlapping triangles are similar. If they are similar, all the corresponding angles in the figure must be congruent.

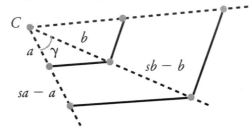

The smaller triangle in this case has sides of lengths a and b and an angle γ between them. The larger triangle has sides of lengths sa (or $sa - a + a = sa$) and sb and an angle γ between them. Thus, by SAS similarity, these two triangles are similar.

Once this reasoning is applied to the other pair of overlapping triangles, it can be shown that angles θ and α are equal. Furthermore, due to the fact that these triangles have been shown to be similar, it is also true that line segments must scale by the same factor, s (this is necessary to maintain the similarity of the triangles above).

As a result of this reasoning, it can be shown that figures that are dilated using an arbitrary scale factor, s, and center of dilation, C, must maintain all angles through the dilation, and all line segments (or sides) of the figure must also scale by s. As a result, figures that are dilated are similar to the original figures.

Since dilations are transformations that maintain similarity of the figures being dilated, they can also be viewed as changes of scale about C. For instance, a dilation of a portion of a map would simply result in a change of the scale of the map.

Multiple Transformations

Multiple transformations (or compositions of transformations) can be performed on a geometrical figure. The order of these transformations may or may not be important. For instance, multiple translations can be performed in any order, as can multiple rotations (around a single fixed point) or reflections (across a single fixed line). The order of the transformations becomes important when several types of transformations are performed or when the point of rotation or the line of reflection changes among transformations. For example, consider a translation of a given distance upward and a clockwise rotation by 90° around a fixed point. Changing the order of these transformations changes the result.

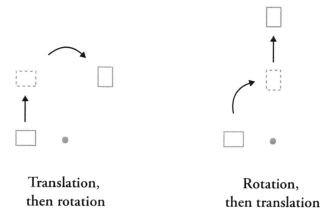

**Translation,
then rotation**

**Rotation,
then translation**

As shown, the final position of the box is different, depending on the order of the transformations. Thus, it is crucial that the proper order of transformations (whether determined by the details of the problem or some other consideration) be followed.

Example: Find the final location of a point at (1, 1) that undergoes the following transformations: rotate 90° counter-clockwise about the origin; translate distance 2 in the negative y direction; reflect about the x-axis.

First, draw a graph of the x and y axes and plot the point at (1, 1).

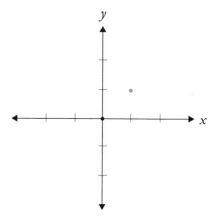

Next, perform the rotation. The center of rotation is the origin and is in the counter-clockwise direction. In this case, the even value of 90° makes the rotation simple to do by inspection. Next, perform a translation of distance 2 in the negative y direction (down). The results of these transformations are shown below.

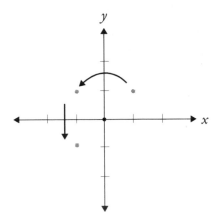

Finally, perform the reflection about the *x*-axis. The final result, shown below, is a point at (1, −1).

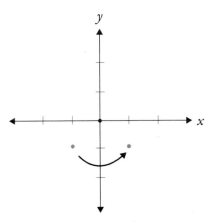

Using this approach, polygons can be transformed on a point-by-point basis.

For some problems, there is no need to work with coordinate axes. For instance, the problem may simply require transformations without respect to any absolute positioning.

Example: Rotate the following regular pentagon by 36° about its center and then reflect it across the horizontal line.

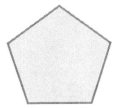

First, perform the rotation. In this case, the direction is not important because the pentagon is symmetric. As it turns out in this case, a rotation of 36° yields the same result as flipping the pentagon vertically (assuming the vertices of the pentagon are indistinguishable).

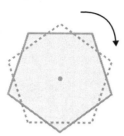

Finally, perform the reflection. Note that the result here is the same as a downward translation (assuming the vertices of the pentagon are indistinguishable).

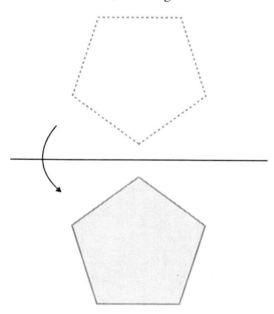

Symmetry

A figure has symmetry when there is an isometry that maps the figure onto itself. A figure has rotational symmetry if there is a rotation of 180 degrees or less that maps the figure onto itself. Point symmetry is where a plane figure can be mapped onto itself by a half-turn or a rotation of 180 degrees around some point. Thus, point symmetry is a specific type of rotational symmetry. An example of a figure with point symmetry is shown below.

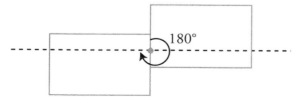

REFLECTIONAL SYMMETRY: an isometry that maps the figure onto itself by reflection across a line

REFLECTIONAL SYMMETRY, or line symmetry, is an isometry that maps the figure onto itself by reflection across a line. An alternative view is that if the figure is folded along a line of symmetry, the two halves will match perfectly. Examples of figures with line symmetry are shown below, with all the potential lines of symmetry marked as broken lines.

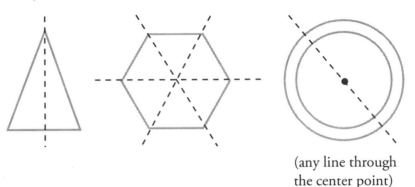

(any line through the center point)

TRANSLATIONAL SYMMETRY: symmetry which allows an image to be translated in a specific direction to produce the same image

TRANSLATIONAL SYMMETRY is where an image can be translated in a specific direction to produce the same image. Necessarily, this requires that the image be infinite in extent and repeating in nature. A **TESSELLATION** is an image with translational symmetry. A tessellation or tiling, consists of a repeating pattern of figures that completely cover an area. Below are a couple of examples of art tessellations.

TESSELLATION: an image with translational symmetry

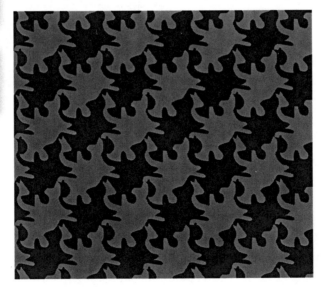

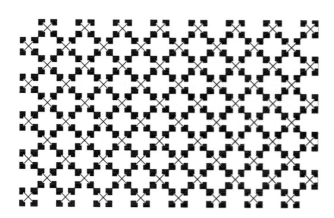

A regular tessellation is made by taking a pattern of polygons that are interlocked and can be extended infinitely. A portion of a tessellation made with hexagons is shown below. This image is made by taking congruent, regular polygons and using them to cover a plane in such a way that there are no holes or overlaps. A semi-regular tessellation is made with polygons arranged exactly the same way at every vertex point. Tessellations occur in frequently in nature. A bee's honeycomb is an example of a tessellation found in nature.

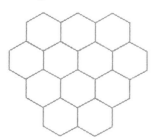

SKILL 10.4 Analyzing the use of the techniques of coordinate geometry in geometric proofs

COORDINATE GEOMETRY involves the application of algebraic methods to geometry. The locations of points in space are expressed in terms of coordinates on a Cartesian plane. The relationships between the coordinates of different points are expressed as equations.

> **COORDINATE GEOMETRY:** the application of algebraic methods to geometry

Proofs using coordinate geometry techniques employ the following commonly used formulae and relationships:

1. Midpoint formula: The midpoint (x, y) of the line joining points (x_1, y_1) and (x_2, y_2) is given by $(x, y) = \left(\dfrac{x_1 + x_2}{2}, \dfrac{y_1 + y_2}{2} \right)$

2. **Distance formula:** The distance between points (x_1, y_1) and (x_2, y_2) is given by $D = \sqrt{(x_2 - x_1)^2 + (y_2 - y_1)^2}$

3. **Slope formula:** The slope m of a line passing through the points (x_1, y_1) and (x_2, y_2) is given by $m = \frac{y_2 - y_1}{x_2 - x_1}$

4. **Equation of a line:** The equation of a line is given by $y = mx + b$, where m is the slope of the line and b is the y-intercept, i.e., the y-coordinate at which the line intersects the y-axis.

5. **Parallel and perpendicular lines:** Parallel lines have the same slope. The slope of a line perpendicular to a line with slope m is $\frac{-1}{m}$.

Example: Prove that quadrilateral ABCD with vertices A (-3, 0), B (-1, 0), C (0, 3), and D (2, 3) is in fact a parallelogram using coordinate geometry:

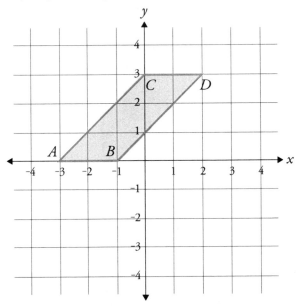

By definition, a parallelogram has diagonals that bisect each other. Using the midpoint formula, $(x, y) = \left(\frac{x_1 + x_2}{2} + \frac{y_1 + y_2}{2}\right)$, find the midpoints of $\overline{AD}$ and $\overline{BC}$.

The midpoint of $\overline{BC} = \left(\frac{-1 + 0}{2}, \frac{0 + 3}{2}\right) = \left(\frac{-1}{2}, \frac{3}{2}\right)$

The midpoint of $\overline{AD} = \left(\frac{-3 + 2}{2}, \frac{0 + 3}{2}\right) = \left(\frac{-1}{2}, \frac{3}{2}\right)$

Since the midpoints of the diagonals are the same, the diagonals bisect each other. Hence the polygon is a parallelogram.

In the above example, the proof involved a specific geometric figure with given coordinates. Coordinate geometry can also be used to prove more general results.

Example: Prove that the diagonals of a rhombus are perpendicular to each other.

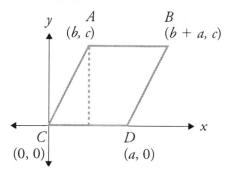

Draw a rhombus *ABCD* with side of length *a* such that the vertex *C* is at the origin and the side *CD* lies along the *x*-axis. The coordinates of the corners of the rhombus can then be written as shown above.

The slope m_1 of the diagonal *AD* is given by $m_1 = \frac{c}{b-a}$.

The slope m_2 of the diagonal *BC* is given by $m_2 = \frac{c}{b+a}$.

The product of the slopes is $m_1 \times m_2 = \frac{c}{b-a} \times \frac{c}{b+a} = \frac{c^2}{b^2-a^2}$.

The length of side $AC = \sqrt{b^2 + c^2} = a$ (since each side of the rhombus is equal to *a*). Therefore,

$b^2 + c^2 = a^2$

$\rightarrow b^2 - a^2 = -c^2$

$\rightarrow \frac{c^2}{b^2 - a^2} = -1$

The product of the slopes of the diagonals $m_1 \times m_2 = -1$.
Hence the two diagonals are perpendicular to each other.

Example: Prove that the line joining the midpoints of two sides of a triangle is parallel to and half the length of the third side.

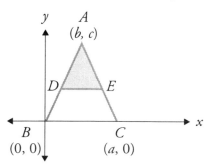

Draw triangle *ABC* on the coordinate plane in such a way that the vertex *B* coincides with the origin and the side *BC* lies along the *x*-axis. Let point *C* have coordinates $(a, 0)$ and point *A* have coordinates (b, c). Point *D* is the midpoint of side *AB* and point *E* is the midpoint of side *AC*.

We need to prove that segment DE is parallel to and half the length of side BC.

Using the midpoint formula, coordinates of $D = \left(\frac{b}{2}, \frac{c}{2}\right)$; coordinates of $E = \left(\frac{b+a}{2}, \frac{c}{2}\right)$.

The slope of the line segment DE is then given by $\dfrac{\frac{c}{2} - \frac{c}{2}}{\frac{b+a}{2} - \frac{b}{2}} = 0$, which is equal to the slope of the x-axis. Thus DE is parallel to BC.

The length of the line segment $DE = \sqrt{\left(\frac{b+a}{2} - \frac{b}{2}\right)^2 + \left(\frac{c}{2} - \frac{c}{2}\right)^2} = \sqrt{\left(\frac{a}{2}\right)^2} = \frac{a}{2}$.

The length of DE is half that of side BC.

DOMAIN IV
DATA, RANDOMNESS, AND UNCERTAINTY

PERSONALIZED STUDY PLAN

KNOWN MATERIAL/ SKIP IT

PAGE	COMPETENCY AND SKILL	
159	**11: Apply knowledge of data investigations**	☐
	11.1: Devising a plan for collecting data using appropriate sampling techniques	☐
	11.2: Selecting an effective format for organizing and describing data distributions	☐
	11.3: Describing data distributions in terms of mean, median, mode, and spread	☐
	11.4: Interpreting data presented in a variety of formats	☐
170	**12: Understand the principles of probability**	☐
	12.1: Analyzing the relationship between randomness and sampling methods in making statistical claims about populations	☐
	12.2: Determining the probabilities of simple and compound events using counting principles and the concept of sample space	☐
	12.3: Solving problems using graphic representations to calculate probabilities	☐
	12.4: Determining probabilities based on data collection, experiments, and simulations	☐

COMPETENCY 11
APPLY KNOWLEDGE OF DATA INVESTIGATIONS

Statistical studies typically involve a large number of people or a large pool of data known as the POPULATION. In most cases, it is impractical or impossible to collect data from every member, and therefore a representative sample has to be chosen. The process of selecting a sample must be undertaken with extreme care to ensure that it truly represents a population.

POPULATION: in a statistical study, a large number of people or a large pool of data

In addition to deciding what kind of sample will be selected, one must also select the sample statistic to be used. Different sample statistics can be used to estimate a particular population parameter. In order to estimate a population mean, for instance, one can use the sample median or the sample mean. One way to evaluate whether a sample statistic accurately reflects the value of a population parameter is by studying the characteristics of a sampling distribution. For a study that involves a sample of size n, for example, different samples of the same size and same type will produce slightly different values for the same statistic. A SAMPLE STATISTIC, therefore, is a random variable that follows a probability distribution. Informal inferences about the shape, symmetry, mean, and variance of this sampling distribution can help in selection of the appropriate sampling statistic or estimator.

SAMPLE STATISTIC: a random variable that follows a probability distribution

For an UNBIASED ESTIMATOR, i.e., a sample statistic that accurately reflects a population parameter, the sampling distribution mean is equal to the estimated population parameter and the distribution is centered at the population parameter. The shape of the sample distribution approaches a normal distribution as the sample size increases. Since consistency between samples is desired in the choice of an estimator, a smaller standard deviation indicates a better estimator.

UNBIASED ESTIMATOR: a sample statistic that accurately reflects a population parameter

Surveys and Sampling

In cases where the number of events or individuals is too large to collect data on each one, scientists collect information from only a small percentage. This is known as SAMPLING or SURVEYING. If sampling is done correctly, it should give the investigator nearly the same information he would have obtained by testing the entire population. The survey must be carefully designed, considering both the sampling technique and the size of the sample.

SAMPLING OR SURVEYING: when scientists collect information from only a small percentage of a numbers of events or individuals because the data pool is too large

There are a variety of sampling techniques, both random and nonrandom. Random sampling is also known as probability sampling, since the methods of probability theory can be used to ascertain the odds that the sample is representative of the whole population. Statistical methods may be used to determine how large a sample is necessary to give an investigator a specified level of certainty (95% is a typical confidence interval). Conversely, if an investigator has a sample of a certain size, those same statistical methods can be used to determine how confident one can be that the sample accurately reflects the whole population.

A truly random sample must choose events or individuals without regard to time, place, or result. Simple random sampling is ideal for populations that are relatively homogeneous with respect to the data being collected.

In some cases an accurate representation of distinct sub-populations requires stratified random sampling or quota sampling. For instance, if men and women are likely to respond very differently to a particular survey, the total sample population can be separated into these two subgroups and then a random group of respondents selected from each subgroup. This kind of sampling not only provides balanced representation of different subgroups, it also allows comparison of data between subgroups.

Stratified sampling is sometimes proportional; i.e., the number of samples selected from each subgroup reflects the fraction of the whole population represented by the subgroup.

Sometimes compromises must be made to save time, money, or effort. For instance, when conducting a phone survey, calls are typically made only in a certain geographical area and at a certain time of day. This is an example of cluster random sampling. There are three stages to cluster, or area, sampling:

1. The target population is divided into many regional clusters (groups).

2. A few clusters are randomly selected for study.

3. A few subjects are randomly chosen from within a cluster.

Systematic random sampling involves the collection of a sample at defined intervals (for instance, every tenth part to come off a manufacturing line). Here, it is assumed that the population is ordered randomly and that there is no hidden pattern that may compromise the randomness of the sampling.

Nonrandom sampling is also known as nonprobability sampling. Convenience sampling is the method of choosing items arbitrarily and in an unstructured manner from the frame. Purposive sampling targets a particular section of the population. Snowball sampling (e.g., having survey participants recommend others) and expert sampling are other types of non-random sampling. Obviously, nonrandom samples are far less representative of the whole population than random ones. They may, however, be the only methods available or may meet the needs of a particular study.

SKILL 11.2 **Selecting an effective format for organizing and describing data distributions**

Displaying Statistical Data

The data obtained from sampling may be categorical (e.g., yes or no responses) or numerical. In both cases, results are displayed using a variety of graphical techniques. Geographical data is often displayed superimposed on maps.

Histograms

The most common form of graphical display used for numerical data obtained from random sampling is the histogram. A trend line can be superposed on a histogram to observe the general shape of the distribution. In some cases, the trend line may also be fitted to a probability density function.

If the data set is large, it may be expressed in compact form as a FREQUENCY DISTRIBUTION. The number of occurrences of each data point is the FREQUENCY of that value. The RELATIVE FREQUENCY is defined as the frequency divided by the total number of data points. Since the sum of the frequencies equals the number of data points, the relative frequencies add up to 1. The relative frequency of a data point, therefore, represents the probability of occurrence of that value. Thus, a distribution consisting of relative frequencies is known as a PROBABILITY DISTRIBUTION. The CUMULATIVE FREQUENCY of a data point is the sum of the frequencies from the beginning up to that point.

A histogram is used to display a discrete frequency distribution graphically. It shows the counts of data in different ranges, the center of the data set, the spread of the data, and whether there are any outliers. It also shows whether the data has a single mode or more than one.

Example: The table below shows the summary of some test results, where people scored points ranging from 0 to 45. The total range of points has been divided into bins 0–5, 6–10, 11–15, and so on. The frequency for the first bin (labeled 5) is the number of people who scored points ranging from 0 to 5; the frequency for the second bin (labeled 10) is the number of people who scored points ranging from 6 to 10; and so on.

FREQUENCY DISTRIBUTION: divides a set of data into classes or intervals

FREQUENCY: the number of occurrences of a certain value in a data set

RELATIVE FREQUENCY: the frequency divided by the total number of data points

PROBABILITY DISTRIBUTION: a distribution consisting of relative frequencies

CUMULATIVE FREQUENCY: the sum of the frequencies from the beginning up to that point

A histogram is used to display a discrete frequency distribution graphically.

Points	Frequency	Cumulative Frequency	Relative Frequency
5	1	1	0.009
10	4	5	0.035
15	12	17	0.105
20	22	39	0.193
25	30	69	0.263
30	25	94	0.219
35	13	107	0.114
40	6	113	0.053
45	1	114	0.009

The histogram of the probability distribution is given below:

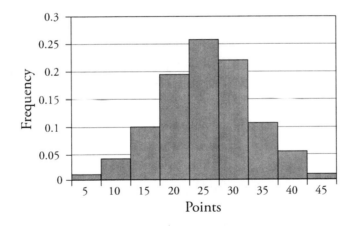

The probability distribution can be used to calculate the probability of a particular test score occurring in a certain range. For instance, the probability of a test score lying between 15 and 30 is given by the sum of the areas (assuming width of 1) of the three middle bins in the histogram above:

$$0.193 + 0.263 + 0.219 = 0.675$$

Bar graphs

> Bar graphs are used to compare various quantities using bars of different lengths.

Bar graphs are used to compare various quantities using bars of different lengths.

Example: A class had the following grades: 4 As, 9 Bs, 8 Cs, 1 D, 3 Fs.
Graph these on a bar graph.

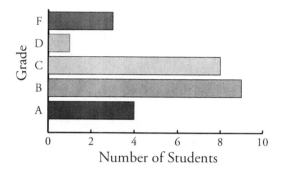

Line graphs

Line graphs are used to show trends, often over a period of time.

Line graphs are used to show trends, often over a period of time.

Example: Graph the following information using a line graph.

THE NUMBER OF NATIONAL MERIT FINALISTS/SCHOOL YEAR						
School	**90-91**	**91-92**	**92-93**	**93-94**	**94-95**	**95-96**
Central	3	5	1	4	6	8
Wilson	4	2	3	2	3	2

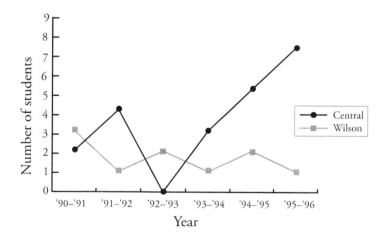

Circle graphs (pie charts)

Circle graphs or pie charts show the relationships of various parts of a data set to each other and to the whole. Each part is shown as a percentage of the total and occupies a proportional sector of the circular area. To make a circle

Circle graphs or pie charts show the relationships of various parts of a data set to each other and to the whole.

graph, total all the information that is to be included on the graph. Determine the central angle to be used for each sector of the graph using the following formula:

$$\frac{\text{information}}{\text{total information}} \times 360° = \text{degrees in central} \measuredangle$$

Lay out the central angles according to these sizes, label each section and include its percentage.

Example: Graph this information on a circle graph:

MONTHLY EXPENSES	
Rent	$400
Food	$150
Utilities	$75
Clothes	$75
Savings	$100
Misc.	$200

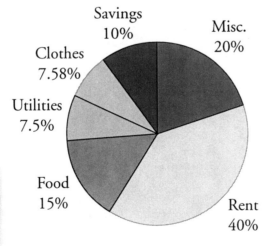

Scatter plots

Scatter plots compare two characteristics of the same group of things or people and usually consist of a large body of data. They show how much one variable is affected by another. The relationship between the two variables is their CORRELATION. The closer the data points come to making a straight line when plotted, the closer the correlation.

Scatter plots compare two characteristics of the same group of things or people and usually consist of a large body of data. They show how much one variable is affected by another.

CORRELATION: the relationship between two variables when comparing statistical data

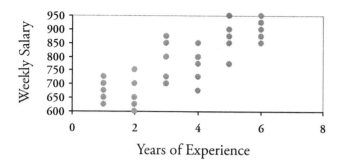

Statistics for Discrete Distributions

Mean, Median, and Mode

The mean, median, and mode are measures of central tendency (i.e., the average or typical value) in a data set. They can be defined both for discrete and continuous data sets. For discrete data, the MEAN is the average of the data items, or the value obtained by adding all the data values and dividing by the total number of data items. For a data set of n items with data values $x_1, x_2, x_3, \ldots, x_n$, the mean is given by

$$\bar{x} = \frac{x_1 + x_2 + x_3 + \ldots + x_n}{n}$$

The WEIGHTED AVERAGE is the mean of a set of data in which each individual datum has an associated probability or weight. For data values $x_1, x_2, x_3, \ldots, x_n$, with associated probabilities (or weights) $p(x_1), p(x_2), p(x_3), \ldots, p(x_n)$, the mean value is

$$\bar{x} = x_1 p(x_1) + x_2 p(x_2) + x_3 p(x_3) + \ldots + x_n p(x_n) = \sum_i x_i p(x_i)$$

This is the most general definition of the mean.

The MEDIAN is found by putting the data in order from smallest to largest and selecting the value in the middle (or the average of the two values in the middle if the number of data items is even). The MODE is the most frequently occurring datum. There can be more than one mode in a data set.

MEAN: for discrete data, the value obtained by adding all the data values and then dividing by the total number of values

WEIGHTED AVERAGE: the mean of a set of data in which each individual datum has an associated probability or weight

MEDIAN: found by putting the data in order from smallest to largest and selecting the value in the middle

MODE: the most frequently occurring datum

Example: Find the mean, median, and mode of the test scores listed below:

85	77	65
92	90	54
88	85	70
75	80	69
85	88	60
72	74	95

Mean: sum of all scores ÷ number of scores = 78

Median: Put the numbers in order from smallest to largest. Pick the middle number.

54 60 65 69 70 72 74 75 | 77 80 | 85 85 85 88 88 90 92 95

Two values are in the middle.

Therefore, the median is average of the two numbers in the middle, or 78.5. The mode is the most frequent number, or 85.

Range, Variance, and Standard Deviation

The **RANGE** is a measure of variability that is calculated by subtracting the smallest value from the largest value in a set of discrete data.

The **VARIANCE** and **STANDARD DEVIATION** are measures of the "spread" of data around the mean. It is noteworthy that descriptive statistics involving such parameters as variance and standard deviation can be applied to a set of data that spans the entire population (population parameters, typically represented using Greek symbols) or to a set of data that only constitutes a portion of the population (sample statistics, typically represented by Latin letters).

When making informal inferences about a population based on sample statistics, it is important to ensure that the sample is collected in a manner that adequately represents the population (see the discussion of surveys and sampling in *Skill 11.1*). The confidence in an inference based on sample statistics can increase when, for instance, the size of the sample space approaches that of the population, or when the sampling approach is designed to take into account known aspects of the population. Insofar as the sample represents the population, sample statistics approach (and can be equal to, in some cases) population parameters.

The mean of a set of data, whether for a population (μ) or for a sample ($\bar{x}$), uses the formula discussed above and can be represented as either a set of individual data or as a set of data with associated frequencies. The variance and standard deviation for the population differ slightly from those of a sample. The population variance (σ^2) and the population standard deviation (σ) are as follows.

$$\sigma^2 = \tfrac{1}{n} \Sigma (x_i - \mu)^2$$
$$\sigma = \sqrt{\sigma^2}$$

> **RANGE:** found by subtracting the smallest data value from the largest

> **VARIANCE:** a measure of the "spread" of data about the mean

> **STANDARD DEVIATION:** also a measure of the "spread" of data about the mean; the standard deviation is the square root of the variance

For a sample, the data does not include the entire population. As a result, it should be expected that the sample data might not be perfectly representative of the population. To account for this shortcoming in the sample variance (s^2) and standard deviation (s), the sum of the squared differences between the data and the mean is divided by ($n - 1$) instead of just n. This increases the variance and standard deviation slightly, which in turn increases slightly the data spread to account for the possibility that the sample may not accurately represent the population.

$$s^2 = \frac{1}{n-1} \Sigma \, (x_i - \bar{x})^2$$
$$s = \sqrt{s^2}$$

Example: Calculate the range, variance, and standard deviation for the following data set: {3, 3, 5, 7, 8, 8, 8, 10, 12, 21}.

The range is simply the largest data value minus the smallest. In this case, the range is $21 - 3 = 18$.

To calculate the variance and standard deviation, first calculate the mean. If it is not stated whether a data set constitutes a population or sample, assume it is a population. (In this case, if the data were labeled as "ages of the 10 people in a room," this would be a population. If the data were labeled "ages of males at a crowded circus event," the data would be a sample.)

$$\mu = \frac{3 + 3 + 5 + 7 + 8 + 8 + 8 + 10 + 12 + 21}{10} = 8.5$$

Use this mean to calculate the variance.

$$\sigma^2 = \frac{1}{10} \Sigma \, (x_i - 8.5)^2$$
$$\sigma^2 = \frac{1}{10} \{(3 - 8.5)^2 + (3 - 8.5)^2 + (5 - 8.5)^2 + \ldots + (21 - 8.5)^2\}$$
$$\sigma^2 = \frac{246.5}{10} = 24.65$$

The standard deviation is
$$\sigma = \sqrt{\sigma^2} = \sqrt{24.65} \approx 4.96$$

Statistics for Continuous Distributions

The *range* for a continuous data distribution is the same as that for a discrete distribution: the largest value minus the smallest value. Calculation of the mean, variance, and standard deviation are similar, but slightly different. Since a continuous distribution does not permit a simple summation, integrals must be used. The mean μ of a distribution function $f(x)$ is expressed below.

$$\mu \int_{-\infty}^{\infty} xf(x)dx$$

The variance σ^2 also has an integral form and has a form similar to that of a discrete distribution.

$$\sigma^2 = \int_{-\infty}^{\infty} (x - \mu)^2 f(x)dx$$

The standard deviation σ is simply

$$\sigma = \sqrt{\sigma^2}$$

Example: Calculate the standard deviation of a data distribution function f(x), where

$$f(x) = \begin{cases} 0 & x < 1 \\ -2x^2 + 2 & -1 \le x \le 1 \\ 0 & x > 1 \end{cases}$$

First calculate the mean of the function. Since the function is zero except between 1 and -1, the integral can likewise be evaluated from -1 to 1.

$$\mu = \int_{-1}^{1} (-2x^2 + 2)x\,dx$$

$$\mu = -2 \int_{-1}^{1} (x^3 - x)\,dx$$

$$\mu = -2 \left[\frac{x^4}{4} - \frac{x^2}{2}\right]_{x=-1}^{x=1}$$

$$\mu = -2 \left\{\left[\frac{(1)^4}{4} - \frac{(1)^2}{2}\right] - \left[\frac{(-1)^4}{4} \cdot 2 \frac{(-1)^2}{2}\right]\right\} = 0$$

The mean can also be seen clearly by the fact that the graph of the function $f(x)$ is symmetric about the y-axis, indicating that its center (or mean) is at $x = 0$. Next, calculate the variance of f.

$$\sigma^2 = \int_{-1}^{1} (x - 0)^2 (-2x^2 + 2)dx = -2 \int_{-1}^{1} x^2(x^2 - 1)dx$$

$$\sigma^2 = -2 \int_{-1}^{1} (x^4 - x^2)dx$$

$$\sigma^2 = -2 \left[\frac{x^5}{5} - \frac{x^3}{3}\right]_{x=-1}^{x=1} = -2\left\{\left[\frac{(1)^5}{5} + \frac{(1)^3}{3}\right] - \left[\frac{(-1)^5}{5} - \frac{(-1)^3}{3}\right]\right\}$$

$$\sigma^2 = -2\left\{\frac{1}{5} - \frac{1}{3} - \left(-\frac{1}{5}\right) + \left(-\frac{1}{3}\right)\right\} = -2\left(\frac{2}{5} - \frac{2}{3}\right)$$

$$\sigma^2 = \frac{8}{15} \approx 0.533$$

The standard deviation is

$$\sigma = \sqrt{\sigma^2} = \sqrt{\frac{8}{15}} \approx 0.730$$

Probability density functions

PROBABILITY DENSITY FUNCTION: the integral of the probability density function over a certain range gives the probability of a data point being in that range of values

A large data set of continuous data is often represented using a probability distribution expressed as a **PROBABILITY DENSITY FUNCTION**. The integral of the probability density function over a certain range gives the probability of a data point being in that range of values. The integral of the probability density function over the whole range of values is equal to 1.

The *mean* value for a distribution of a variable x represented by a probability density function $f(x)$ is given by

$$\int_{-\infty}^{+\infty} xf(x)\,dx$$

(Compare this with its discrete counterpart $\bar{x} = \sum x_i f_i'$).

The *median* is the upper bound for which the integral of the probability density function is equal to 0.5; i.e., if $\int_{-\infty}^{a} f(x)\,dx = 0.5$, then a is the median of the distribution.

The *mode* is the maximum value or values of the probability density function within the range of the function.

As mentioned before, the mean and median are very close together for symmetric distributions. If a distribution is skewed to the right, the mean is greater than the median. If a distribution is skewed to the left, the mean is smaller than the median.

> *If a distribution is skewed to the right, the mean is greater than the median. If a distribution is skewed to the left, the mean is smaller than the median.*

Example: Find the mean, median, and mode for the distribution given by the probability density function

$$f(x) = \begin{cases} 4x(1 - x^2) & 0 \le x \le 1 \\ 0 & \text{otherwise} \end{cases}$$

$$\text{Mean} = \int_{0}^{1} 4x^2(1 - x^2)\,dx = \frac{4x^3}{3}\Big|_0^1 - \frac{4x^5}{5}\Big|_0^1 = \frac{4}{3} - \frac{4}{5} = \frac{20 - 12}{15} = \frac{8}{15} = 0.53$$

If $x = a$ is the median, then

$$\int_{0}^{a} 4x(1 - x^2)\,dx = 0.5$$
$$\rightarrow \frac{4x^2}{2}\Big|_0^a - \frac{4x^4}{4}\Big|_0^a = 0.5$$
$$\rightarrow 2a^2 - a^4 = 0.5$$
$$\rightarrow 2a^4 - 4a^2 + 1 = 0$$

Solving for a yields

$$a^2 = \frac{4 \pm \sqrt{16 - 8}}{4} = 1 \pm \frac{2\sqrt{2}}{4} = 1 - \frac{\sqrt{2}}{2} \text{ (to keep } x \text{ within the range 0 to 1)}$$

$$a = \sqrt{1 - \frac{1}{\sqrt{2}}} = 0.54$$

The mode is obtained by taking the derivative of the probability density function and setting it to zero as shown below. (Notice that the second derivative is negative at $x = 0.58$, and, hence, this is clearly a maximum.)

$$\frac{d}{dx}(4x - 4x^3) = 4 - 12x^2 = 0$$
$$\rightarrow 12x^2 = 4$$
$$\rightarrow x^2 = \frac{1}{3}$$
$$\rightarrow x = \frac{1}{\sqrt{3}} = 0.58$$

SKILL Interpreting data presented in a variety of formats
11.4

See Skill 11.2

COMPETENCY 12
UNDERSTAND THE PRINCIPLES OF PROBABILITY

SKILL Analyzing the relationship between randomness and sampling
12.1 methods in making statistical claims about populations

See Skill 11.1

SKILL Determining the probabilities of simple and compound events
12.2 using counting principles and the concept of sample space

---

PROBABILITY: given a random experiment, the relative frequency of an outcome

RANDOM EXPERIMENT: a structured, repeatable experiment for which the outcome cannot be predicted

RELATIVE FREQUENCY: the number of times an experiment yields a certain outcome for a very large number of trials

---

The **PROBABILITY** of an outcome, given a **RANDOM EXPERIMENT** (a structured, repeatable experiment for which the outcome cannot be predicted or, alternatively, for which the outcome is dependent on "chance"), is the relative frequency of the outcome. The **RELATIVE FREQUENCY** of an outcome is the number of times an experiment yields a certain outcome for a very large (ideally, infinite) number of trials. For instance, if a "fair" coin is tossed a very large number of times, then the relative frequency of a "heads-up" outcome is 0.5, or 50% (that is, one out of every two trials, on average, should be heads up). The probability is this relative frequency.

In probability theory, the **SAMPLE SPACE** is a list of all possible outcomes of an experiment. For example, the sample space of tossing two coins is the set {HH, HT, TT, TH}, where H is heads and T is tails, and the sample space of rolling a six-sided die is the set {1, 2, 3, 4, 5, 6}. When conducting experiments with a large number of possible outcomes, it is important to determine the size of the sample space. The size of the sample space can be determined by using the fundamental counting principles and the rules of combinations and permutations.

A RANDOM VARIABLE is a function that corresponds to the outcome of some experiment or event, which is in turn dependent on "chance." For instance, the result of a tossed coin is a random variable: the outcome is either heads or tails, and each outcome has an associated probability. A DISCRETE VARIABLE is one that can only take on certain specific values. For instance, the number of students in a class can only be a whole number (e.g., 15 or 16, but not 15.5).

A CONTINUOUS VARIABLE, such as the weight of an object, can take on a continuous range of values.

The probabilities for the possible values of a random variable constitute the PROBABILITY DISTRIBUTION for that random variable. Probability distributions can be discrete, as with the case of the tossing of a coin (there are only two possible distinct outcomes), or they can be continuous, as with the outside temperature at a given time of day. In the latter case, the probability is represented as a continuous function over a range of possible temperatures, and finite probabilities can only be measured in terms of ranges of temperatures rather than specific temperatures. That is to say, for a continuous distribution, it is not meaningful to say "the probability that the outcome is x"; instead, only "the probability that the outcome is between x and $\triangle x$" is meaningful. (Note that if each potential outcome in a continuous distribution has a non-zero probability, then the sum of all the probabilities would be greater than 1, since there are an infinite number of potential outcomes.)

> **SAMPLE SPACE:** a list of all possible outcomes of an experiment

> **RANDOM VARIABLE:** a function that corresponds to the outcome of some experiment or event

> **DISCRETE VARIABLE:** can take on only certain specific values

> **CONTINUOUS VARIABLE:** can take on a continuous range of values

> **PROBABILITY DISTRIBUTION:** the probabilities for the possible values of a random variable

Example: Find the sample space and construct a probability distribution for tossing a six-sided die (with numbers 1 through 6) for which even numbers are twice as likely as odd numbers to come up on a given roll (assume the even numbers are equally likely and the odd numbers are equally likely).

The sample space is simply the set of all possible outcomes that can arise in a given trial. For this die, the sample space is {1, 2, 3, 4, 5, 6}. To construct the associated probability distribution, note first that the sum of the probabilities must equal 1. Let the probability of rolling an odd number (1, 3, or 5) be x; the probability of rolling an even number (2, 4, or 6) is then $2x$.

$$1 = p(1) + p(2) + p(3) + p(4) + p(5) + p(6) = 3x + 6x = 9x$$

$$x = \frac{1}{9}$$

The probability distribution can be shown as a histogram below.

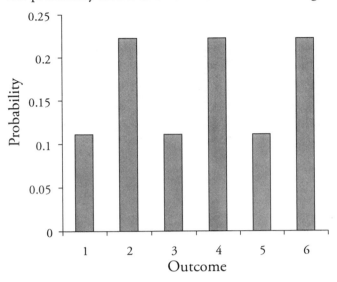

The sum of the probabilities for all the possible outcomes of a discrete distribution (or the integral of the continuous distribution over all possible values) must be equal to unity. The expected value of a probability distribution is the same as the mean value of a probability distribution. The EXPECTED VALUE is thus a measure of the central tendency or average value for a random variable with a given probability distribution.

A BERNOULLI TRIAL is an experiment whose outcome is random and can be either of two possible outcomes, which are called "success" or "failure." Tossing a coin would be an example of a Bernoulli trial. The probability of success is represented by p, with the probability of failure being $q = 1 - p$. Bernoulli trials can be applied to any real-life situation in which there are only two possible outcomes. For example, concerning the birth of a child, the only two possible outcomes for the sex of the child are male or female.

Probability can also be expressed in terms of odds. ODDS are defined as the ratio of the number of favorable outcomes to the number of unfavorable outcomes. The sum of the favorable outcomes and the unfavorable outcomes should always equal the total possible outcomes.

For example, given a bag of 12 red marbles and 7 green marbles, compute the odds of randomly selecting a red marble.

Odds of red = $\frac{12}{7}$

Odds of not getting red = $\frac{7}{12}$

In the case of flipping a coin, it is equally likely that a head or a tail will be tossed. The odds of tossing a head are 1:1. This is called even odds.

EXPECTED VALUE: a measure of the central tendency or average value for a random variable with a given probability distribution

BERNOULLI TRIAL: an experiment whose outcome is random and can be either of two possible outcomes, which are called "success" or "failure"

ODDS: the ratio of the number of favorable outcomes to the number of unfavorable outcomes

A SIMPLE EVENT is a single event such as a coin toss. A COMPOUND EVENT is a combination of two or more simple events that may or may not be dependent on each other. The counting principles described below are used to calculate probabilities for compound events.

The following discussion uses the symbols ∩ to mean "and," ∪ to mean "or," and $P(x)$ to mean "the probability of x." Also, $N(x)$ means "the number of ways that x can occur."

The Addition Rule

The ADDITION PRINCIPLE OF COUNTING states that if A and B are arbitrary events, then

$$N(A \cup B) = N(A) + N(B) - N(A \cap B)$$

Furthermore, if A and B are MUTUALLY EXCLUSIVE EVENTS, then

$$N(A \cup B) = N(A) + N(B)$$

Correspondingly, the probabilities associated with arbitrary events are

$$P(A \cup B) = P(A) + P(B) - P(A \cap B)$$

For mutually exclusive events, the probabilities are

$$P(A \cup B) = P(A) + P(B)$$

Example: In how many ways can you select a black card or a jack from an ordinary deck of playing cards?

Let B denote selection of a black card and let J denote selection of a jack. Then, since half the cards (26) are black and four are jacks,

$$N(B) = 26$$
$$N(J) = 4.$$

Also, since a card can be both black and a jack (the jack of spades and the jack of clubs),

$$N(B \cap J) = 2$$

Thus, the solution is

$$N(B \cup J) = N(B) + N(J) - N(B \cap J) = 26 + 4 - 2 = 28$$

Example: A travel agency offers 40 possible trips: 14 to Asia, 16 to Europe, and 10 to South America. In how many ways can you select a trip to Asia or to Europe through this agency?

Let A denote selection of a trip to Asia and let E denote selection of a trip to Europe. Since these are mutually exclusive events, then

$$N(A \cup E) = N(A) + N(E) = 14 + 16 = 30$$

Therefore, there are 30 ways you can select a trip to Asia or to Europe.

Sidebar definitions:

SIMPLE EVENT: a single event such as a coin toss

COMPOUND EVENT: a combination of two or more simple events that may or may not be dependent on each other

ADDITION PRINCIPLE OF COUNTING: if A and B are arbitrary events, then $N(A \cup B) = N(A) + N(B) - N(A \cap B)$

MUTUALLY EXCLUSIVE EVENTS: events that cannot occur together or have no outcomes in common

The Multiplication Rule

The MULTIPLICATION PRINCIPLE OF COUNTING FOR DEPENDENT EVENTS states that if A and B are arbitrary events, then the number of ways that A and B can occur in a two-stage experiment is given by

$$N(A \cap B) = N(A)N(B \mid A),$$

where $N(B \mid A)$ is the number of ways B can occur given that A has already occurred. This expression is also known as the joint probability of events A and B. If A and B are independent events (events for which the probability of one event is not dependent on the outcome of another event), then

$$N(A \cap B) = N(A)N(B).$$

Also, the probabilities associated with arbitrary events are

$$P(A \cap B) = P(A)P(B \mid A).$$

For independent events, the probabilities are

$$P(A \cap B) = P(A)P(B).$$

> MULTIPLICATION PRINCIPLE OF COUNTING FOR DEPENDENT EVENTS: if A and B are arbitrary events, then the number of ways that A and B can occur in a two-stage experiment is given by $N(A \cap B) = N(A)N(B \mid A)$ where $N(B \mid A)$ is the number of ways B can occur given that A has already occurred

Example: In how many ways can two jacks from an ordinary deck of 52 cards be drawn in succession if the first card is not replaced into the deck before the second card is drawn (that is, without replacement)?

This is a two-stage experiment. Let A be selection of a jack in the first draw and let B be selection of a jack in the second draw. It is clear that

$$N(A) = 4.$$

If the first card drawn is a jack, however, then there are only three jacks remaining for the second draw. Thus, drawing two cards without replacement means the events A and B are dependent, and

$$N(B \mid A) = 3.$$

The solution is

$$N(A \cap B) = N(A)N(B \mid A) = (4)(3) = 12.$$

Example: How many six-letter code "words" can be formed if repetition of letters is not allowed?

Since these are code words, a word does not have to be in the dictionary; for example, *abcdef* could be a code word. Since the experiment requires choosing each letter without replacing the letters from previous selections, the experiment has six stages.

Repetition is not allowed; thus, there are 26 choices for the first letter, 25 for the second, 24 for the third, 23 for the fourth, 22 for the fifth, and 21 for the sixth. Therefore, if A is the selection of a six-letter code word without repetition, then

$$N(A) = (26)(25)(24)(23)(22)(21) = 165{,}765{,}600.$$

There are over 165 million ways to choose a six-letter code word with six unique letters.

Finite Probability

Using the fundamental counting principles described above, finite probability problems can be solved. Generally, finding the probability of a particular event or set of events involves dividing the number of ways the particular event can take place by the total number of possible outcomes for the experiment. Thus, by appropriately counting these possible outcomes using the above rules, probabilities can be determined.

Example: Determine the probability of rolling three even numbers on three successive rolls of a six-sided die.

This is a three-stage experiment. First, determine the total number of possible outcomes for three rolls of a die. For each roll,

$$N(\text{roll}) = 6.$$

There are three possible even rolls for a die: 2, 4, and 6.

$$N(\text{even}) = 3$$

The probability of rolling an even number on any particular roll is

$$P(\text{even}) = \frac{N(\text{even})}{N(\text{roll})} = \frac{3}{6} = \frac{1}{2}.$$

For three successive rolls, use the multiplication rule for mutually exclusive events.

$$P(3 \text{ even rolls}) = P(\text{even})^3 = \left(\tfrac{1}{2}\right)^3 = \frac{1}{8} = 0.125$$

Thus, the probability of rolling three successive even numbers using a six-sided die is 0.125.

Dependent and Independent Events

Dependent events occur when the probability of the second event depends on the outcome of the first event. For example, consider these two events: the home team wins the semifinal round (event A) and the home team wins the final round (event B). The probability of event B is contingent on the probability of event A. If the home team fails to win the semifinal round, it has a zero probability of winning in the final round. On the other hand, if the home team wins the semifinal round, it may have a finite probability of winning in the final round. Symbolically, the probability of event B, given event A, is written $P(B \mid A)$. The conditional probability can be calculated according to the following definition, in which the symbol $\cap$ means "and," the symbol $\cup$ means "or," and the notation $P(x)$ means "the probability of x."

> *Dependent events occur when the probability of the second event depends on the outcome of the first event.*

$$P(B|A) = \frac{P(A \cap B)}{P(A)}$$

Consider a pair of dice, one red and one green. First the red die is rolled, followed by the green die. It is apparent that these events do not depend on each other, since the outcome of the roll of the green die is not affected by the outcome of the roll of the red die. The total probability of the two independent events can be found by multiplying the separate probabilities.

$$P(A \cap B) = P(A)P(B)$$
$$P(A \cap B) = \left(\frac{1}{6}\right)\left(\frac{1}{6}\right) = \frac{1}{36}$$

In many instances, however, events are not independent. Suppose a jar contains 12 red marbles and 8 blue marbles. If a marble is selected at random and then replaced, the probability of picking a certain color is the same in the second trial as it is in the first trial. If the marble is not replaced, then the probability of picking a certain color is not the same in the second trial, because the total number of marbles is decreased by one. This is an illustration of conditional probability. If R_n signifies selection of a red marble on the nth trial and B_n signifies selection of a blue marble on the nth trial, the probability of selecting a red marble in two trials *with replacement* is

$$P(R_1 \cap R_2) = P(R_1)P(R_2) = \left(\frac{12}{20}\right)\left(\frac{12}{20}\right) = \frac{144}{400} = 0.36$$

The probability of selecting a red marble in two trials *without replacement* is

$$P(R_1 \cap R_2) = P(R_1)P(R|R_1) = \left(\frac{12}{20}\right)\left(\frac{11}{19}\right) = \frac{132}{360} \approx 0.367$$

Example: A car has a 75% probability of traveling 20,000 miles without breaking down. It has a 50% probability of traveling 10,000 additional miles without breaking down if it first reaches 20,000 miles without breaking down. What is the probability that the car reaches 30,000 miles without breaking down?

Let event A be that the car reaches 20,000 miles without breaking down.

$$P(A) = 0.75$$

Event B is that the car travels an additional 10,000 miles without breaking down (assuming it didn't break down for the first 20,000 miles). Since event B is contingent on event A, write the probability

$$P(B|A) = 0.50$$

Use the conditional probability formula to find the probability that the car travels 30,000 miles ($A \cap B$) without breaking down.

$$P(B|A) = \frac{P(A \cap B)}{P(A)}$$
$$P(B|A) = \frac{P(A \cap B)}{0.75}$$
$$P(A \cap B) = (0.50)(0.75) = 03.75$$

Thus, the car has a 37.5% probability of traveling 30,000 consecutive miles without breaking down.

SKILL Solving problems using graphic representations to calculate
12.3 probabilities

Probabilities can be calculated by finding the ratios of areas of geometric regions. In the context of probability distributions, probabilities correspond to areas under the probability density function. For instance, the total area under the probability density curve should be unity (since the probability of some outcome for an experiment must be one). The ratio of the area under the curve for some particular value or range of values for the random variable to the total area (unity) is the probability of that value or range of values.

Likewise, probabilities can be represented using the **VENN DIAGRAM**, which represents events or sets of events as shapes that depict the relationships of these events by overlapping (or not overlapping). For example, let the rectangle below represent all the possible outcomes of the random selection of a card from a standard deck. Let oval A be all the outcomes for which a spade is chosen, and let oval B be all the outcomes for which a jack is chosen. Since there is one choice that falls within both of these categories (the jack of spades), the ovals overlap.

> **VENN DIAGRAM:**
> represents events or sets of events as shapes that depict the relationships of these events by overlapping (or not overlapping)

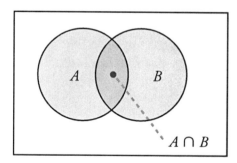

$A \cap B$

If the shapes correspond to areas that are to scale with their probabilities, then a Venn diagram can be used to calculate probabilities using ratios of these areas. Consider, for instance, the flip of a fair coin. The diagram for this case is shown below. (Although this may not be strictly considered a Venn diagram, depending on the definition of such, it does relay the same idea.)

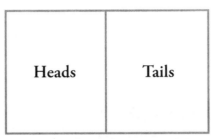

Notice that the total area A is divided evenly between "heads" $\left(\frac{A}{2}\right)$ and "tails" $\left(\frac{A}{2}\right)$. Thus, the probability of heads (or tails) is

$$\frac{\frac{A}{2}}{2} = \frac{1}{2}.$$

Another Venn diagram is shown below for a six-sided die.

1	4
2	5
3	6

Again, the possibility of a particular outcome or range of outcomes can be found by using ratios of the associated areas. In both the cases above, there are no possible outcomes beyond those shown, so the Venn diagram does not show any area outside these outcomes.

Geometric probability describes situations that involve shapes and measures. For example, given a 10-inch string, we can determine the probability of cutting the string so that one piece is at least 8 inches long. If the cut occurs in the first or last two inches of the string, one of the pieces will be at least 8 inches long.

String

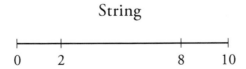

Thus, the probability of such a cut is $\frac{2+2}{10} = \frac{4}{10} = \frac{2}{5}$ or 40%.

Other geometric probability problems involve the ratio of areas. For example, to determine the likelihood of randomly hitting a defined area of a dartboard (pictured below) we determine the ratio of the target area to the total area of the board.

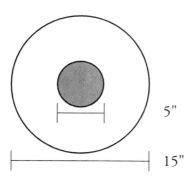

5"

15"

Given that a randomly thrown dart lands somewhere on the board, the probability that it hits the target area is the ratio of the areas of the two circles. Thus, the probability, P, of hitting the target is

$$P = \frac{(2.5)^2\pi}{(7.5)^2\pi} \times 100 = \frac{6.25}{56.25} \times 100 = 11.1\%.$$

<h3>SKILL 12.4 — Determining probabilities based on data collection, experiments, and simulations</h3>

Probability Simulations

Simulations of random events or variables can be helpful in making informal inferences about theoretical probability distributions. Although simulations can involve use of physical situations that bear some similarity to the situation of interest, oftentimes simulations involve computer modeling.

Pseudorandom numbers

One of the crucial aspects of modeling probability using a computer program is the need for a random number that can be used to "randomize" the aspect of the program that corresponds to the event or variable. Although there is no function on a computer that can provide a truly random number, most programming languages have some function designed to produce a pseudorandom number. A PSEUDORANDOM NUMBER is not truly random, but it is sufficiently unpredictable that it can be used as a random number in many contexts.

Pseudorandom numbers can serve as the basis for simulation of rolling a die, flipping a coin, selecting an object from a collection of different objects, and a range of other situations. If, for instance, the pseudorandom number generator produces a number between 0 and 1, simply divide up that range in accordance with the probabilities of each particular outcome. (For instance, assign 0 to 0.5 as heads and 0.5 to 1 as tails for the flip of a fair coin.) By performing a number of simulated trials and tallying the results, empirical probability distributions can be created.

PSEUDORANDOM NUMBER: a number that is not truly random but that is sufficiently unpredictable that it can be used as a random number in many contexts

Ideally, as the number of trials goes to infinity, the empirical probability distribution should approach the theoretical distribution. As a result, by performing a sufficiently large number of trials (this number must be at least somewhat justified for the particular situation), one should be able to make informal inferences based on the data. Such inferences, however, must take into account the limitations of the computer, such as the inability to perform an infinite number of trials in finite time and the numerical inaccuracies that are an inherent part of computer programming.

D O M A I N   V
DISCRETE MATHEMATICS AND READING

PERSONALIZED STUDY PLAN

KNOWN MATERIAL/ SKIP IT

COMPETENCY 13
UNDERSTAND THE PROCESSES AND APPLICATIONS OF DISCRETE MATHEMATICS

SKILL 13.1 **Applying the concept of patterns** *(e.g., series and sequences, iteration and recursion, inductive reasoning, finite differences)* **to model situations and solve problems**

See Skills 4.1 and 4.2 for a discussion of patterns.

See Skill 9.4 for a discussion of inductive reasoning.

SKILL 13.2 **Applying systematic counting techniques**

Example: Suppose you want to order a pizza. You have a choice of three sizes (small, medium, or large), three types of crust (thin, pan, or hand-tossed), four choices of meat (pepperoni, sausage, both, or none), and three choices of cheese (regular, double, or stuffed with cheese). How many different types of pizza could you order?

$3 \times 3 \times 4 \times 3 = 108$ different types of pizza

Another method of basic counting is the tree diagram.

Example: Suppose you want to look at the possible sequence of events for having two children in a family. Since a child will be either a boy or a girl, you would have the following tree diagram to illustrate the possible outcomes:

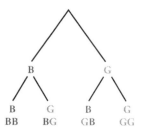

From the diagram, you see that there are four possible outcomes, two of which are the same.

Using Pascal's Triangle to Solve Problems

Pascal's triangle looks like the following:

$$
\begin{array}{ccccccccccc}
 & & & & & 1 & & & & & \\
 & & & & 1 & & 1 & & & & \\
 & & & 1 & & 2 & & 1 & & & \\
 & & 1 & & 3 & & 3 & & 1 & & \\
 & 1 & & 4 & & 6 & & 4 & & 1 & \\
1 & & 5 & & 10 & & 10 & & 5 & & 1
\end{array}
$$

where the sum of Row 1 $= 2^0$, Row 2 $= 2^1$, Row 3 $= 2^2$, Row 4 $= 2^3$, Row 5 $= 2^4$, Row 6 $= 2^5$. From this, we can see that the sum of row n would be 2^n.

Pascal's Triangle is useful in experiments in which there are only two equally likely possibilities, such as coin tosses.

Example: Find the probability of getting at least 5 heads when tossing 6 coins.

Solution: The fundamental counting property tells us that there are 2^6 possible outcomes when tossing 6 coins. We then construct the row of Pascal's Triangle that begins 1, 6:

$$
\begin{array}{ccccccc}
1 & 6 & 15 & 20 & 15 & 6 & 1
\end{array}
$$

The first five numbers, 1, 6, 15, 20, and 15, represent the number of outcomes for which there are at least 5 heads. Therefore, we find the probability of tossing at least 5 heads with 6 coins as:

$$
\frac{(1 + 6 + 15 + 20 + 15)}{2^6} = \frac{57}{64}
$$

Permutations and Combinations

A PERMUTATION is the number of possible arrangements of n items, without repetition, where order of selection is important.

A COMBINATION is the number of possible arrangements of n items, without repetition, where order of selection is not important.

PERMUTATION: the number of possible arrangements of n items, without repetition, where order of selection is important

COMBINATION: the number of possible arrangements of n items, without repetition, where order of selection is not important

Example: If any two numbers are selected from the set {1, 2, 3, 4}, list the possible permutations and combinations.

Combinations	Permutations
12, 13, 14, 23, 24, 34: six ways	12, 21, 13, 31, 14, 41, 23, 32, 24, 42, 34, 43: twelve ways

Note that the list of permutations includes 12 and 21 as separate possibilities since the order of selection is important. In the case of combinations, however, the order of selection is not important and, therefore, 12 is the same combination as 21. Hence, 21 is not listed separately as a possibility.

The number of permutations and combinations may also be found by using the formulae given below.

The number of possible permutations in selecting r objects from a set of n is given by

$$_nP_r = \frac{n!}{(n-r)!}$$ The notation $_nP_r$ is read "the number of permutations of n objects taken r at a time."

In our example, two objects are being selected from a set of four.

$$_4P_2 = \frac{4!}{(4-2)!}$$ Substitute known values.

$$_4P_2 = 12$$

The number of possible combinations in selecting r objects from a set of n is given by

$$_nC_r = \frac{n!}{(n-r)!r!}$$ The number of combinations when r objects are selected from n objects.

In our example,

$$_4C_2 = \frac{4!}{(4-2)!2!}$$ Substitute known values.

$$_4C_2 = 6$$

Objects arranged in a row

It can be shown that $_nP_n$, the number of ways n objects can be arranged in a row, is equal to $n!$. We can think of the problem as n positions being filled, one at a time. The first position can be filled in n ways using any one of the n objects. Since one of the objects has already been used, the second position can be filled only in $n-1$ ways. Similarly, the third position can be filled in $n-2$ ways, and so on. Hence, the total number of possible arrangements of n objects in a row is given by

$$_nP_n = n(n-1)(n-2)........1 = n!.$$

Example: Five books are placed in a row on a bookshelf. In how many different ways can they be arranged?

The number of possible ways in which 5 books can be arranged in a row is $5! = 1 \times 2 \times 3 \times 4 \times 5 = 120$.

The formula given above for $_nP_r$, *the number of possible permutations of* r *objects selected from* n *objects,* can also be proven in a similar manner. If r positions are filled by selecting from n objects, the first position can be filled in n ways, the second position can be filled in $n - 1$ ways, and so on (as shown before). The rth position can be filled in $n - (r - 1) = n - r + 1$ ways. Hence,

$$_nP_r = n(n - 1)(n - 2)\ldots(n - r + 1) = \frac{n!}{(n - r)!}$$

The formula for the *number of possible combinations of* r *objects selected from* n, $_nC_r$, may be derived by using the above two formulae. For the same set of r objects, the number of permutations is $r!$. All of these permutations, however, correspond to the same combination. Hence,

$$_nC_r = \frac{_nP_r}{r!} = \frac{n!}{(n - r)!r!}$$

Objects arranged in a ring

The number of permutations of n *objects in a ring is given by* (n − 1)!. This can be demonstrated by considering the fact that the number of permutations of n objects in a row is $n!$. When the objects are placed in a ring, moving every object one place to its left will result in the same arrangement. Moving each object two places to its left will also result in the same arrangement. We can continue this kind of movement up to n places to get the same arrangement. Thus the count $n!$ is n times too many when the objects are arranged in a ring. Hence, the number of permutations of n objects in a ring is given by $\frac{n!}{n} = (n - 1)!$.

Example: There are 20 people at a meeting. Five of them are selected to lead a discussion. How many different combinations of five people can be selected from the group? If the five people are seated in a row, how many different seating permutations are possible? If the five people are seated around a circular table, how many possible permutations are there?

The number of possible combinations of 5 people selected from the group of 20 is

$$_{20}C_5 = \frac{20!}{15!5!} = \frac{16 \times 17 \times 18 \times 19 \times 20}{1 \times 2 \times 3 \times 4 \times 5} = \frac{1860480}{120} = 15504.$$

The number of possible permutations of the five seated in a row is

$$_{20}P_5 = \frac{20!}{15!} = 16 \times 17 \times 18 \times 19 \times 20 = 1860480.$$

The number of possible permutations of the five seated in a circle is

$$\frac{_{20}P_5}{5} = \frac{20!}{5 \times 15!} = \frac{16 \times 17 \times 18 \times 19 \times 20}{5} = 372096.$$

Sets containing like objects

If the set of n objects contains some objects that are exactly alike, the number of permutations will again be different than $n!$. For instance, if n_1 of the n objects are exactly alike, then switching those objects among themselves will result in the same arrangement. Since we already know that n_1 objects can be arranged in $n_1!$ ways, n! must be reduced by a factor of $n_1!$ to get the correct number of permutations. Thus, the number of permutations of n objects of which n_1 are exactly alike is given by $\frac{n!}{n_1!}$. Generalizing this, *we can say that the number of different permutations of* n *objects of which* n_1 *are alike,* n_2 *are alike,* …, n_j *are alike, is*

$$\frac{n!}{n_1! \, n_2! \dots n_j!} \text{ where } n_1 + n_2 \dots + n_j = n.$$

Example: A box contains 3 red, 2 blue, and 5 green marbles. If all the marbles are taken out of the box and arranged in a row, how many different permutations are possible?

The number of possible permutations is

$$\frac{10!}{3!2!5!} = \frac{6 \times 7 \times 8 \times 9 \times 10}{6 \times 2} = 2520$$

SKILL 13.3 **Analyzing algorithms designed to accomplish a task**

Algorithms

An **ALGORITHM** is a method of calculating; simply put, it can be multiplication, subtraction, or a combination of operations. When we work with computers and calculators, we employ algorithmic thinking, which means performing mathematical tasks by creating a sequential and often repetitive set of steps. A simple example would be to create an algorithm to generate the Fibonacci numbers utilizing the MR and M+ keys found on most calculators. The table below shows the entry made in the calculator, the value x seen in the display, and the value M contained in the memory.

> **ALGORITHM:** a method of calculating

ENTRY	ON/AC	1	M+	+	M+	MR	+	M+	MR	+	...
x	0	1	1	1	1	2	3	3	5	8	...
M	0	0	1	1	2	2	2	5	5	5	...

This eliminates the need to repeatedly enter required numbers.

Computers have to be programmed and many advanced calculators are programmable. A **PROGRAM** is the steps of an algorithm that are entered into a computer or calculator. The main advantage of using a program is that, once the algorithm is entered, a result may be obtained by merely using a single keystroke to select the program, thereby eliminating the need to continually enter a large number of steps. Teachers find that programmable calculators are excellent for investigating "what if?" situations.

> **PROGRAM:** the steps of an algorithm that are entered into a computer or calculator

Using graphing calculators or computer software has many advantages. The technology is better able to handle large data sets, such as the results of a science experiment, and it is much easier to edit and sort the data and to change the style of the graph to find its best representation. Furthermore, graphing calculators also provide a tool to plot statistics.

Concrete and visual representations can help demonstrate the logic behind operational algorithms. Blocks or other objects modeled on the base ten system are useful concrete tools. Base ten blocks represent ones, tens, and hundreds. For example, modeling the partial sums algorithm with base ten blocks helps clarify the thought process. Consider the sum of 242 and 193. We represent 242 with 2 one hundred blocks, 4 ten blocks, and 2 one blocks. We represent 193 with 1 one hundred block, 9 ten blocks, and 3 one blocks. In the partial sums algorithm, we manipulate each place value separately and total the results. Thus, we group the hundred blocks, ten blocks, and one blocks and derive a total for each place value. We combine the place values to complete the sum.

An example of a visual representation of an operational algorithm is the modeling of a two-term multiplication as the area of a rectangle. For example, consider the product of 24 and 39. We can represent the product in geometric form. Note that the four sections of the rectangle equate to the four products of the partial products method.

	30	9
20	A = 600	A = 180
4	A = 120	A = 36

Thus, the final product is the sum of the areas or $600 + 180 + 120 + 36 = 936$.

Flowcharts

A flowchart is a kind of diagram that represents the sequential steps in an algorithm or a process. Flowcharts are commonly used in computer programming. In general, a flow chart is typically used to represent a process that includes decision points where the process branches out into alternate paths.

Example: Create a flow chart to represent plans for a field day at a school. Morning classes will be followed by a pizza lunch and then outdoor sports for two hours before dismissal. If it rains, children will play indoor games after lunch. If the temperature is higher than 90°F, tents will be set up outside before the sports activities.

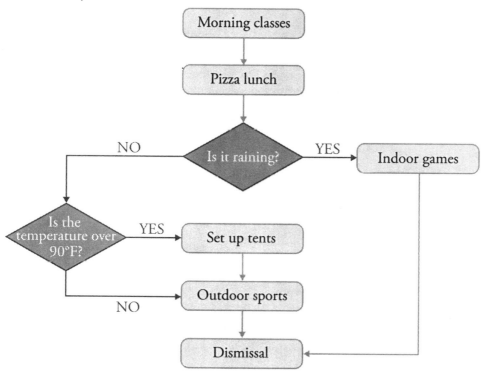

SKILL **Applying a variety of models** *(e.g., vertex-edge graphs, trees, arrays,*
13.4 *matrices)* **to solve problems**

Difference Equations

A **DIFFERENCE EQUATION** is a discrete analog for a differential equation, with "differences" being analogous to derivatives. For a sequence of numbers $\{a_n\}$, the first difference is defined as

$$d(a_n) = a_n - a_{n-1}$$

The second difference is given by

$$d^2(a_n) = d(a_n) - d(a_{n-1}) = a_n - 2a_{n-1} + a_{n-2}$$

Subsequent differences are defined in a similar fashion.

DIFFERENCE EQUATION: a discrete analog for a differential equation, with "differences" being analogous to derivatives

A difference equation is an equation composed of a discrete variable a_n and its differences of different orders. It is clear from the above definitions that a difference equation is nothing but a recurrence relation, and many people use the two terms interchangeably.

Graphs

GRAPH: a set of points (or nodes) and lines (or edges) that connect some subset of these points

FINITE GRAPH: a graph with a limited number of both nodes and edges

A GRAPH is a set of points (or nodes) and lines (or edges) that connect some subset of these points. A FINITE GRAPH has a limited number of both nodes and edges. An example graph follows. Note that not all of the nodes in a graph need be connected to other nodes.

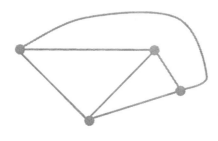

The edges of a graph may or may not have a specified direction or orientation; also, the edges (and nodes) may or may not have some assigned label or value. For instance, a graph representing airline flight paths might include nodes that represent cities and edges the represent the direction and distance of the paths between the cities.

Trees

TREE: a graph that does not include any closed loops or unconnected nodes

FINITE TREE: a tree with a limited number of edges and nodes

NETWORK: a graph (directed or undirected) in which each edge is assigned a positive real number in accordance with a specific function

A TREE is a graph that does not include any closed loops. In addition, a tree has no unconnected nodes (separate nodes or groups of connected nodes constitute a separate tree—groups of several trees are called a forest). In addition, the edges that connect the nodes of a tree do not have a direction or orientation. A FINITE TREE, like a finite graph, has a limited number of edges and nodes. The graph shown above is not a tree, but it takes the form of a tree with a few alterations:

Networks

A NETWORK is a graph (directed or undirected) in which each edge is assigned a positive real number in accordance with a specific function. The function may correspond to the distance between two points on a map, for instance.

Solving Problems Using Trees and Graphs

Trees and graphs can be used to represent a wide variety of types of information. They can also be useful tools for solving problems that involve maps, hierarchies, directories, structures, communications networks and a range of other objects.

Example: Find the shortest path between points A and B on the following directed graph.

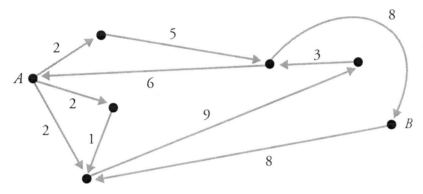

Taking careful note of the direction of the edges, find the possible routes through the graph from *A* to *B*. Only two paths are possible; choose the path with the smallest sum of the values along the associated edges.

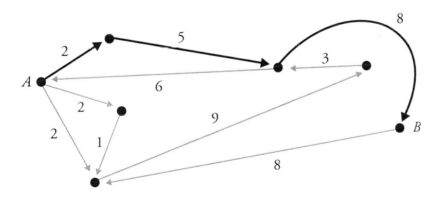

The total distance for the shortest path is 2 + 5 + 8 = 15.

Matrices

Properties of Matrices

A **MATRIX** is an array of an ordered set of numbers called elements. An example matrix is shown below. The **DIMENSIONS** of a matrix are written as the number of rows by the number of columns ($r \times c$).

$$\begin{pmatrix} 0 & 3 & 1 \\ 4 & 2 & 3 \\ 1 & 0 & 2 \end{pmatrix}$$

MATRIX: an array of an ordered set of numbers called elements

DIMENSIONS: written as the number of rows by the number of columns ($r \times c$)

Since this matrix has three rows and three columns, it is called a 3 × 3 matrix. The element in the second row of the third column would be denoted as $3_{2,3}$.

$$\begin{pmatrix} 1 & 2 & 3 \\ 4 & 5 & 6 \end{pmatrix} \text{ is a 2 × 3 matrix (2 rows by 3 columns)}$$

$$\begin{pmatrix} 1 & 2 \\ 3 & 4 \\ 5 & 6 \end{pmatrix} \text{ is a 3 × 2 matrix (3 rows by 2 columns)}$$

Matrices can be added or subtracted only if their dimensions are the same. To add (subtract) compatible matrices, simply add (subtract) the corresponding elements, as with the example below for 2 × 2 matrices.

$$\begin{pmatrix} a_{11} & a_{12} \\ a_{21} & a_{22} \end{pmatrix} + \begin{pmatrix} a_{11} & a_{12} \\ a_{21} & a_{22} \end{pmatrix} = \begin{pmatrix} a_{11} + b_{11} & a_{11} + b_{12} \\ a_{21} + b_{21} & a_{22} + b_{22} \end{pmatrix}$$

Scalar Multiplication of Matrices

SCALAR MULTIPLICATION is the product of the scalar (the outside number) and each element inside the matrix.

> **SCALAR MULTIPLICATION:** the product of the scalar (the outside number) and each element inside the matrix

Example: Given:

$$A = \begin{pmatrix} 4 & 0 \\ 3 & -1 \end{pmatrix}, \text{ find } 2A.$$

$$2A = 2 \begin{pmatrix} 4 & 0 \\ 3 & -1 \end{pmatrix}$$

$$\begin{pmatrix} 2 \times 4 & 2 \times 0 \\ 2 \times 3 & 2 \times -1 \end{pmatrix} \qquad \text{Multiply each element in the matrix by the scalar.}$$

$$\begin{pmatrix} 8 & 0 \\ 6 & -2 \end{pmatrix} \qquad \text{Simplify.}$$

The variable in a matrix equation represents a matrix. When solving for the answer use the adding, subtracting, and scalar multiplication properties.

Example: Solve the matrix equation for the variable x.

$$2x + \begin{pmatrix} 4 & 8 & 2 \\ 7 & 3 & 4 \end{pmatrix} = 2 \begin{pmatrix} 1 & -2 & 0 \\ 3 & -5 & 7 \end{pmatrix}$$

$$2x = 2 \begin{pmatrix} 1 & -2 & 0 \\ 3 & -5 & 7 \end{pmatrix} - \begin{pmatrix} 4 & 8 & 2 \\ 7 & 3 & 4 \end{pmatrix} \qquad \text{Subtract } \begin{pmatrix} 4 & 8 & 2 \\ 7 & 3 & 4 \end{pmatrix} \text{ from both sides.}$$

$$2x = \begin{pmatrix} 2 & -4 & 0 \\ 6 & -10 & 14 \end{pmatrix} + \begin{pmatrix} -4 & -8 & -2 \\ -7 & -3 & -4 \end{pmatrix} \qquad \begin{array}{l} \text{Scalar multiplication and} \\ \text{matrix subtraction.} \end{array}$$

$$2x = \begin{pmatrix} -2 & -12 & -2 \\ -1 & -13 & 10 \end{pmatrix} \qquad \text{Matrix addition.}$$

$$x = \begin{pmatrix} -1 & -6 & -1 \\ -\frac{1}{2} & -\frac{13}{2} & 5 \end{pmatrix}$$

Multiply both sides by $\frac{1}{2}$ or divide by 2.

Solve for the unknown values of the elements in the matrix.

$$\begin{pmatrix} x+3 & y-2 \\ z+3 & w-4 \end{pmatrix} + \begin{pmatrix} -2 & 4 \\ 2 & 5 \end{pmatrix} = \begin{pmatrix} 4 & 8 \\ 6 & 1 \end{pmatrix}$$

$$\begin{pmatrix} x+1 & y+2 \\ z+5 & w+1 \end{pmatrix} = \begin{pmatrix} 4 & 8 \\ 6 & 1 \end{pmatrix}$$

Matrix addition.

$x + 1 = 4 \quad y + 2 = 8 \quad z + 5 = 6 \quad w + 1 = 1$

$x = 3 \qquad y = 6 \qquad z = 1 \qquad w = 0$

Definition of equal matrices.

Matrices are often used to solve systems of equations. They are also used by physicists, mathematicians, and biologists to organize and study data such as population growth, and they are used in finance for such purposes as investment growth and portfolio analysis. Matrices are easily translated into computer code in high-level programming languages and can be easily expressed in electronic spreadsheets.

The following is an example of using a matrix to solve a simple financial problem. A company has two stores. The incomes and expenses (in dollars) for the two stores, for three months, are shown in the matrices.

April	Income	Expenses
Store 1	190,000	170,000
Store 2	100,000	110,000

May	Income	Expenses
Store 1	210,000	200,000
Store 2	125,000	120,000

June	Income	Expenses
Store 1	220,000	215,000
Store 2	130,000	115,000

The owner wants to know what his first-quarter income and expenses were, so he adds the three matrices.

1st Quarter	Income	Expenses
Store 1	620,000	585,000
Store 2	355,000	345,000

Then, to find the profit for each store:

Profit for Store 1 = \$620,000 − \$585,000 = \$35,000

Profit for Store 2 = \$355,000 − \$345,000 = \$10,000

When given the following system of equations

$ax + by = e$

$cx + dy = f,$

the matrix equation is written in the form

$$\begin{pmatrix} a & b \\ c & d \end{pmatrix} \begin{pmatrix} x \\ y \end{pmatrix} = \begin{pmatrix} e \\ f \end{pmatrix}.$$

The solution is found using the inverse of the matrix of coefficients. The inverse of a 2 × 2 matrix can be written as follows:

$$A^{-1} = \frac{1}{|A|}\begin{pmatrix} d & -b \\ -c & a \end{pmatrix}.$$

Example: Write the matrix equation of the following system of equations and solve for x and y.

$$3x - 4y = 2$$
$$2x - y = 5$$

$$\begin{pmatrix} 3 & -4 \\ 2 & 1 \end{pmatrix}\begin{pmatrix} x \\ y \end{pmatrix} = \begin{pmatrix} 2 \\ 5 \end{pmatrix}$$ Definition of matrix equation.

$$\begin{pmatrix} x \\ y \end{pmatrix} = \frac{1}{11}\begin{pmatrix} 1 & 4 \\ -2 & 1 \end{pmatrix}\begin{pmatrix} 2 \\ 5 \end{pmatrix}$$ Multiply by the inverse of the coefficient matrix.

$$\begin{pmatrix} x \\ y \end{pmatrix} = \frac{1}{11}\begin{pmatrix} 22 \\ 11 \end{pmatrix}$$ Matrix multiplication.

$$\begin{pmatrix} x \\ y \end{pmatrix} = \begin{pmatrix} 2 \\ 1 \end{pmatrix}$$ Scalar multiplication.

The solution is $x = 2$ and $y = 1$.

COMPETENCY 14
UNDERSTAND THE CONTENT AND METHODS FOR DEVELOPING STUDENTS' CONTENT-AREA READING SKILLS TO SUPPORT THEIR READING AND LEARNING IN MIDDLE LEVEL MATHEMATICS

> **SKILL 14.1** **Demonstrating knowledge of key components and processes involved in reading** *(e.g., vocabulary knowledge, including orthographic and morphological knowledge; background knowledge; knowledge of academic discourse, including the syntactic and organizational structures used in print and digital academic texts; print processing abilities, including decoding skills; use of cognitive and metacognitive skills and strategies)*

In 2000, the National Reading Panel released its now well-known report on teaching children to read. This report partially put to rest the debate between phonics and whole language. It essentially argued that word–letter recognition is as important as understanding what the text means. The report's "Big 5" critical areas of reading instruction are explained in the following sections.

Phonemic Awareness

PHONEMIC AWARENESS is the acknowledgement of sounds and words; for example, a child's realization that some words rhyme is one of the skills that fall under this category. *Onset* and *rhyme* are skills that might help students learn that the sound of the first letter "b" in the word "bad" can be changed with the sound "d" to make it "dad." The key in phonemic awareness is that it can be taught with the students' eyes closed; in other words, it's all about understanding sounds, not ascribing written letters to sounds.

PHONEMIC AWARE-NESS: the acknowledge-ment of sounds and words

Phonics

As opposed to phonemic awareness, the study of phonics must be done with the eyes open. PHONICS is the connection between sounds and the letters on a page. In other words, students learning phonics might see the word "bad" and sound each letter out slowly until they recognize that they just said the word.

PHONICS: the connection between sounds and the letters on a page

Fluency

When students practice FLUENCY, they practice reading connected pieces of text. In other words, instead of looking at a word as just a word, they might read a sentence straight through. The point of fluency is for the student to comprehend what he or she is reading by putting words in a sentence together quickly. If a student is NOT fluent in reading, he or she would sound each letter or word out slowly and pay more attention to the phonics of each word. A fluent reader, on the other hand, might read a sentence out loud using appropriate intonations.

FLUENCY: reading con-nected pieces of text

The best way to test for fluency is to have a student read something out loud, preferably a few sentences in a row. Most students just learning to read will not be very fluent right away, but with practice, they will increase their fluency. Even though fluency is not the same as comprehension, fluency is a good predictor of comprehension; when the student is freed from focusing on sounding out each word, he or she can shift attention to the meaning of the words.

Comprehension

COMPREHENSION simply means that the reader can ascribe meaning to text. Even though students may be good with phonics, and may know what many words on a page mean, some of them are not able to demonstrate comprehension because they do not have the tools to help them comprehend. For example, students should know that stories often have structures (beginning, middle, and end). They should also know that when they are reading something and it does not make sense, they will need to employ "fix-up" strategies where they go back into the text

COMPREHENSION: when the reader can ascribe meaning to text

they just read and look for clues. Teachers can use many strategies to teach comprehension, including questioning, asking students to paraphrase or summarize, utilizing graphic organizers, and focusing on mental images.

Vocabulary

Students will be better at comprehension if they have a stronger working vocabulary. Research has shown that students learn more vocabulary when it is presented in context, rather than in vocabulary lists, for example. Furthermore, the more students get to use particular words in context, the more they will remember each word and utilize the words in the comprehension of sentences that contain the words.

See also Skill 14.4

SKILL 14.2 **Demonstrating ability to plan instruction and select strategies to support all students' content-area reading** (e.g., *differentiating instruction to meet the needs of students with varying reading proficiency levels and linguistic backgrounds, identifying and addressing gaps in students' background knowledge, scaffolding reading tasks for students who experience comprehension difficulties*)

ASSESSMENT: the practice of collecting information about children's progress

EVALUATION: the process of judging the children's responses to determine how well they are achieving particular goals or demonstrating reading skills

FORMAL ASSESSMENT: composed of standardized tests and procedures carried out under prescribed conditions

Reading Assessment

ASSESSMENT is the practice of collecting information about children's progress, and EVALUATION is the process of judging the children's responses to determine how well they are achieving particular goals or demonstrating reading skills.

Assessment and evaluation are intricately connected in the literacy classroom. Assessment is necessary because teachers need ways to determine what students are learning and how they are progressing. In addition, assessment is a tool that can also help students take ownership of their own learning and become partners in their ongoing development as readers and writers. In this day of public accountability, clear, definite, and reliable assessment creates confidence in public education. There are two broad categories of assessment.

FORMAL ASSESSMENT is composed of standardized tests and procedures carried out under prescribed conditions. Formal assessments include state tests, standardized achievement tests, NAEP tests, and the like.

INFORMAL ASSESSMENT is the use of observation and other non-standardized procedures to compile anecdotal and observational data/evidence of children's progress. Informal assessment includes but is not limited to checklists, observations, and performance tasks.

INFORMAL ASSESS-MENT: the use of observation and other non-standardized procedures to compile anecdotal and ob-servational data/evidence of children's progress

Skills to be evaluated

- The ability to use syntactic cues when encountering an unknown word. Good readers will expect the word to fit the syntax they are familiar with. Poor readers may substitute a word that does not fit the syntax and will not correct themselves.

- The ability to use semantic cues to determine the meaning of an unknown word. Good readers will consider the meanings of all the known words in the sentence. Poor readers may read one word at a time with no regard for the other words.

- The ability to use schematic cues to connect words with prior knowledge. Good readers will incorporate what they know with what the text says or implies. Poor readers may think only of the word they are reading without associating it with prior knowledge.

- The ability to use phonics cues to improve ease and efficiency in reading. Good readers will apply letter and sound associations almost subconsciously. Poor readers may have one of two kinds of problems:

  A. They may have underdeveloped phonics skills, and use only an initial clue without analyzing vowel patterns before quickly guessing the word.

  B. They may use phonics skills in isolation, becoming so absorbed in the word "noises" that they ignore or forget the message of the text.

- The ability to process information from the text. Good readers should be able to get information from the text as well as store, retrieve, and integrate it for later use.

- The ability to use interpretive thinking to make logical predictions and inferences.

- The ability to use critical thinking to make decisions and insights about the text.

- The ability to use appreciative thinking to respond to the text, whether emotionally, mentally, or ideologically.

Methods of evaluation

- Assess students at the beginning of each year to determine grouping for instruction.

- Judge whether a student recognizes that a word does not make sense.

- Monitor whether the student knows when to ignore a reading mistake and read on or when to reread a sentence.

- Look for skills such as recognizing cause and effect, finding main ideas, and using comparison and contrast techniques.

- Keep dated records to follow individual progress. Focus on a few students each day. Grade them on a scale of one to five according to how well they perform certain reading abilities (such as making logical predictions). Include informal observations such as, "Ed was able to determine the meaning of the word 'immigrant' by examining the other words in the sentence."

- Remember that evaluation is important but fostering an enjoyment of reading is the ultimate goal. Keep reading pressure-free and fun so that students do not become intimidated by reading. Even if the students are not meeting standards, if they continue to want to read each day, that is a success!

Differentiation of Instruction

Teachers can differentiate instruction in order to address the needs of students with varying levels of reading proficiency.

DIFFERENTIATION OF INSTRUCTION occurs when the teacher will vary the content, process, or product used in instruction (Tomlinson, 1995).

There are three primary ways to differentiate:

- Content: The specifics of what is learned. This does not mean that whole units or concepts should be modified. However, within certain topics, specifics can be modified.

- Process: The route to learning the content. All students do not have to learn the content using exactly the same method.

- Product: The result of the learning. Usually, a product is the result or assessment of learning. For example, not all students are going to demonstrate complete learning on a quiz; likewise, not all students will demonstrate complete learning on a written paper.

> **DIFFERENTIATION OF INSTRUCTION:** when the teacher varies the content, process, or product used in instruction

There are two keys to successful differentiation:

- Knowing what is essential in the curriculum: Although certain things can be modified, other things must remain intact and in a specific order. Disrupting central components of a curriculum can actually damage a student's ability to learn something successfully.

- Knowing the needs of the students: While this can take quite some time to figure out, it is very important that teachers pay attention to the interests, tendencies, and abilities of their students so that they understand how each of their students will best learn.

Many students will need certain concepts explained in greater depth; others may pick up on concepts rather quickly. For this reason, teachers will want to adapt the curriculum in a way that gives students the opportunity to learn at their own pace while also keeping the class together as a community. Although this can be difficult, the more creative a teacher is with the ways in which students can demonstrate mastery, the more fun the experience will be for students and teachers. Furthermore, teachers will reach students more successfully if they tailor lesson plans, activities, groupings, and other elements of curriculum to each student's need. The reasons for differentiating instruction are based on two important differences in children: interest and ability.

Differentiating Reading Instruction

Differentiating reading instruction is a bit complex. When a teacher wants to ensure that each student in his class is getting the most out of the reading instruction, the teacher will need to consider the level at which the student is proficient in reading—as well as the specific areas in which each student struggles. It is first important to use a variety of sources of data to make decisions on differentiation, rather than rely on just one test, for example.

When teachers have proficient readers in their classrooms, they usually feel that these students need less attention and less work. This is a mistake. If these students are not provided appropriate instruction and challenging activities to increase their reading abilities further, they may become disengaged with school. These students benefit greatly from integrating classroom reading with other types of reading, perhaps complementing the whole-class novel with some additional short stories or nonfiction pieces.

They also benefit from sustained silent reading, in which they can choose their own books and read independently. Discussion groups and teacher-led discussion activities are also very useful for these students. It is important, however, to ensure that these students do not feel that they have to do more work than everyone else.

When teachers have proficient readers in their classrooms, they usually feel that these students need less attention and less work. If these students are not provided appropriate instruction and challenging activities to increase their reading abilities further, they may become disengaged with school.

Remember, differentiation does not distinguish differences in quantity; it distinguishes differences in types of work.

Average readers may benefit from many of the things that highly proficient readers do; however, they may need more skill instruction. Most likely, they will not need as much skill instruction as weak readers, but they will benefit highly from having a teacher who knows which skills they are lacking and teaches them to use those skills in their own reading.

Weak readers need to focus highly on skills. Teachers will want to encourage them to make predictions, connect ideas, outline concepts, evaluate, and summarize. The activities that these students engage in should be developed to instill reading strategies that they can use in their independent reading and to propel them toward higher levels of reading.

Alternatives to Textbooks

There is a wide variety of materials available to today's teachers. Personal computers with Internet connections are becoming more commonplace in classrooms, and teachers can bring alive the content of a reference book in text, motion, and sound. Textbook publishers often provide video, recordings, and software to accompany the text, as well as overhead transparencies and colorful posters to help students visualize what is being taught. To stay current in the field, teachers can scan the educational publishers' brochures that arrive at their principal's or department head's office or attend workshops, conferences, and presentations by educational publishers.

> **SKILL 14.3** Demonstrating knowledge of explicit strategies for facilitating students' comprehension before, during, and after reading content-area texts and for promoting their use of comprehension strategies

Content-area texts are usually nonfiction. Therefore, students can use specific strategies to better comprehend the text. Content-area subjects often have texts with a great deal of information. More information is included than is necessary for students to know at one time. Therefore, it is necessary for students to develop specific skills to help them take in the important information while weeding out the less important.

- Highlighting is a difficult strategy for students to master. Even at the college level, it seems that students have a hard time determining what is most important. Students have a tendency to highlight too much information. Encourage students to highlight less: Key ideas and vocabulary are a good place to start.

- Outlining is a skill that many teachers use to help students understand the important facts. Creating outlines can be difficult for some students though, so teachers may want to provide the outline to the students to use as a guide when taking their own notes. In this way, the students know what to focus on when reading.

- Summarizing helps students identify key information. To create a summary, a student should identify the main idea of a passage and then find the details that support the main idea. Using this information, the student can write a short summary.

- Textual features facilitate the location of pertinent information. Headings, bold text, text in boxes, diagrams, photos, and captions bring attention to important information and clarify key concepts and ideas. The table of contents and the index allow students to search for information, and the glossary lists key terms and their definitions.

The point of comprehension instruction is not necessarily to focus just on the text(s) students are using at the very moment of instruction, but rather to help them learn the strategies that they can use independently with any other text.

COMMON METHODS OF TEACHING INSTRUCTION	
Summarization	Students go over the main point of the text, along with strategically chosen details that highlight the main point. This is not the same as paraphrasing, which is saying the same thing in different words. Teaching students how to summarize is very important because it will help them look for the most critical areas in a text and in nonfiction. For example, it will help them distinguish between main arguments and examples. In fiction, it helps students to learn how to focus on the main characters and events and distinguish those from the lesser characters and events.
Question Answering	While this tends to be overused in many classrooms, it is still a valid method of teaching students to comprehend. Students answer questions regarding a text, either out loud, in small groups, or individually on paper. The best questions are those that cause students to think about the text (rather than just find an answer within the text).
Question Generating	This is the opposite of question answering, although students can then be asked to answer their own questions or the questions of peers. In general, we want students to constantly question texts as they read. This is important because it causes students to become more critical readers. To teach students to generate questions helps them to learn the types of questions they can ask and it gets them thinking about how best to be critical of texts.

Continued on next page

Graphic Organizers	Graphic organizers are graphical representations of content within a text. For example, Venn diagrams can be used to highlight the difference between two characters in a novel or two similar political concepts in a social studies textbook. Or a teacher can use flow-charts with students to talk about the steps in a process, such as the steps of setting up a science experiment or the chronological events of a story. Semantic organizers are similar in that they graphically display information. The difference, usually, is that semantic organizers focus on words or concepts. For example, a word web can help students make sense of a word by mapping out from the central word all the similar and related concepts to that word.
Text Structure	Often in nonfiction—particularly in textbooks—and sometimes in fiction, text structures will give important clues to readers about what to look for. Students may not know how to make sense of all the types of headings in a textbook and do not realize that, for example, the side-bar story about a character in history is not the main text on a particular page in the history textbook. Teaching students how to interpret text structures gives them tools with which to tackle similar texts.
Monitoring Comprehension	Students need to be aware of their comprehension, or lack of it, in particular texts. So, it is important to teach students what to do when suddenly text stops making sense. For example, students can go back and reread the description of a character. Or they can go back to the table of contents or the first paragraph of a chapter to see where they are headed.
Textual Marking	This is where students interact with the text as they read. For example, armed with sticky notes, students can insert questions or comments regarding specific sentences or paragraphs within the text. This helps students focus on the importance of the small things, particularly when they are reading larger works (such as novels in high school). It also gives students a reference point on which to go back into the text when they need to review something.
Discussion	Small group or whole-class discussion stimulates thoughts about texts and gives students a larger picture of the impact of those texts. For example, teachers can strategically encourage students to discuss related concepts to the text. This helps students learn to consider texts within larger societal and social concepts. Or teachers can encourage students to provide personal opinions in discussion. By listening to various students' opinions, this will help all students in a class to see the wide range of possible interpretations and thoughts regarding one text.

SKILL 14.4 Demonstrating knowledge of explicit strategies for promoting students' academic language and vocabulary development, including their knowledge of domain-specific vocabulary words

Here are some strategies that teachers can use to increase the development of vocabulary skills in students:

CONTEXT: the text that surrounds the word

- Context clues help readers determine the meanings of words they are not familiar with. The **CONTEXT** of a word is the text that surrounds the word. Context clues can appear within the sentence itself, within the preceding and/

or following sentences, or within the passage as a whole. Read the following sentences and attempt to determine the meaning of the word in bold print:

> The **luminosity** of the room was so incredible that there was no need for lights.

If there was no need for lights, then one must assume that the word luminosity has something to do with giving off light. The definition of luminosity, therefore, is "the emission of light."

- Word classification helps students draw comparisons between different types of words. Young children might begin by looking at parts of speech. Older students might begin by classifying the words in more specific categories based on the content area or other classification system.

- ETYMOLOGY is the study of the history of words. Understanding the language basis of words can help in determining the meaning and in building comprehension. It is particularly useful to know the definitions of prefixes, suffixes, and root words; these can help determine the meaning of several other words. For example, the Latin root "bene" means "good" or "well." English words from this root include "benefit," "beneficial," and "beneficiary." In math, knowing Greek and Latin roots can help students learn the names of geometrical shapes and other mathematical terms.

- Application of vocabulary words in new situations. Understanding what a word means in one context helps the student for that one reading passage. Learning to transfer that understanding to new and varied situations helps the student become a life-long learner and reader. This transfer of knowledge can be done by asking students to think of other situations where the word can be used, or by providing examples from other content areas.

> **ETYMOLOGY:** the study of the history of words

CONTENT AREA VOCABULARY is the specific vocabulary related to particular concepts of various academic disciplines (social science, science, math, art, etc).

While teachers tend to think of content area vocabulary as something that should be focused on just at the secondary level (middle and high school), even elementary school students studying various subjects will understand concepts better when the vocabulary used to describe them is explicitly explained. But it is true that at the secondary level, where students go to different teachers for each subject, content area vocabulary becomes more emphasized.

Often, educators believe that vocabulary should just be taught in a language arts class, not realizing that there is not enough time for students to learn the enormous vocabulary in only one class in order to be successful with a standards-based education and that the teaching of vocabulary related to a particular subject is a very good way to help students understand the subject better.

> **CONTENT AREA VOCABULARY:** the specific vocabulary related to particular concepts of various academic disciplines (social science, science, math, art, etc.)

First and foremost, teachers should teach strategies to determine the meanings for difficult vocabulary when students encounter it on their own. Teachers can do this by teaching students how to identify the meanings of words in context (usually through activities where the word is taken out, and the students have to figure out a way to make sense of the sentence). In addition, dictionary skills must be taught in all subject areas. Teachers should also consider that teaching vocabulary is not just the teaching of words; rather, it is the teaching of complex concepts, each with histories and connotations.

When teachers explicitly teach vocabulary, it is best if they can connect new words to ideas, words, and experiences with which students are already familiar. This will help to reduce the strangeness of the new words. Furthermore, the more concrete the examples, the more likely students will be able to use the word in context.

Finally, students need plenty of exposure to the new words. They need to be able to hear and use the new words in many naturally produced sentences. The more one hears and uses a sentence in context, the more the word is solidified in the person's long-term vocabulary.

See also Skill 14.1

SKILL 14.5 **Demonstrating ability to plan instruction and select strategies that support students' reading and understanding of middle level mathematics texts** *(e.g., asking students to translate between different mathematical representations, asking students to describe in words or sentences the relationship between symbols and the situation being modeled, matching mathematical representations to differences in learning styles)*

According to Piaget, there are four primary cognitive structures or development stages: sensorimotor, preoperations, concrete operations, and formal operations. In the sensorimotor stage (0-2 years), intelligence takes the form of motor actions. In the preoperation stage (3-7 years), intelligence is intuitive in nature. Intelligence in the concrete operational stage (8-11 years) is logical but depends upon concrete referents. In the final stage of formal operations (12-15 years), thinking involves abstractions.

> Research has shown that learning is most effective when information is presented through multiple modalities or representations.

Even though middle-school students are typically ready to approach mathematics in abstract ways, some of them still require concrete referents such as manipulatives. It is useful to keep in mind that the developmental stages of individuals vary. In addition, different people have different learning styles, some tending more towards the visual and others relatively verbal. Research has shown that learning is most effective when information is presented through multiple modalities or representations. Most mathematics textbooks now use this multimodal approach.

When introducing a new mathematical concept to students, teachers should utilize the concrete-to-representational-to-abstract sequence of instruction. The first step of the instructional progression is the introduction of a concept modeled with concrete materials. The second step is the translation of concrete models into representational diagrams or pictures. The third and final step is the translation of representational models into abstract models using only numbers and symbols.

Teachers should first use concrete models to introduce a mathematical concept because they are easiest to understand. For example, teachers can allow students to use counting blocks to learn basic arithmetic. Teachers should give students ample time and many opportunities to experiment, practice, and demonstrate mastery with the concrete materials.

The second step in the learning process is the translation of concrete materials to representational models. For example, students may use tally marks or pictures to represent the counting blocks they used in the previous stage. Once again, teachers should give students ample time to master the concept on the representational level.

The final step in the learning process is the translation of representational models into abstract numbers and symbols. For example, students represent the processes carried out in the previous stages using only numbers and arithmetic symbols.

To ease the transition, teachers should associate numbers and symbols with the concrete and representational models throughout the learning progression.

Throughout this guide, mathematical operations and situations are represented through words, algebraic symbols, geometric diagrams, and graphs. A few commonly used representations are discussed below.

The basic mathematical operations are addition, subtraction, multiplication and division. In word problems, these are represented by the following typical expressions.

Operation	Descriptive Words
Addition	plus, combine, sum, total, put together
Subtraction	minus, less, take away, difference
Multiplication	product, times, groups of
Division	quotient, into, split into equal groups

Symbolic representation is the basic language of mathematics. Converting data to symbols allows for easy manipulation and problem solving. Students should have the ability to recognize what the symbolic notation represents and to convert verbal information into symbolic form. For example, from the graph of a line, students should have the ability to determine the slope and intercepts and derive the line's equation from the observed data. Another possible application of symbolic representation is the formulation of algebraic expressions and relations from data presented in word-problem form.

Some verbal and symbolic representations of basic mathematical operations include the following:

Verbal	Symbolic
7 added to a number	$n + 7$
a number decreased by 8	$n - 8$
12 times a number divided by 7	$12n \div 7$
28 less than a number	$n - 28$
the ratio of a number to 55	$\dfrac{n}{55}$
4 times the sum of a number and 21	$4(n + 21)$

Multiplication can be shown using arrays. For instance, 3×4 can be expressed as 3 rows of 4 each.

□ □ □ □
□ □ □ □
□ □ □ □

In a similar manner, addition and subtraction can be demonstrated with symbols.

ψψψζζζζ
$3 + 4 = 7$
$7 - 3 = 4$

Fractions can be represented using pattern blocks, fraction bars, or paper folding.

Diagrams of arithmetic operations can present mathematical data in visual form. For example, a number line can be used to add and subtract, as illustrated below.

Five added to negative four on the number line, or $-4 + 5 = 1$.

Pictorial representations can also be used to explain the arithmetic processes.

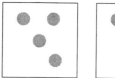

The diagram above shows that two groups of four equal eight, or $2 \times 4 = 8$. The next diagram illustrates the addition of two objects to three objects, resulting in five objects.

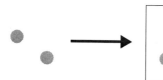

Concrete examples are real-world applications of mathematical concepts. For example, measuring the shadow produced by a tree or a building is a real-world application of trigonometric functions, the acceleration or velocity of a car is an application of derivatives, and finding the volume or the area of a swimming pool is a real-world application of geometric principles.

Pictorial illustrations of mathematic concepts help clarify difficult ideas and simplify problem solving. The following example illustrates the use of pictures.

Rectangle R represents the 300 students in School A. Circle P represents the 150 students that participate in band. Circle Q represents the 170 students that participate in a sport. 70 students participate in both band and a sport.

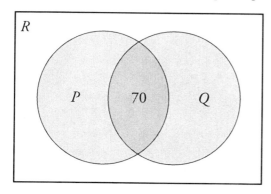

Although symbolic and verbal presentations of mathematical concepts and data can be both useful and informative, they are not always the most lucid representations of that information. The use of visual media can be helpful in numerous cases. Graphs and tables of data can, in many cases, provide a clearer representation of that data than can, for instance, a symbolic expression (for some form of regression, for example). Diagrams can also be extremely helpful, especially in problem-solving contexts. One of the chief rules of solving a problem is to draw a diagram (where appropriate) illustrating the problem; this approach helps organize information and it provides a perspective that often makes the information more accessible than it would be in words and mathematical expressions alone. Animations can also be helpful. Although animations generally require more technology (typically a computer) to construct than do diagrams, they provide an additional dimension to the visual presentation.

Throughout this guide, the concepts and examples that are presented often include graphs, tables, and diagrams to illustrate the information presented.

SAMPLE TEST

SAMPLE TEST

Formulas

Formula	Description
$V = \frac{1}{3}Bh$	Volume of a right cone or a pyramid
$A = 4\pi r^2$	Surface area of a sphere
$V = \frac{4}{3}\pi r^3$	Volume of a sphere
$A = \pi r\sqrt{r^2 + h^2} = \pi r l$	Lateral surface area of a right cone
$S_n = \frac{n}{2}[2a_1 + (n-1)d] = \frac{n(a_1 + a_n)}{2}$	Sum of an arithmetic series
$S_n = \frac{a(1 - r^n)}{1 - r}$	Sum of a finite geometric series
$\sum_{n=0}^{\infty} ar^n = \frac{a}{1 - r}, \ |r| < 1$	Sum of an infinite geometric series
$d = \sqrt{(x_2 - x_1)^2 + (y_2 - y_1)^2}$	Distance formula
$\frac{x_1 + x_2}{2}, \frac{y_1 + y_2}{2}$	Midpoint formula
$\frac{a}{\sin A} = \frac{b}{\sin B} = \frac{c}{\sin C}$	Law of sines
$c^2 = a^2 + b^2 - 2ab \cos C$	Law of cosines
$s^2 = \frac{\sum_{i=1}^{n} (x_i - \overline{x})^2}{n - 1}$	Variance
$s = r\theta$	Arc length
$x = \frac{-b \pm \sqrt{b^2 - 4ac}}{2a}$	Quadratic formula
$\overline{A}$ is the complement of set A	Set theory
$_nP_r = P(n,r) = \frac{n!}{(n - r)!}$	Permutations
$_nC_r = C(n,r) = \frac{n!}{(n - r)!r!}$	Combinations

Number Sense

(Easy) (Skill 1.1)

1. Mr. Brown feeds his cat premium cat food which costs $40 per month. Approximately how much will it cost to feed her for one year?

    A. $500

    B. $400

    C. $80

    D. $4800

(Average) (Skill 1.1)

2. The mass of a chocolate chip cookie is about:

    A. 1 kilogram

    B. 1 gram

    C. 15 grams

    D. 15 milligrams

(Average) (Skill 1.2)

3. Given W = whole numbers
    N = natural numbers
    Z = integers
    R = rational numbers
     I = irrational numbers,

    which of the following is not true?

    A. $R \subset I$

    B. $W \subset Z$

    C. $Z \subset R$

    D. $N \subset W$

(Average) (Skill 1.2)

4. Which of the following is an irrational number?

    A. .362626262...

    B. $4\frac{1}{3}$

    C. $\sqrt{5}$

    D. $-\sqrt{16}$

(Easy) (Skill 1.2)

5. The conjugate of $4 + 5i$ is:

    A. $-4 + 5i$

    B. $4 - 5i$

    C. $4i + 5$

    D. $4i - 5$

(Average) (Skill 1.2)

6. Simplify: $(6 + 3i) - (4 - 2i)$

    A. $2 + 5i$

    B. $2 + i$

    C. $10 + 5i$

    D. $2 - 2i$

(Average) (Skill 1.3)

7. Choose the set in which the members are not equivalent.

    A. $\frac{1}{2}$, 0.5, 50%

    B. $\frac{10}{5}$, 2.0, 200%

    C. $\frac{3}{8}$, 0.385, 38.5%

    D. $\frac{7}{10}$, 0.7, 70%

(Rigorous) (Skill 1.3)

8. Change $.\overline{63}$ into a fraction in simplest form.

   A. $\frac{63}{100}$

   B. $\frac{7}{11}$

   C. $6\frac{3}{10}$

   D. $\frac{2}{3}$

(Average) (Skill 2.1)

9. Find the LCM of 27, 90, and 84.

   A. 90

   B. 3,780

   C. 204,120

   D. 1,260

(Average) (Skill 2.1)

10. Find the GCF of $2^2 \times 3^2 \times 5$ and $2^2 \times 3 \times 7$.

   A. $2^5 \times 3^3 \times 5 \times 7$

   B. $2 \times 3 \times 5 \times 7$

   C. $2^2 \times 3$

   D. $2^3 \times 3^2 \times 5 \times 7$

(Rigorous) (Skill 2.1)

11. Given even numbers x and y, which could be the LCM of x and y?

   A. $\frac{xy}{2}$

   B. $2xy$

   C. $4xy$

   D. xy

(Average) (Skill 2.2)

12. A student had 60 days to appeal the results of an exam. If the results were received on March 23, what was the last day that the student could appeal?

   A. May 21

   B. May 22

   C. May 23

   D. May 24

(Average) (Skill 2.2)

13. $24 - 3 \times 7 + 2 =$

   A. 5

   B. 149

   C. -3

   D. 189

(Average) (Skill 2.3)

14. Which of the following illustrates an inverse property?

   A. $a + b = a - b$

   B. $a + b = b + a$

   C. $a + 0 = a$

   D. $a + (-a) = 0$

(Rigorous) (Skill 2.3)

15. Which of the following sets is closed under division?
   I) $\{\frac{1}{2}, 1, 2, 4\}$
   II) $\{-1, 1\}$
   III) $\{-1, 0, 1\}$

   A. I only

   B. II only

   C. III only

   D. I and II

(Rigorous) (Skill 2.3)

16. Which axiom is incorrectly applied?

    $3x + 4 = 7$

    Step a. $3x + 4 - 4 = 7 - 4$
    additive equality

    Step b. $3x + 4 - 4 = 3$
    commutative axiom of addition

    Step c. $3x + 0 = 3$
    additive inverse

    Step d. $3x = 3$
    additive identity

    A. Step a

    B. Step b

    C. Step c

    D. Step d

(Easy) (Skill 3.1)

17. Front-end estimation of the expression $\frac{363 \times 3362}{42 \times 27}$ would produce the answer:

    A. 1008

    B. 1000

    C. 1125

    D. 1512

(Easy) (Skill 3.2)

18. The range of heights in a class is from 4 ft. 7 in. to 5 ft. 5 in. The average height cannot be:

    A. 4 ft. 5 in.

    B. 4 ft. 11 in.

    C. 5 ft. 1 in.

    D. 5 ft. 2 in.

(Rigorous) (Skill 3.2)

19. Mr. Lacey is using problem solving to help students develop their math skills. He gives the class a box of pencils. He says that the pencils have to be divided so that each student has the same number of pencils. What step should come first in problem solving?

    A. Find a strategy to solve the problem

    B. Identify the problem

    C. Count the number of pencils

    D. Make basic calculations

(Rigorous) (Skill 3.3)

20. What is the total cost of the purchase of a suit for $295.99 and a pair of shoes for $69.95 including 6.5% sales tax?

    A. $389.73

    B. $398.37

    C. $237.86

    D. $315.23

(Rigorous) (Skill 3.3)

21. The volume of water flowing through a pipe varies directly with the square of the radius of the pipe. If the water flows at a rate of 80 liters per minute through a pipe with a radius of 4 cm, at what rate would water flow through a pipe with a radius of 3 cm?

    A. 45 liters per minute

    B. 6.67 liters per minute

    C. 60 liters per minute

    D. 4.5 liters per minute

(Average) (Skill 3.3)

22. Express .0000456 in scientific notation.

   A. 4.56×10^{-4}

   B. 45.6×10^{-6}

   C. 4.56×10^{-6}

   D. 4.56×10^{-5}

Patterns, Relations, and Functions (Skills 4.1 – 7.4)

(Average) (Skill 4.1)

23. Given the series of examples below, what is $5 \notin 4$?

   $4 \notin 3 = 13$ $7 \notin 2 = 47$

   $3 \notin 1 = 8$ $1 \notin 5 = -4$

   A. 20

   B. 29

   C. 1

   D. 21

(Average) (Skill 4.2)

24. Which of the following is a recursive definition of the sequence $\{1, 2, 2, 4, 8, 32, ...\}$?

   A. $N_i = 2N_{i-1}$

   B. $N_i = 2N_{i-2}$

   C. $N_i = N^2_{i-1}$

   D. $N_i = N_{i-1}N_{i-2}$

(Average) (Skill 4.4)

25. What is the sum of the first 20 terms of the geometric sequence (2, 4, 8, 16, 32, …)?

   A. 2,097,150

   B. 1,048,575

   C. 524,288

   D. 1,048,576

(Rigorous) (Skill 4.4)

26. Find the sum of the first one hundred terms in the progression (6, -2, 2, …).

   A. 19,200

   B. 19,400

   C. -604

   D. 604

(Average) (Skill 5.1)

27. State the domain of the function $f(x) = \frac{3x-6}{x^2-25}$.

   A. $x \neq 2$

   B. $x \neq 5, -5$

   C. $x \neq 2, -2$

   D. $x \neq 5$

(Average) (Skill 5.1)

28. Find the domain of the function $\sqrt{6 - x^2}$.

   A. $x \geq \sqrt{6}$

   B. $-\sqrt{6} \leq x \leq \sqrt{6}$

   C. $0 \leq x \leq \sqrt{6}$

   D. $x \geq 0$

(Rigorous) (Skill 5.2)

29. Which of the following is a factor of
    $6 + 48m^3$?

    A. $(1 + 2m)$

    B. $(1 - 8m)$

    C. $(1 + m - 2m)$

    D. $(1 - m + 2m)$

(Rigorous) (Skill 5.2)

30. Factor completely:

    $8(x - y) + a(y - x)$

    A. $(8 + a)(y - x)$

    B. $(8 - a)(y - x)$

    C. $(a - 8)(y - x)$

    D. $(a - 8)(y + x)$

(Rigorous) (Skill 5.2)

31. Simplify: $\dfrac{\frac{3}{4}x^2y^{-3}}{\frac{2}{3}xy}$

    A. $\frac{1}{2}xy^{-4}$

    B. $\frac{1}{2}x^{-1}y^{-4}$

    C. $\frac{9}{8}xy^{-4}$

    D. $\frac{9}{8}xy^{-2}$

(Average) (Skill 5.2)

32. Which of the following is incorrect?

    A. $(x^2y^3)^2 = x^4y^6$

    B. $m^2(2n)^3 = 8m^2n^3$

    C. $\dfrac{(m^3n^4)}{(m^2n^2)} = mn^2$

    D. $(x + y^2)^2 = x^2 + y^4$

(Easy) (Skill 5.3)

33. The function $y = 3x - 2$ is represented
    by which of the following ordered pairs?

    A. $(0, -2), (1, 1), (2, 4), (3, 7)$

    B. $(0, -2), (1, 1), (2, 4), (3, -2)$

    C. $(0, -2), (1, -3), (2, -4), (3, -5)$

    D. $(0, 0), (1, 3), (2, 6), (3, 9)$

(Rigorous) (Skill 5.6)

34. If y varies directly as x, and x is 2 when
    y is 6, what is x when y is 18?

    A. 3

    B. 6

    C. 26

    D. 36

(Rigorous) (Skill 5.6)

35. If y varies inversely as x, and x is 4 when
    y is 6, what is the constant of variation?

    A. 2

    B. 12

    C. $\frac{3}{2}$

    D. 24

(Average) (Skill 6.1)

36. What is the equation of the graph shown
    below?

    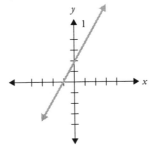

    A. $2x + y = 2$

    B. $2x - y = -2$

    C. $2x - y = 2$

    D. $2x + y = -2$

(Average) (Skill 6.1)

37. Which equation is represented by the graph below?

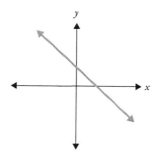

A. $x - y = 3$

B. $x - y = -3$

C. $x + y = 3$

D. $x + y = -3$

(Rigorous) (Skill 6.1)

38. What is the slope of any line parallel to the line $2x + 4y = 4$?

A. -2

B. -1

C. $-\frac{1}{2}$

D. 2

(Easy) (Skill 6.2)

39. The inequality $x > 7$ is bounded graphically on the coordinate plane by:

A. A vertical solid line

B. A vertical dotted line

C. A horizontal solid line

D. A horizontal dotted line

(Average) (Skill 6.3)

40. Find the height of a box with surface area of 94 sq. ft. with a width of 3 feet and a depth of 4 feet.

A. 3 ft.

B. 4 ft.

C. 5 ft.

D. 6 ft.

(Rigorous) (Skill 6.3)

41. A boat travels 30 miles upstream in three hours. It makes the return trip in one and a half hours. What is the speed of the boat in still water?

A. 10 mph

B. 15 mph

C. 20 mph

D. 30 mph

(Rigorous) (Skill 6.3)

42. Cindy bought a package of cookies. She ate half of them and gave one-third of the remainder to a friend. She then had 20 fewer cookies than she did in the beginning. This information can be expressed symbolically in which of the following ways?

A. $\frac{n}{2} - \frac{n}{3} = n - 20$

B. $\frac{n}{2} - \frac{n}{6} = n - 20$

C. $\frac{n}{2}\left(1 - \frac{1}{3}\right) = n - 20$

D. $\frac{n}{2} - \frac{n}{3} = n + 20$

(Average) (Skill 7.1)

43. Which graph represents the equation of $y = x^2 + 3x$?

A.

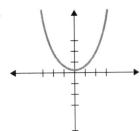

B.

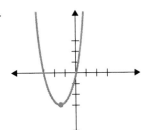

C.

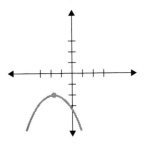

D.

(Rigorous) (Skill 7.1)

44. Which equation is graphed below?

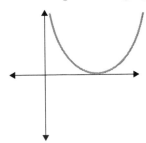

A. $y = 4(x + 3)^2$

B. $y = 4(x - 3)^2$

C. $y = 3(x - 4)^2$

D. $y = 3(x + 4)^2$

(Rigorous) (Skill 7.1)

45. Which of the following is the graph of the function $3^x - 4$?

A.

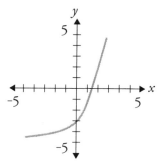

B.

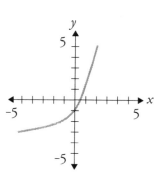

C.

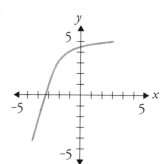

D.

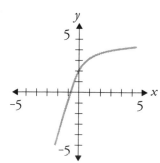

(Rigorous) (Skill 7.3)

46. The length of a picture frame is 2 inches greater than its width. If the area of the frame is 143 square inches, what is its width?

A. 11 inches

B. 13 inches

C. 12 inches

D. 10 inches

(Rigorous) (Skill 7.3)

47. Ralph and Rhonda can paint a barn together in 4 hours. If Ralph needs 6 more hours than Rhonda to paint the barn by himself, how many hours does Rhonda need to paint the barn by herself?

A. 5

B. 6

C. 7

D. 8

(Rigorous) (Skill 7.3)

48. After 5730 years, a given amount of carbon-14 decays to half its original amount. If A_0 is the original amount, A is the current amount, and t is the number of years elapsed, the exponential decay model for carbon-14 is:

A. $A = A_0 e^{-\frac{t}{5730}}$

B. $A = A_0 e^{-5730t}$

C. $A = A_0 e^{\frac{ln0.5}{5730}t}$

D. $A = A_0 e^{\frac{t}{5730}}$

(Average) (Skill 7.3)

49. Three less than four times a number is five times the sum of that number and 6. Which equation could be used to solve this problem?

   A. $3 - 4n = 5(n + 6)$

   B. $3 - 4n + 5n = 6$

   C. $4n - 3 = 5n + 6$

   D. $4n - 3 = 5(n + 6)$

(Rigorous) (Skill 7.4)

50. Find the first derivative of the function: $f(x) = x^3 - 6x^2 + 5x + 4.$

   A. $3x^2 - 12x^2 + 5x$

   B. $3x^2 - 12x - 5$

   C. $3x^2 - 12x + 9$

   D. $3x^2 - 12x + 5$

(Rigorous) (Skill 7.4)

51. If the distance traveled by a car t seconds after it starts is given by $4 + t^2$ meters, what is the velocity of the car after 5 seconds?

   A. 29 m/s

   B. 10 m/s

   C. 5.8 m/s

   D. 14 m/s

Shape and Space (Skills 8.1 – 10.4)

(Average) (Skill 8.1)

52. The term "cubic feet" indicates which kind of measurement?

   A. Volume

   B. Mass

   C. Length

   D. Distance

(Rigorous) (Skill 8.1)

53. Given that M is a mass, V is a velocity, A is an acceleration, and T is a time, what type of unit corresponds to the overall expression $\frac{AMT}{V}$?

   A. Mass

   B. Time

   C. Velocity

   D. Acceleration

(Average) (Skill 8.2)

54. Find the surface area of a box that is 3 feet wide, 5 feet tall, and 4 feet deep.

   A. 47 sq. ft.

   B. 60 sq. ft.

   C. 94 sq. ft.

   D. 188 sq. ft.

(Rigorous) (Skill 8.2)

55. Find the area of the figure pictured below.

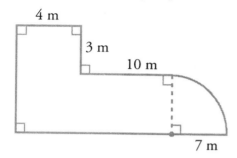

A. 136.47 m²

B. 148.48 m²

C. 293.86 m²

D. 178.47 m²

(Rigorous) (Skill 8.2)

56. Compute the area of the shaded region, given a radius of 5 meters. Point *O* is the center.

A. 7.13 cm²

B. 7.13 m²

C. 78.5 m²

D. 19.63 m²

(Rigorous) (Skill 8.2)

57. Determine the area of the shaded region of the trapezoid in terms of *x* and *y*.

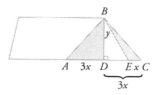

A. 4*xy*

B. 2*xy*

C. 3*x²y*

D. There is not enough information given

(Average) (Skill 8.3)

58. If a ship sails due south 6 miles, then due west 8 miles, how far is it from the starting point?

A. 100 miles

B. 10 miles

C. 14 miles

D. 48 miles

(Rigorous) (Skill 8.3)

59. If the area of the base of a cone is tripled, the volume will be:

A. The same as the original

B. 9 times the original

C. 3 times the original

D. 3π times the original

(Rigorous) (Skill 8.3)

60. If the radius of a right circular cylinder is doubled, how does its volume change?

    A. No change

    B. It is doubled

    C. It is 4 times the original

    D. π times the original

(Easy) (Skill 9.1)

61. A portion of a line that has one end point and continues infinitely in the other direction is called a:

    A. Point

    B. Ray

    C. Line

    D. Plane

(Easy) (Skill 9.2)

62. Given that $QO \perp NP$ and $QO = NP$, quadrilateral $NOPQ$ can most accurately be described as a:

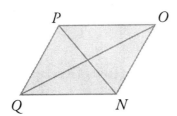

    A. Parallelogram

    B. Rectangle

    C. Square

    D. Rhombus

(Average) (Skill 9.2)

63. Which of the following statements about a trapezoid is incorrect?

    A. It has one pair of parallel sides.

    B. The parallel sides are called bases.

    C. If the two bases are the same length, the trapezoid is called isosceles.

    D. The median is parallel to the bases.

(Rigorous) (Skill 9.2)

64. What is the measure of minor arc AD, given the measure of arc PS is 40° and $m\angle K = 10°$?

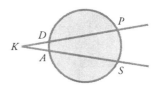

    A. 50°

    B. 20°

    C. 30°

    D. 25°

(Average) (Skill 9.2)

65. What is the degree measure of an interior angle of a regular 10-sided polygon?

    A. 18°

    B. 36°

    C. 144°

    D. 54°

(Average) (Skill 9.3)

66. Which theorem can be used to prove $\triangle BAK \cong \triangle MKA$?

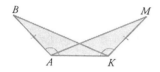

A. SSS

B. ASA

C. SAS

D. AAS

(Average) (Skill 9.3)

67. Which postulate could be used to prove $\triangle ABD \cong \triangle CEF$, given $BC \cong DE$, $\angle C \cong \angle D$, and $AD \cong CF$?

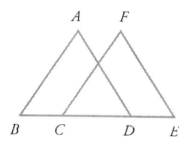

A. ASA

B. SAS

C. SAA

D. SSS

(Easy) (Skill 9.4)

68. When you begin by assuming the conclusion of a theorem is false, then show that through a sequence of logically correct steps you contradict an accepted fact, this is known as:

A. Inductive reasoning

B. Direct proof

C. Indirect proof

D. Exhaustive proof

(Rigorous) (Skill 10.2)

69. Compute the distance from $(-2, 7)$ to the line $x = 5$.

A. -9

B. -7

C. 5

D. 7

(Rigorous) (Skill 10.2)

70. Given $K(-4, y)$ and $L(2, -3)$ with midpoint $M(x, 1)$, determine the values of x and y.

A. $x = -1, y = 5$

B. $x = 3, y = 2$

C. $x = 5, y = -1$

D. $x = -1, y = -1$

(Easy) (Skill 10.3)

71. A glide reflection involves:

A. A translation and a dilation

B. A reflection and a dilation

C. A translation and a reflection

D. A reflection and a rotation

(Average) (Skill 10.3)

72. A point at (1, 2) on a Cartesian coordinate plane is translated two units to the left, reflected in the *y*-axis and then reflected in the *x*-axis. What is its final position?

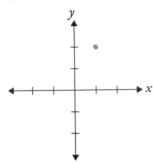

A. (3, 2)

B. (–1, 2)

C. (–2, 1)

D. (1, –2)

(Average) (Skill 10.3)

73. Kindergarten students are doing a butterfly art project. They fold paper in half. On one half, they paint a design. Then they fold the paper closed and reopen. The resulting picture is a butterfly with matching sides. What math principle does this demonstrate?

A. Slide

B. Rotate

C. Symmetry

D. Transformation

Data, Randomness, and Uncertainty (Skills 11.1 – 12.4)

(Average) (Skill 11.1)

74. Which of the following is not a valid method of collecting statistical data?

A. Random sampling

B. Systematic sampling

C. Cluster sampling

D. Cylindrical sampling

(Easy) (Skill 11.1)

75. Systematic random sampling involves:

A. Choosing items arbitrarily and in an unstructured manner

B. Targeting a particular section of the population

C. The collection of a sample at defined intervals

D. Proportional sampling from subgroups

(Easy) (Skill 11.2)

76. Which type of graph uses symbols to represent quantities?

A. Bar graph

B. Line graph

C. Pictograph

D. Circle graph

(Average) (Skill 11.2)

77. **What conclusion can be drawn from the graph below?**

MLK Elementary School
Student Enrollment

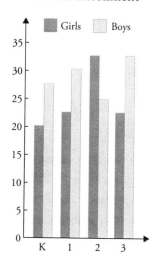

A. The number of students in first grade exceeds the number in second grade.

B. There are more boys than girls in the entire school.

C. There are more girls than boys in the first grade.

D. Third grade has the largest number of students.

(Easy) (Skill 11.2)

78. **The pie chart below shows sales at an automobile dealership for the first four months of a year. What percentage of the vehicles were sold in April?**

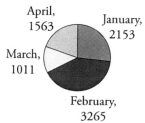

A. More than 50%

B. Less than 25%

C. Between 25% and 50%

D. None

(Easy) (Skill 11.3)

79. **Compute the median for the following data set:**

{12, 19, 13, 16, 17, 14}

A. 14.5

B. 15.17

C. 15

D. 16

(Rigorous) (Skill 11.3)

80. **Compute the standard deviation for the following set of temperatures:**
(37, 38, 35, 37, 38, 40, 36, 39)

A. 37.5

B. 1.5

C. 0.5

D. 2.5

(Rigorous) (Skill 11.3)

81. Half the students in a class scored 80% on an exam; most of the rest scored 85% except for one student who scored 10%. Which would be the best measure of central tendency for the test scores?

   A. Mean

   B. Median

   C. Mode

   D. Either the median or the mode because they are equal

(Easy) (Skill 12.2)

82. A jar contains 3 red marbles, 5 white marbles, 1 green marble, and 15 blue marbles. If one marble is picked at random from the jar, what is the probability that it will be red?

   A. $\frac{1}{3}$

   B. $\frac{1}{8}$

   C. $\frac{3}{8}$

   D. $\frac{1}{24}$

(Rigorous) (Skill 12.2)

83. A die is rolled several times. What is the probability that a 3 will not appear before the third roll of the die?

   A. $\frac{1}{3}$

   B. $\frac{25}{216}$

   C. $\frac{25}{36}$

   D. $\frac{1}{216}$

(Rigorous) (Skill 12.2)

84. If there are three people in a room, what is the probability that at least two of them will share a birthday? (Assume a year has 365 days.)

   A. 0.67

   B. 0.05

   C. 0.008

   D. 0.33

(Average) (Skill 12.2)

85. Given a drawer with 5 black socks, 3 blue socks, and 2 red socks, what is the probability that you will draw two black socks in two draws in a dark room?

   A. $\frac{2}{9}$

   B. $\frac{1}{4}$

   C. $\frac{17}{18}$

   D. $\frac{1}{18}$

(Average) (Skill 12.3)

86. A rectangular garden 20 ft. by 15 ft. has a 5 ft. by 5 ft. vegetable plot within it. If a ball is thrown at random into the garden, what is the probability that it will fall into the vegetable plot?

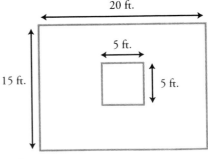

   A. $\frac{1}{3}$

   B. $\frac{1}{4}$

   C. $\frac{1}{12}$

   D. $\frac{1}{7}$

(Rigorous) (Skill 12.3)

87. A circular disc with a radius of 1 ft. is placed on a 6 ft. by 6 ft. square table. The center of the disc may be placed on any point on the table top. What is the probability that the entire disk will be on top of the table without any portion hanging over the edge?

   A. $\frac{4}{9}$

   B. $\frac{25}{36}$

   C. $\frac{1}{2}$

   D. $\frac{16}{25}$

(Rigorous) (Skill 12.4)

88. Ann flips a coin 10 times. She gets 7 heads in a row followed by 3 tails. From this we can conclude:

   A. The coin has a theoretical probability of coming up heads $\frac{7}{10}$th of the time.

   B. There is something wrong with the way the coin was flipped since there were 7 heads in a row.

   C. The number of flips is too few to draw any definite conclusion.

   D. None of the above.

Discrete Mathematics and Reading (Skills 13.1 – 14.5)

(Easy) (Skill 13.2)

89. The number of permutations of m out of n objects is:

   A. Greater than the number of combinations of m out of n objects

   B. Fewer than the number of combinations of m out of n objects

   C. Equal to the number of combinations of m out of n objects

   D. Sometimes fewer and sometimes greater than the number of combinations of m out of n objects

(Average) (Skill 13.2)

90. A school has 15 male teachers and 35 female teachers. In how many ways can they form a committee with 2 male teachers and 4 female teachers?

   A. 525

   B. 5,497,800

   C. 88

   D. 263,894,400

(Average) (Skill 13.4)

91. The population of geese in a city is given by the difference equation:

$$p_{n+1} = p_n + 0.1p_n$$

where p_n is the population in the nth year since the counting was begun.

If the initial number of geese in the year $n = 0$ was 1000, what will the population be after 2 years?

A. 1200

B. 1210

C. 1100

D. 1150

(Easy) (Skill 13.4)

92. The scalar multiplication of the number 3 with the matrix $\begin{pmatrix} 2 & 1 \\ 3 & 5 \end{pmatrix}$ yields:

A. 33

B. $\begin{pmatrix} 6 & 1 \\ 9 & 5 \end{pmatrix}$

C. $\begin{pmatrix} 2 & 3 \\ 3 & 15 \end{pmatrix}$

D. $\begin{pmatrix} 6 & 3 \\ 9 & 15 \end{pmatrix}$

(Easy) (Skill 13.4)

93. Find the sum of the following matrices:

$$\begin{pmatrix} 6 & 3 \\ 9 & 15 \end{pmatrix} \begin{pmatrix} 4 & 7 \\ 1 & 0 \end{pmatrix}$$

A. $\begin{pmatrix} 10 & 10 \\ 10 & 15 \end{pmatrix}$

B. $\begin{pmatrix} 13 & 7 \\ 9 & 16 \end{pmatrix}$

C. 45

D. $\begin{pmatrix} 20 \\ 25 \end{pmatrix}$

(Rigorous) (Skill 13.4)

94. Solve the following matrix equation:

$$3x + \begin{pmatrix} 1 & 5 & 2 \\ 0 & 6 & 9 \end{pmatrix} = \begin{pmatrix} 7 & 17 & 5 \\ 3 & 9 & 9 \end{pmatrix}$$

A. $\begin{pmatrix} 2 & 4 & 1 \\ 1 & 1 & 0 \end{pmatrix}$

B. 2

C. $\begin{pmatrix} 8 & 23 & 7 \\ 3 & 15 & 18 \end{pmatrix}$

D. $\begin{pmatrix} 9 \\ 2 \end{pmatrix}$

(Average) (Skill 14.1)

95. Mr. Sanchez is having his students work with one-syllable words, removing the first consonant and substituting another, as in changing *mats* to *hats*. What reading skill are they working on?

A. Morphemic inflections

B. Pronouncing short vowels

C. Invented spelling

D. Phonemic awareness

(Rigorous) (Skill 14.2)

96. Which of the following is not a primary way to differentiate instruction?

A. Product

B. Content

C. Quantity

D. Process

(Average) (Skill 14.3)

97. To summarize a passage, a student should:

   A. Answer the key questions raised in the passage

   B. Paraphrase the main idea

   C. Create a list of key words in the passage

   D. State the main idea and supporting details

(Easy) (Skill 14.3)

98. A Venn diagram is an example of which type of comprehension strategy?

   A. Text structure

   B. Graphic organizer

   C. Summarization

   D. Textual marking

(Easy) (Skill 14.4)

99. Which of the following is true about content-area vocabulary?

   A. Content-area vocabulary should be taught by connecting new words to familiar ideas, words, and experiences.

   B. Content-area vocabulary should be taught beginning in middle school.

   C. Content-area vocabulary should be taught primarily in language-arts classes.

   D. Content-area vocabulary should be introduced once and then used occasionally for review.

(Average) (Skill 14.5)

100. According to Piaget, at which developmental level would a child be able to learn formal algebra?

   A. Pre-operational

   B. Sensorimotor

   C. Formal operational

   D. Concrete operational

Answer Key

ANSWER KEY						
1. A	16. B	31. C	46. A	61. B	76. C	91. B
2. C	17. B	32. D	47. B	62. C	77. B	92. D
3. A	18. A	33. A	48. C	63. C	78. B	93. A
4. C	19. B	34. B	49. D	64. B	79. C	94. A
5. B	20. A	35. D	50. D	65. C	80. B	95. D
6. A	21. A	36. B	51. B	66. C	81. B	96. C
7. C	22. D	37. C	52. A	67. B	82. B	97. D
8. B	23. D	38. C	53. A	68. C	83. C	98. B
9. B	24. D	39. B	54. C	69. D	84. C	99. A
10. C	25. A	40. C	55. B	70. A	85. A	100. C
11. A	26. A	41. B	56. B	71. C	86. C	
12. B	27. B	42. B	57. B	72. D	87. A	
13. A	28. B	43. C	58. B	73. C	88. C	
14. D	29. A	44. B	59. C	74. D	89. A	
15. B	30. C	45. A	60. C	75. C	90. B	

Rigor Table

RIGOR TABLE	
Rigor level	**Questions**
Easy 20%	1, 5, 17, 18, 33, 39, 60, 61, 67, 70, 73, 74, 76, 77, 80, 87, 90, 91, 96, 98
Average 40%	2, 3, 4, 6, 7, 9, 10, 12, 13, 14, 22, 23, 24, 25, 27, 28, 32, 36, 37, 40, 43, 51, 53, 57, 62, 64, 65, 66, 71, 72, 75, 83, 84, 88, 89, 93, 95, 97, 99, 100
Rigorous 40%	8, 11, 15, 16, 19, 20, 21, 26, 29, 30, 31, 34, 35, 38, 41, 42, 44, 45, 46, 47, 48, 49, 50, 52, 54, 55, 56, 58, 59, 63, 68, 69, 78, 79, 81, 82, 85, 86, 92, 94

Sample Test with Rationales

Formulas

Formula	Description
$V = \frac{1}{3}Bh$	Volume of a right cone or a pyramid
$A = 4\pi r^2$	Surface area of a sphere
$V = \frac{4}{3}\pi r^3$	Volume of a sphere
$A = \pi r\sqrt{r^2 + h^2} = \pi r l$	Lateral surface area of a right cone
$S_n = \frac{n}{2}[2a_1 + (n-1)d] = \frac{n(a_1 + a_n)}{2}$	Sum of an arithmetic series
$S_n = \frac{a(1 - r^n)}{1 - r}$	Sum of a finite geometric series
$\displaystyle\sum_{n=0}^{\infty} ar^n = \frac{a}{1 - r},\ |r| < 1$	Sum of an infinite geometric series
$d = \sqrt{(x_2 - x_1)^2 + (y_2 - y_1)^2}$	Distance formula
$\frac{x_1 + x_2}{2}, \frac{y_1 + y_2}{2}$	Midpoint formula
$\frac{a}{\sin A} = \frac{b}{\sin B} = \frac{c}{\sin C}$	Law of sines
$c^2 = a^2 + b^2 - 2ab\cos C$	Law of cosines
$s^2 = \dfrac{\displaystyle\sum_{i=1}^{n}(x_i - \bar{x})^2}{n - 1}$	Variance
$s = r\theta$	Arc length
$x = \frac{-b \pm \sqrt{b^2 - 4ac}}{2a}$	Quadratic formula
$\overline{A}$ is the complement of set A	Set theory
$_nP_r = P(n,r) = \frac{n!}{(n - r)!}$	Permutations
$_nC_r = C(n,r) = \frac{n!}{(n - r)!r!}$	Combinations

Number Sense

(Easy) (Skill 1.1)

1. Mr. Brown feeds his cat premium cat food which costs $40 per month. Approximately how much will it cost to feed her for one year?

    A. $500

    B. $400

    C. $80

    D. $4800

    Answer: A. $500

    $12(40) = 480$, which is closest to $500.

(Average) (Skill 1.1)

2. The mass of a chocolate chip cookie is about:

    A. 1 kilogram

    B. 1 gram

    C. 15 grams

    D. 15 milligrams

    Answer: C. 15 grams

    Since an ordinary cookie would not weigh as much as 1 kilogram or as little as 1 gram or 15 milligrams, the only reasonable answer is 15 grams.

(Average) (Skill 1.2)

3. Given W = whole numbers
    N = natural numbers
    Z = integers
    R = rational numbers
    I = irrational numbers,

    which of the following is not true?

    A. $R \subset I$

    B. $W \subset Z$

    C. $Z \subset R$

    D. $N \subset W$

    Answer: A. $R \subset I$

    The rational numbers are not a subset of the irrational numbers. All of the other statements are true.

(Average) (Skill 1.2)

4. Which of the following is an irrational number?

    A. .362626262...

    B. $4\frac{1}{3}$

    C. $\sqrt{5}$

    D. $-\sqrt{16}$

    Answer: C. $\sqrt{5}$

    5 is an irrational number A and B can both be expressed as fractions. D can be simplified to -4, an integer and rational number.

(Easy) (Skill 1.2)

5. **The conjugate of $4 + 5i$ is:**

   A. $-4 + 5i$

   B. $4 - 5i$

   C. $4i + 5$

   D. $4i - 5$

Answer: B. $4 - 5i$

By definition, the conjugate of a complex number is obtained by changing the sign of its imaginary part.

(Average) (Skill 1.2)

6. **Simplify: $(6 + 3i) - (4 - 2i)$**

   A. $2 + 5i$

   B. $2 + i$

   C. $10 + 5i$

   D. $2 - 2i$

Answer: A. $2 + 5i$

Use the rules of addition and subtraction for complex numbers. $(6 + 3i) - (4 - 2i)$ $= 6 + 3i - 4 + 2i = 2 + 5i$

(Average) (Skill 1.3)

7. **Choose the set in which the members are not equivalent.**

   A. $\frac{1}{2}$, 0.5, 50%

   B. $\frac{10}{5}$, 2.0, 200%

   C. $\frac{3}{8}$, 0.385, 38.5%

   D. $\frac{7}{10}$, 0.7, 70%

Answer: C. $\frac{3}{8}$, 0.385, 38.5%

$\frac{3}{8}$ is equivalent to .375 and 37.5%.

(Rigorous) (Skill 1.3)

8. **Change $.\overline{63}$ into a fraction in simplest form.**

   A. $\frac{63}{100}$

   B. $\frac{7}{11}$

   C. $6\frac{3}{10}$

   D. $\frac{2}{3}$

Answer: B. $\frac{7}{11}$

Let $N = .636363\ldots$. Then multiplying both sides of the equation by 100 or 10² (because there are 2 repeated numbers), we get $100N = 63.636363\ldots$. Then subtracting the two equations gives $99N = 63$ or $N = \frac{63}{99} = \frac{7}{11}$.

(Average) (Skill 2.1)

9. **Find the LCM of 27, 90, and 84.**

   A. 90

   B. 3,780

   C. 204,120

   D. 1,260

Answer: B. 3,780

To find the LCM of the above numbers, factor each into its prime factors and multiply each common factor the maximum number of times it occurs. Thus,
$27 = 3 \times 3 \times 3$
$90 = 2 \times 3 \times 3 \times 5$
$84 = 2 \times 2 \times 3 \times 7$
$LCM = 2 \times 2 \times 3 \times 3 \times 3 \times 5 \times 7 = 3,780$.

(Average) (Skill 2.1)

10. **Find the GCF of $2^2 \times 3^2 \times 5$ and $2^2 \times 3 \times 7$.**

    A. $2^5 \times 3^3 \times 5 \times 7$

    B. $2 \times 3 \times 5 \times 7$

    C. $2^2 \times 3$

    D. $2^3 \times 3^2 \times 5 \times 7$

    Answer: C. $2^2 \times 3$

    Choose the number of each prime factor that is in common.

(Rigorous) (Skill 2.1)

11. **Given even numbers x and y, which could be the LCM of x and y?**

    A. $\frac{xy}{2}$

    B. $2xy$

    C. $4xy$

    D. xy

    Answer: A. $\frac{xy}{2}$

    Although choices B, C and D are common multiples, when both numbers are even, the product can be divided by two to obtain the least common multiple.

(Average) (Skill 2.2)

12. **A student had 60 days to appeal the results of an exam. If the results were received on March 23, what was the last day that the student could appeal?**

    A. May 21

    B. May 22

    C. May 23

    D. May 24

Answer: B. May 22

Recall: 30 days in April and 31 in March. 8 days in March + 30 days in April + 22 days in May brings him to a total of 60 days on May 22.

(Average) (Skill 2.2)

13. $24 - 3 \times 7 + 2 =$

    A. 5

    B. 149

    C. -3

    D. 189

Answer: A. 5

According to the order of operations, multiplication is performed first, and then addition and subtraction from left to right.

(Average) (Skill 2.3)

14. **Which of the following illustrates an inverse property?**

    A. $a + b = a - b$

    B. $a + b = b + a$

    C. $a + 0 = a$

    D. $a + (-a) = 0$

Answer: D. $a + (-a) = 0$

The correct answer is D because $a + (-a) = 0$ is a statement of the additive inverse property.

(Rigorous) (Skill 2.3)

15. **Which of the following sets is closed under division?**
    I) $\{\frac{1}{2}, 1, 2, 4\}$
    II) $\{-1, 1\}$
    III) $\{-1, 0, 1\}$

    A. I only

    B. II only

    C. III only

    D. I and II

    Answer: B. II only

    Set I is not closed because $\frac{4}{.5} = 8$ and 8 is not in the set. Set III is not closed because $\frac{1}{0}$ is undefined. Set II is closed because $\frac{-1}{1} = -1, \frac{1}{-1} = -1, \frac{1}{1} = 1, \frac{-1}{-1} = 1$, and all the quotients are in the set.

(Rigorous) (Skill 2.3)

16. **Which axiom is incorrectly applied?**
    $3x + 4 = 7$

    Step a. $3x + 4 - 4 = 7 - 4$
    additive equality

    Step b. $3x + 4 - 4 = 3$
    commutative axiom of addition

    Step c. $3x + 0 = 3$
    additive inverse

    Step d. $3x = 3$
    additive identity

    A. Step a

    B. Step b

    C. Step c

    D. Step d

Answer: B. Step b

In simplifying from step a to step b, 3 replaced $7 - 4$; therefore, the correct justification would be subtraction or substitution.

(Easy) (Skill 3.1)

17. **Front-end estimation of the expression $\frac{363 \times 3362}{42 \times 27}$ would produce the answer:**

    A. 1008

    B. 1000

    C. 1125

    D. 1512

    Answer: B. 1000

    Front-end estimation involves rounding each number to the place value of the first digit in the number. Hence,

    $$\frac{363 \times 3362}{42 \times 27} = \frac{400 \times 3000}{40 \times 30} = 1000.$$

(Easy) (Skill 3.2)

18. **The range of heights in a class is from 4 ft. 7 in. to 5 ft. 5 in. The average height cannot be:**

    A. 4 ft. 5 in.

    B. 4 ft. 11 in.

    C. 5 ft. 1 in.

    D. 5 ft. 2 in.

    Answer: A. 4 ft. 5 in.

    The average height cannot be 4 ft. 5 in. since it is smaller than the minimum height. Hence, choice A is not a reasonable answer.

(Rigorous) (Skill 3.2)

19. Mr. Lacey is using problem solving to help students develop their math skills. He gives the class a box of pencils. He says that the pencils have to be divided so that each student has the same number of pencils. What step should come first in problem solving?

    A. Find a strategy to solve the problem

    B. Identify the problem

    C. Count the number of pencils

    D. Make basic calculations

    Answer: B. Identify the problem

    The first step in problem solving is always to identify the problem.

(Rigorous) (Skill 3.3)

20. **What is the total cost of the purchase of a suit for $295.99 and a pair of shoes for $69.95 including 6.5% sales tax?**

    A. $389.73

    B. $398.37

    C. $237.86

    D. $315.23

    Answer: A. $389.73

    Before the tax, the total comes to $365.94. Then, the tax is .065($365.94) = $23.79. With the tax added on, the total bill is $365.94 + $23.79 = $389.73. (The same answer can be found in a quicker way: 1.065($365.94) = $389.73.)

(Rigorous) (Skill 3.3)

21. The volume of water flowing through a pipe varies directly with the square of the radius of the pipe. If the water flows at a rate of 80 liters per minute through a pipe with a radius of 4 cm, at what rate would water flow through a pipe with a radius of 3 cm?

    A. 45 liters per minute

    B. 6.67 liters per minute

    C. 60 liters per minute

    D. 4.5 liters per minute

    Answer: A. 45 liters per minute

    Set up the direct variation: $\frac{V}{r^2} = \frac{V}{r^2}$. Substitution yields $\frac{80}{16} = \frac{V}{9}$. Solve for V to get 45 liters per minute.

(Average) (Skill 3.3)

22. **Express .0000456 in scientific notation.**

    A. 4.56×10^{-4}

    B. 45.6×10^{-6}

    C. 4.56×10^{-6}

    D. 4.56×10^{-5}

    Answer: D. 4.56×10^{-5}

    In scientific notation, the decimal point belongs to the right of the 4, the first significant digit. To get from 4.56×10^{-5} back to 0.0000456, we would move the decimal point 5 places to the left.

Patterns, Relations, and Functions (Skills 4.1 – 7.4)

(Average) (Skill 4.1)

23. Given the series of examples below, what is $5 \not\subset 4$?

    $4 \not\subset 3 = 13$ $7 \not\subset 2 = 47$

    $3 \not\subset 1 = 8$ $1 \not\subset 5 = -4$

    A. 20

    B. 29

    C. 1

    D. 21

Answer: D. 21

By inspection of the examples given, $a \not\subset b = a^2 - b$. Therefore, $5 \not\subset 4 = 25 - 4 = 21$.

(Average) (Skill 4.2)

24. Which of the following is a recursive definition of the sequence $\{1, 2, 2, 4, 8, 32, ...\}$?

    A. $N_i = 2N_{i-1}$

    B. $N_i = 2N_{i-2}$

    C. $N_i = N^2_{i-1}$

    D. $N_i = N_{i-1}N_{i-2}$

Answer: D. $N_i = N_{i-1}N_{i-2}$

Test each answer, or look at the pattern of the numbers in the sequence. Note that each number (with the exception of the first two) is the product of the preceding two numbers. In recursive form using index i, the expression is $N_i = N_{i-1} N_{i-2}$ and the correct answer is D.

(Average) (Skill 4.4)

25. What is the sum of the first 20 terms of the geometric sequence (2, 4, 8, 16, 32, ...)?

    A. 2,097,150

    B. 1,048,575

    C. 524,288

    D. 1,048,576

Answer: A. 2,097,150

For a geometric sequence $a, ar, ar^2, ..., ar^n$, the sum of the first n terms is given by $\frac{a(r^n - 1)}{r - 1}$. In this case $a = 2$ and $r = 2$. Thus, the sum of the first 20 terms of the sequence is $\frac{2(2^{20} - 1)}{2 - 1} = 2,097,150$.

(Rigorous) (Skill 4.4)

26. Find the sum of the first one hundred terms in the progression (-6, -2, 2, ...).

    A. 19,200

    B. 19,400

    C. -604

    D. 604

Answer: A. 19,200

To find the 100th term: $t_{100} = -6 + 99(4) = 390$. To find the sum of the first 100 terms, use $S = \frac{100}{2}(-6 + 390) = 19,200$.

(Average) (Skill 5.1)

27. State the domain of the function $f(x) = \frac{3x - 6}{x^2 - 25}$.

    A. $x \neq 2$

    B. $x \neq 5, -5$

    C. $x \neq 2, -2$

    D. $x \neq 5$

Answer: B. $x \neq 5, -5$

The values of 5 and -5 must be omitted from the domain of all real numbers because if x took on either of those values, the denominator of the fraction would have a value of 0, and therefore the fraction would be undefined.

(Average) (Skill 5.1)

28. **Find the domain of the function** $\sqrt{6 - x^2}$.

    A. $x \geq \sqrt{6}$

    B. $-\sqrt{6} \leq x \leq \sqrt{6}$

    C. $0 \leq x \leq \sqrt{6}$

    D. $x \geq 0$

    Answer: B. $-\sqrt{6} \leq x \leq \sqrt{6}$

    The expression under the square root sign cannot be negative. Hence, we must have $6 - x^2 \geq 0; \rightarrow x^2 \leq 6; \rightarrow x \leq \sqrt{6}$ and $x \geq -\sqrt{6}$

(Rigorous) (Skill 5.2)

29. **Which of the following is a factor of** $6 + 48m^3$?

    A. $(1 + 2m)$

    B. $(1 - 8m)$

    C. $(1 + m - 2m)$

    D. $(1 - m + 2m)$

    Answer: A. $(1 + 2m)$

    Removing the common factor of 6 and then factoring the sum of two cubes gives $6 + 48m^3 = 6(1 + 8m^3) = 6(1 + 2m)$ $(12 - 2m^3 + (2m)^2)$.

(Rigorous) (Skill 5.2)

30. **Factor completely:**

    $$8(x - y) + a(y - x)$$

    A. $(8 + a)(y - x)$

    B. $(8 - a)(y - x)$

    C. $(a - 8)(y - x)$

    D. $(a - 8)(y + x)$

    Answer: C. $(a - 8)(y - x)$

    Glancing first at the solution choices, factor $(y - x)$ from each term. This leaves -8 from the first term and a from the second term: $(a - 8)(y - x)$.

(Rigorous) (Skill 5.2)

31. **Simplify:** $\dfrac{\frac{3}{4}x^2y^{-3}}{\frac{2}{3}xy}$

    A. $\frac{1}{2}xy^{-4}$

    B. $\frac{1}{2}x^{-1}y^{-4}$

    C. $\frac{9}{8}xy^{-4}$

    D. $\frac{9}{8}xy^{-2}$

    Answer: C. $\frac{9}{8}xy^{-4}$

    Simplify the complex fraction by inverting the denominator and multiplying: $\frac{3}{4}\left(\frac{3}{2}\right) = \frac{9}{8}$, then subtract exponents to obtain the correct answer.

(Average) (Skill 5.2)

32. **Which of the following is incorrect?**

    A. $(x^2y^3)^2 = x^4y^6$

    B. $m^2(2n)^3 = 8m^2n^3$

    C. $\frac{(m^3n^4)}{(m^2n^2)} = mn^2$

    D. $(x + y^2)^2 = x^2 + y^4$

Answer: D. $(x + y^2)^2 = x^2 + y^4$

Using FOIL to do the expansion, we get $(x + y^2)^2 = (x + y^2)(x + y^2) = x^2 + 2xy^2 + y^4$.

(Easy) (Skill 5.3)

33. The function $y = 3x - 2$ is represented by which of the following ordered pairs?

    A. (0, -2), (1, 1), (2, 4), (3, 7)

    B. (0, -2), (1, 1), (2, 4), (3, -2)

    C. (0, -2), (1, -3), (2, -4), (3, -5)

    D. (0, 0), (1, 3), (2, 6), (3, 9)

    Answer: A. (0, -2), (1, 1), (2, 4), (3, 7)

    Substituting the x-values 0, 1, 2, and 3 in the expression $3x - 2$, we see that the corresponding y-values are -2, 1, 4, and 7. This matches choice A.

(Rigorous) (Skill 5.6)

34. If y varies directly as x, and x is 2 when y is 6, what is x when y is 18?

    A. 3

    B. 6

    C. 26

    D. 36

    Answer: B. 6

    The equation for direct variation is $y = kx$. In this case, $k = \frac{y}{x} = \frac{6}{2} = 3$. Substitute 18 for y and 3 for k and solve: $18 = 3x$, $x = 6$.

(Rigorous) (Skill 5.6)

35. If y varies inversely as x, and x is 4 when y is 6, what is the constant of variation?

    A. 2

    B. 12

    C. $\frac{3}{2}$

    D. 24

    Answer: D. 24

    The constant of variation for an inverse proportion is xy.

(Average) (Skill 6.1)

36. What is the equation of the graph shown below?

    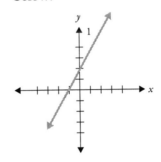

    A. $2x + y = 2$

    B. $2x - y = -2$

    C. $2x - y = 2$

    D. $2x + y = -2$

    Answer: B. $2x - y = -2$

    By observation, we see that the graph has a y-intercept of 2 and a slope of $\frac{2}{1} = 2$. Therefore, its equation is $y = mx + b = 2x + 2$. Rearranging the terms yields $2x - y = -2$.

(Average) (Skill 6.1)

37. **Which equation is represented by the graph below?**

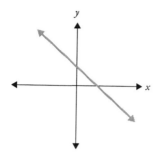

A. $x - y = 3$

B. $x - y = -3$

C. $x + y = 3$

D. $x + y = -3$

Answer: C. $x + y = 3$

By looking at the graph, we can determine the slope to be -1 and the y-intercept to be 3. Write the slope intercept form of the line as $y = -1x + 3$. Add x to both sides to obtain $x + y = 3$, the equation in standard form.

(Rigorous) (Skill 6.1)

38. **What is the slope of any line parallel to the line $2x + 4y = 4$?**

A. -2

B. -1

C. $-\frac{1}{2}$

D. 2

Answer: C. $-\frac{1}{2}$

The formula for slope is $y = mx + b$, where m is the slope. Lines that are parallel have the same slope.

$2x + 4y = 4$
$4y = -2x + 4$
$y = \frac{-2x}{4} + 1$
$y = \frac{-1}{2}x + 1$

(Easy) (Skill 6.2)

39. **The inequality $x > 7$ is bounded graphically on the coordinate plane by:**

A. A vertical solid line

B. A vertical dotted line

C. A horizontal solid line

D. A horizontal dotted line

Answer: B. A vertical dotted line

Since the boundary $x = 7$ is marked by a fixed value of x for all y, this is a vertical line.

Since x is "greater" than 7 and not "greater than or equal to," the solution does not include $x = 7$ and therefore is represented by a dotted line.

(Average) (Skill 6.3)

40. **Find the height of a box with surface area of 94 sq. ft. with a width of 3 feet and a depth of 4 feet.**

A. 3 ft.

B. 4 ft.

C. 5 ft.

D. 6 ft.

Answer: C. 5 ft.

Use the expression for surface area and solve for the unknown value h.

$94 = 2(3h) + 2(4h) + 2(12)$
$94 = 6h + 8h + 24$
$94 = 14h + 24$
$70 = 14h$
$5 = h$

Thus, the height of the box is 5 feet.

(Rigorous) (Skill 6.3)

41. A boat travels 30 miles upstream in three hours. It makes the return trip in one and a half hours. What is the speed of the boat in still water?

    A. 10 mph

    B. 15 mph

    C. 20 mph

    D. 30 mph

Answer: B. 15 mph

Let x = the speed of the boat in still water and c = the speed of the current.

	Rate	Time	Distance
Upstream	$x - c$	3	30
Downstream	$x + c$	1.5	30

Solve the system:
$3x - 3c = 30$
$1.5x + 1.5c = 30$

(Rigorous) (Skill 6.3)

42. Cindy bought a package of cookies. She ate half of them and gave one-third of the remainder to a friend. She then had 20 fewer cookies than she did in the beginning. This information can be expressed symbolically in which of the following ways?

    A. $\frac{n}{2} - \frac{n}{3} = n - 20$

    B. $\frac{n}{2} - \frac{n}{6} = n - 20$

    C. $\frac{n}{2}(1 - \frac{1}{3}) = n - 20$

    D. $\frac{n}{2} - \frac{n}{3} = n + 20$

Answer: B. $\frac{n}{2} - \frac{n}{6} = n - 20$

If Cindy started out with n cookies, she ate $\frac{n}{2}$ and had $\frac{n}{2}$ left. Of these, she gave her friend $\frac{1}{3} \times \frac{n}{2} = \frac{n}{6}$ cookies.

(Average) (Skill 7.1)

43. Which graph represents the equation of $y = x^2 + 3x$?

A.

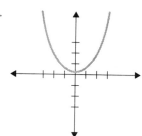

B.

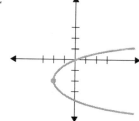

C.

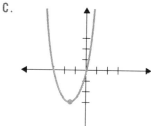

D.

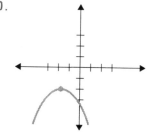

Answer: C.

Answer B is not the graph of a function. Answer D is the graph of a parabola where the coefficient of x^2 is negative. Answer A appears to be the graph of $y = x^2$. To find the x-intercepts of $y = x^2 + 3x$, set $y = 0$ and solve for x: $0 = x^2 + 3x = x(x + 3)$ to get $x = 0$ or $x = -3$. Therefore, the graph of the function intersects the x-axis at $x = 0$ and $x = -3$. The correct answer is C.

(Rigorous) (Skill 7.1)

44. Which equation is graphed below?

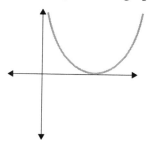

A. $y = 4 (x + 3)^2$

B. $y = 4 (x - 3)^2$

C. $y = 3 (x - 4)^2$

D. $y = 3 (x + 4)^2$

Answer: B. $y = 4 (x - 3)^2$

Since the vertex of the parabola is three units to the left, we choose the solution where 3 is subtracted from x, and then the quantity is squared.

(Rigorous) (Skill 7.1)

45. Which of the following is the graph of the function $3^x - 4$?

A.

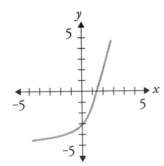

B.

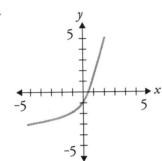

C.

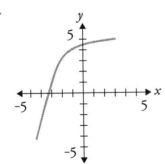

D.

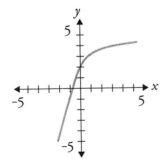

Answer: A.

Note the x and y intercepts. When $x = 0$, $y = -3$, and $y = 0$ when $x = 1.25$.

(Rigorous) (Skill 7.3)

46. The length of a picture frame is 2 inches greater than its width. If the area of the frame is 143 square inches, what is its width?

A. 11 inches

B. 13 inches

C. 12 inches

D. 10 inches

Answer: A. 11 inches

First set up the equation for the problem. If the width of the picture frame is w, then $w(w + 2) = 143$. Next, solve the equation to obtain w. Using the method of completing squares we have
$w^2 + 2w + 1 = 144$
$(w + 1)^2 = 144$
$w + 1 = \pm 12$.
Thus, w is 11 or -13. Since the width cannot be negative, the correct answer is 11 inches.

(Rigorous) (Skill 7.3)

47. Ralph and Rhonda can paint a barn together in 4 hours. If Ralph needs 6 more hours than Rhonda to paint the barn by himself, how many hours does Rhonda need to paint the barn by herself?

A. 5

B. 6

C. 7

D. 8

Answer: B. 6

Let the number of hours Rhonda needs to paint the barn by herself be x. Then Ralph needs $x + 6$ hours to paint the barn by himself.

In 1 hour Rhonda paints $\frac{1}{x}$ of the barn and Ralph paints $\frac{1}{(x + 6)}$ of the barn.

In 4 hours Rhonda paints $\frac{4}{x}$ of the barn and Ralph paints $\frac{4}{(x + 6)}$ of the barn.

Since both of them together paint the whole barn in 4 hours, we can write

$$\frac{4}{x} + \frac{4}{x + 6} = 1$$
$$\rightarrow \frac{4x + 24 + 4x}{x(x + 6)} = 1$$
$$\rightarrow 8x + 24 = x^2 + 6x$$
$$\rightarrow x^2 - 2x - 24 = 0$$
$$\rightarrow (x - 6)(x + 4) = 0$$

The solutions to the above equation are $x = 6$, and $x = -4$. Since in this case we cannot have a negative answer, the number of hours Rhonda needs to paint the barn by herself is 6.

(Rigorous) (Skill 7.3)

48. After 5730 years, a given amount of carbon-14 decays to half its original amount. If A_0 is the original amount, A is the current amount, and t is the number of years elapsed, the exponential decay model for carbon-14 is:

A. $A = A_0 e^{\frac{-t}{5730}}$

B. $A = A_0 e^{-5730t}$

C. $A = A_0 e^{\frac{ln0.5}{5730}t}$

D. $A = A_0 e^{\frac{t}{5730}}$

Answer: C. $A = A_0 e^{\frac{ln0.5}{5730}t}$

The general form of the exponential decay model is $A = A_0 e^{rt}$. We can use the fact that the half life of carbon-14 is 5730 years to find the constant r.

When $t = 5730$, $A = \frac{A_0}{2}$. Therefore

$$\frac{A_0}{2} = A_0 e^{5730r}$$
$$\rightarrow \frac{1}{2} = e^{5730r}$$

Taking the natural logarithm of both sides

$$ln\frac{1}{2} = 5730r$$
$$\rightarrow r = \frac{ln0.5}{5730}$$

(Average) (Skill 7.3)

49. Three less than four times a number is five times the sum of that number and 6. Which equation could be used to solve this problem?

A. $3 - 4n = 5(n + 6)$

B. $3 - 4n + 5n = 6$

C. $4n - 3 = 5n + 6$

D. $4n - 3 = 5(n + 6)$

Answer: D. $4n - 3 = 5(n + 6)$

Be sure to enclose the sum of the number and 6 in parentheses.

(Rigorous) (Skill 7.4)

50. Find the first derivative of the function:
$f(x) = x^3 - 6x^2 + 5x + 4.$

A. $3x^2 - 12x^2 + 5x$

B. $3x^2 - 12x - 5$

C. $3x^2 - 12x + 9$

D. $3x^2 - 12x + 5$

Answer: D. $3x^2 - 12x + 5$

Use the Power Rule for polynomial differentiation: if $y = ax^n$, then $y' = nax^{n-1}$. Then, $f'(x) = 3x^2 - 12x + 5$.

(Rigorous) (Skill 7.4)

51. If the distance traveled by a car t seconds after it starts is given by $4 + t^2$ meters, what is the velocity of the car after 5 seconds?

    A. 29 m/s

    B. 10 m/s

    C. 5.8 m/s

    D. 14 m/s

Answer: B. 10 m/s

Since velocity is the rate of change of distance, the velocity of the car at any time t is given by the derivative of the distance:

$$\frac{d}{dt}(4 + t^2) = 2t$$

When $t = 5$, $2t = 10$. Hence, the velocity of the car after 5 seconds is 10 m/s.

Shape and Space (Skills 8.1 – 10.4)

(Average) (Skill 8.1)

52. The term "cubic feet" indicates which kind of measurement?

    A. Volume

    B. Mass

    C. Length

    D. Distance

Answer: A. Volume

The word *cubic* indicates that this is a term describing volume.

(Rigorous) (Skill 8.1)

53. Given that M is a mass, V is a velocity, A is an acceleration and T is a time, what type of unit corresponds to the overall expression $\frac{AMT}{V}$?

    A. Mass

    B. Time

    C. Velocity

    D. Acceleration

Answer: A. Mass

Use unit analysis to find the simplest expression for the units associated with the expression. Choose any unit system: for example, the metric system.

$$\frac{AMT}{V} - \frac{\left(\frac{m}{s^2}\right)(kg)(s)}{\left(\frac{m}{s}\right)}$$

Simplify the units in the expression

$$\frac{AMT}{V} - \frac{\left(\frac{m}{s}\right)(kg)}{\left(\frac{m}{s}\right)} = kg$$

Kilograms is a unit of mass, and thus the correct answer is A.

(Average) (Skill 8.2)

54. Find the surface area of a box that is 3 feet wide, 5 feet tall, and 4 feet deep.

    A. 47 sq. ft.

    B. 60 sq. ft.

    C. 94 sq. ft.

    D. 188 sq. ft.

Answer: C. 94 sq. ft.

Let's assume the base of the rectangular solid (box) is 3 by 4 and the height is 5. Then, the surface area of the top and bottom together is 2(12) = 24. The sum of the areas of the front and back are 2(15) = 30, and the sum of the areas of the sides are 2(20) = 40. The total surface area is therefore 94 square feet.

(Rigorous) (Skill 8.2)

55. **Find the area of the figure pictured below.**

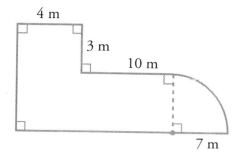

A. 136.47 m²

B. 148.48 m²

C. 293.86 m²

D. 178.47 m²

Answer: B. 148.48 m²

Divide the figure into two rectangles and one quarter circle. The tall rectangle on the left has dimensions 10m by 4m and, thus, an area of 40m². The center rectangle has dimensions 7m by 10m and, thus, an area of 70m². The quarter circle has an area of .25(π)(7m)² = 38.48m². The total area is therefore approximately 148.48m².

(Rigorous) (Skill 8.2)

56. **Compute the area of the shaded region, given a radius of 5 meters. Point O is the center.**

A. 7.13 cm²

B. 7.13 m²

C. 78.5 m²

D. 19.63 m²

Answer: B. 7.13 m²

The area of triangle AOB is .5(5)(5) = 12.5 square meters. Since $\frac{90}{360}$ = .25, the area of sector AOB (the pie-shaped piece) is approximately .25(π)5² = 19.63. Subtracting the triangle area from the sector area to get the area of segment AB yields approximately 19.63 − 12.5 = 7.13 square meters.

(Rigorous) (Skill 8.2)

57. **Determine the area of the shaded region of the trapezoid in terms of x and y.**

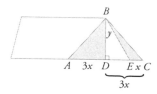

A. $4xy$

B. $2xy$

C. $3x^2y$

D. There is not enough information given

Answer: B. 2*xy*

To find the area of the shaded region, find the area of triangle *ABC* and then subtract the area of triangle *DBE*. The area of triangle *ABC* is .5(6*x*)(*y*) = 3*xy*. The area of triangle *DBE* is .5(2*x*)(*y*) = *xy*. The difference is 2*xy*.

(Average) (Skill 8.3)

58. If a ship sails due south 6 miles, then due west 8 miles, how far is it from the starting point?

 A. 100 miles

 B. 10 miles

 C. 14 miles

 D. 48 miles

Answer: B. 10 miles

Draw a right triangle with legs of 6 and 8. Find the hypotenuse using the Pythagorean Theorem:
$6^2 + 8^2 = c^2 = 36 + 64 = 100$
Therefore, $c = 10$ miles.

(Rigorous) (Skill 8.3)

59. If the area of the base of a cone is tripled, the volume will be:

 A. The same as the original

 B. 9 times the original

 C. 3 times the original

 D. 3π times the original

Answer: C. 3 times the original

The formula for the volume of a cone is $V = \frac{1}{3}Bh$, where B is the area of the circular base and h is the height. If the area of the base is tripled, the volume becomes $V = \frac{1}{3}(3B)h = Bh$, or three times the original area.

(Rigorous) (Skill 8.3)

60. If the radius of a right circular cylinder is doubled, how does its volume change?

 A. No change

 B. It is doubled

 C. It is 4 times the original

 D. π times the original

Answer: C. It is 4 times the original

If the radius of a right circular cylinder is doubled, the volume is multiplied by four because in the formula, the radius is squared, therefore the new volume is 2 × 2, or four times the original.

(Easy) (Skill 9.1)

61. A portion of a line that has one end point and continues infinitely in the other direction is called a:

 A. Point

 B. Ray

 C. Line

 D. Plane

Answer: B. Ray

By definition, a ray is a portion of a line that has only one endpoint and continues infinitely in one direction. Rays are named using the endpoint as the first point and any other point on the ray as the second. The symbol for a ray includes only one arrow indicating that it has one endpoint.

(Easy) (Skill 9.2)

62. Given that $QO \perp NP$ and $QO = NP$, quadrilateral $NOPQ$ can most accurately be described as a:

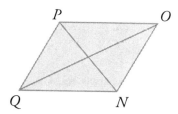

A. Parallelogram

B. Rectangle

C. Square

D. Rhombus

Answer: C. Square

In an ordinary parallelogram, the diagonals are not perpendicular or equal in length. In a rectangle, the diagonals are not necessarily perpendicular. In a rhombus, the diagonals are not equal in length. In a square, the diagonals are both perpendicular and congruent.

(Average) (Skill 9.2)

63. Which of the following statements about a trapezoid is incorrect?

A. It has one pair of parallel sides.

B. The parallel sides are called bases.

C. If the two bases are the same length, the trapezoid is called isosceles.

D. The median is parallel to the bases.

Answer: C. If the two bases are the same length, the trapezoid is called isosceles.

A trapezoid is isosceles if the two legs (not bases) are the same length.

(Rigorous) (Skill 9.2)

64. What is the measure of minor arc AD, given the measure of arc PS is 40° and $m\angle K = 10°$?

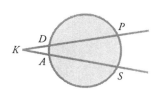

A. 50°

B. 20°

C. 30°

D. 25°

Answer: B. 20°

The formula relating the measure of angle K and the two arcs it intercepts is $m\angle K = \frac{1}{2}(mPS - mAD)$. Substituting the known values yields $10 = \frac{1}{2}(40 - mAD)$. Solving for mAD gives an answer of 20 degrees.

(Average) (Skill 9.2)

65. What is the degree measure of an interior angle of a regular 10-sided polygon?

   A. 18°

   B. 36°

   C. 144°

   D. 54°

Answer: C. 144°

The formula for finding the measure of each interior angle of a regular polygon with n sides is $\frac{(n-2)180}{n}$. For $n = 10$, $\frac{8(180)}{10} = 144$.

(Average) (Skill 9.3)

66. Which theorem can be used to prove $\triangle BAK \cong \triangle MKA$?

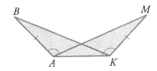

   A. SSS

   B. ASA

   C. SAS

   D. AAS

Answer: C. SAS

Since side AK is common to both triangles, the triangles can be proved congruent by using the Side-Angle-Side Postulate.

(Average) (Skill 9.3)

67. Which postulate could be used to prove $\triangle ABD \cong \triangle CEF$, given $BC \cong DE$, $\angle C \cong \angle D$, and $AD \cong CF$?

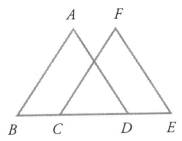

   A. ASA

   B. SAS

   C. SAA

   D. SSS

Answer: B. SAS

To obtain the final side, add CD to both BC and ED.

(Easy) (Skill 9.4)

68. When you begin by assuming the conclusion of a theorem is false, then show that through a sequence of logically correct steps you contradict an accepted fact, this is known as:

   A. Inductive reasoning

   B. Direct proof

   C. Indirect proof

   D. Exhaustive proof

Answer: C. Indirect proof

By definition this describes the procedure of an indirect proof.

(Rigorous) (Skill 10.2)

69. Compute the distance from (-2, 7) to the line $x = 5$.

  A. -9

  B. -7

  C. 5

  D. 7

Answer: D. 7

The line $x = 5$ is a vertical line passing through (5, 0) on the Cartesian plane. By observation, the distance along the horizontal line from the point (-2, 7) to the line $x = 5$ is 7 units.

(Rigorous) (Skill 10.2)

70. Given $K(-4, y)$ and $L(2, -3)$ with midpoint $M(x, 1)$, determine the values of x and y.

  A. $x = -1, y = 5$

  B. $x = 3, y = 2$

  C. $x = 5, y = -1$

  D. $x = -1, y = -1$

Answer: A. $x = -1, y = 5$

The formula for finding the midpoint (a, b) of a segment passing through the points (x_1, y_1) and (x_2, y_2) is $(a, b) = (\frac{x_1 + x_2}{2}, \frac{y_1 + y_2}{2})$. Setting up the corresponding equations from this information yields $x = \frac{-4 + 2}{2}$ and $1 = \frac{y - 3}{2}$. Solving for x and y yields $x = -1$ and $y = 5$.

(Easy) (Skill 10.3)

71. A glide reflection involves:

  A. A translation and a dilation

  B. A reflection and a dilation

  C. A translation and a reflection

  D. A reflection and a rotation

Answer: C. A translation and a reflection

A glide reflection involves a combined translation along and a reflection across a single specified line. The characteristic that defines a glide reflection as opposed to a simple combination of an arbitrary translation and arbitrary reflection is that the direction of translation is parallel with the line of reflection.

(Average) (Skill 10.3)

72. A point at (1, 2) on a Cartesian coordinate plane is translated two units to the left, reflected in the y-axis and then reflected in the x-axis. What is its final position?

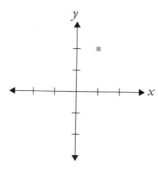

  A. (3, 2)

  B. (-1, 2)

  C. (-2, 1)

  D. (1, -2)

Answer: D. (1, -2)

After translation 2 units to the left, the point is at (-1, 2). After reflection in the y-axis, it is back in its original position (1, 2). After reflection in the x-axis it is at (1, -2).

(Average) (Skill 10.3)

73. Kindergarten students are doing a butterfly art project. They fold paper in half. On one half, they paint a design. Then they fold the paper closed and reopen. The resulting picture is a butterfly with matching sides. What math principle does this demonstrate?

    A. Slide

    B. Rotate

    C. Symmetry

    D. Transformation

Answer: C. Symmetry

By folding the painted paper in half, the design is mirrored on the other side, creating symmetry and reflection. The butterfly design is symmetrical about the center.

Data, Randomness, and Uncertainty (Skills 11.1 – 12.4)

(Average) (Skill 11.1)

74. Which of the following is not a valid method of collecting statistical data?

    A. Random sampling

    B. Systematic sampling

    C. Cluster sampling

    D. Cylindrical sampling

Answer: D. Cylindrical sampling

There is no such method as cylindrical sampling.

(Easy) (Skill 11.1)

75. Systematic random sampling involves:

    A. Choosing items arbitrarily and in an unstructured manner

    B. Targeting a particular section of the population

    C. The collection of a sample at defined intervals

    D. Proportional sampling from subgroups

Answer: C. The collection of a sample at defined intervals

Systematic random sampling involves the collection of a sample at defined intervals (for instance, every tenth part to come off a manufacturing line). Here, it is assumed that the population is ordered randomly and there is no hidden pattern that may compromise the randomness of the sampling.

(Easy) (Skill 11.2)

76. Which type of graph uses symbols to represent quantities?

    A. Bar graph

    B. Line graph

    C. Pictograph

    D. Circle graph

Answer: C. Pictograph

A pictograph shows comparison of quantities using symbols. Each symbol represents a number of items.

(Average) (Skill 11.2)

77. **What conclusion can be drawn from the graph below?**

MLK Elementary School
Student Enrollment

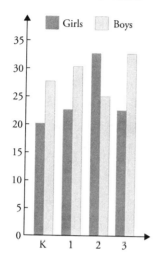

A. The number of students in first grade exceeds the number in second grade.

B. There are more boys than girls in the entire school.

C. There are more girls than boys in the first grade.

D. Third grade has the largest number of students.

Answer: B. There are more boys than girls in the entire school.

In kindergarten, first grade and third grade, there are more boys than girls. The number of extra girls in grade two is more than compensated by the extra boys in all the other grades put together.

(Easy) (Skill 11.2)

78. **The pie chart below shows sales at an automobile dealership for the first four months of a year. What percentage of the vehicles were sold in April?**

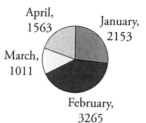

A. More than 50%

B. Less than 25%

C. Between 25% and 50%

D. None

Answer: B. Less than 25%

It is clear from the chart that the April segment covers less than a quarter of the pie.

(Easy) (Skill 11.3)

79. **Compute the median for the following data set:**

{12, 19, 13, 16, 17, 14}

A. 14.5

B. 15.17

C. 15

D. 16

Answer: C. 15

Arrange the data in ascending order: 12, 13, 14, 16, 17, 19. The median is the middle value in a list with an odd number of entries. When there is an even number of entries, the median is the mean of the two center entries. Here the average of 14 and 16 is 15.

(Rigorous) (Skill 11.3)

80. **Compute the standard deviation for the following set of temperatures:**
(37, 38, 35, 37, 38, 40, 36, 39)

A. 37.5

B. 1.5

C. 0.5

D. 2.5

Answer: B. 1.5

First find the mean: $\frac{300}{8} = 37.5$. Then, using the formula for standard deviation yields

$$\sqrt{\frac{2(37.5 - 37)^2 + 2(37.5 - 38)^2 + (37.5 - 35)^2 + (37.5 - 40)^2 + (37.5 - 36)^2 + (37.5 - 39)^2}{8}}.$$

This expression has a value of 1.5.

(Rigorous) (Skill 11.3)

81. **Half the students in a class scored 80% on an exam; most of the rest scored 85% except for one student who scored 10%. Which would be the best measure of central tendency for the test scores?**

A. Mean

B. Median

C. Mode

D. Either the median or the mode because they are equal

Answer: B. Median

In this set of data, the median would be the most representative measure of central tendency because the median is independent of extreme values. Because of the 10% outlier, the mean (average) would be disproportionately skewed. In this data set, it is true that the median and the mode (number which occurs most often) are the same, but the median remains the best choice because of its special properties.

(Easy) (Skill 12.2)

82. **A jar contains 3 red marbles, 5 white marbles, 1 green marble, and 15 blue marbles. If one marble is picked at random from the jar, what is the probability that it will be red?**

A. $\frac{1}{3}$

B. $\frac{1}{8}$

C. $\frac{3}{8}$

D. $\frac{1}{24}$

Answer: B. $\frac{1}{8}$

The total number of marbles is 24 and the number of red marbles is 3. Thus the probability of picking a red marble from the jar is $\frac{3}{24} = \frac{1}{8}$.

(Rigorous) (Skill 12.2)

83. A die is rolled several times. What is the probability that a 3 will not appear before the third roll of the die?

   A. $\frac{1}{3}$

   B. $\frac{25}{216}$

   C. $\frac{25}{36}$

   D. $\frac{1}{216}$

Answer: C. $\frac{25}{36}$

The probability that a 3 will not appear before the third roll is the same as the probability that the first two rolls will consist of numbers other than 3. Since the probability of any one roll resulting in a number other than 3 is $\frac{5}{6}$, the probability of the first two rolls resulting in a number other than 3 is $\left(\frac{5}{6}\right) \times \left(\frac{5}{6}\right) = \frac{25}{36}$.

(Rigorous) (Skill 12.2)

84. If there are three people in a room, what is the probability that at least two of them will share a birthday? (Assume a year has 365 days.)

   A. 0.67

   B. 0.05

   C. 0.008

   D. 0.33

Answer: C. 0.008

The best way to approach this problem is to use the fact that the probability of an event plus the probability of the event not happening is unity. First, find the probability that no two people will share a birthday and then subtract the result from 1. The probability that two of the people will not share a birthday is $\frac{364}{365}$ (since the second person's birthday can be one of the 364 days other than the birthday of the first person). The probability that the third person will also not share either of the first two birthdays is $\left(\frac{364}{365}\right)\left(\frac{363}{365}\right) = 0.992$. Therefore, the probability that at least two people will share a birthday is $1 - 0.992 = 0.008$.

(Average) (Skill 12.2)

85. Given a drawer with 5 black socks, 3 blue socks, and 2 red socks, what is the probability that you will draw two black socks in two draws in a dark room?

   A. $\frac{2}{9}$

   B. $\frac{1}{4}$

   C. $\frac{17}{18}$

   D. $\frac{1}{18}$

Answer: A. $\frac{2}{9}$

In this example of conditional probability, the probability of drawing a black sock on the first draw is $\frac{5}{10}$. It is implied in the problem that there is no replacement, therefore the probability of obtaining a black sock in the second draw is $\frac{4}{9}$. Multiply the two probabilities and reduce to lowest terms.

(Average) (Skill 12.3)

86. A rectangular garden 20 ft. by 15 ft. has a 5 ft. by 5 ft. vegetable plot within it. If a ball is thrown at random into the garden, what is the probability that it will fall into the vegetable plot?

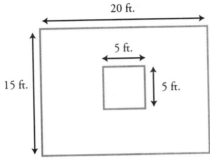

A. $\frac{1}{3}$

B. $\frac{1}{4}$

C. $\frac{1}{12}$

D. $\frac{1}{7}$

Answer: C. $\frac{1}{12}$

The area of the garden is $15 \times 20 = 300$ sq. ft. The area of the vegetable plot is $5 \times 5 = 25$ sq. ft. Since the area of the vegetable plot is $\frac{25}{300} = \frac{1}{12}$ of the area of the whole garden, the probability of the ball falling with in it is $\frac{1}{12}$.

(Rigorous) (Skill 12.3)

87. A circular disc with a radius of 1 ft. is placed on a 6 ft. by 6 ft. square table. The center of the disc may be placed on any point on the table top. What is the probability that the entire disk will be on top of the table without any portion hanging over the edge?

A. $\frac{4}{9}$

B. $\frac{25}{36}$

C. $\frac{1}{2}$

D. $\frac{16}{25}$

Answer: A. $\frac{4}{9}$

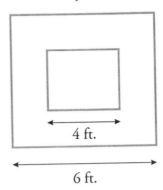

The disk will stay entirely on top of the table if the center is placed at least 1 ft. away from each edge. Therefore the center must be within a square of side 4ft in the middle of the table. Thus, the probability of the disc lying entirely on the table top $= \frac{\text{area of 4 ft. square}}{\text{area of 6 ft. square}} = \frac{16}{36} = \frac{4}{9}$.

(Rigorous) (Skill 12.4)

88. Ann flips a coin 10 times. She gets 7 heads in a row followed by 3 tails. From this we can conclude:

A. The coin has a theoretical probability of coming up heads $\frac{7}{10}$th of the time.

B. There is something wrong with the way the coin was flipped since there were 7 heads in a row.

C. The number of flips is too few to draw any definite conclusion.

D. None of the above.

Answer: C. The number of flips is too few to draw any definite conclusion.

Ideally, as the number of trials goes to infinity, the empirical probability distribution should approach the theoretical distribution. For a fair coin, the number of heads will get closer to half as the number of flips increases. A large number of flips is needed to judge whether the experimental probability in this case deviates from the theoretical probability of getting heads.

Discrete Mathematics and Reading (Skills 13.1 – 14.5)

(Easy) (Skill 13.2)

89. The number of permutations of m out of n objects is:

A. Greater than the number of combinations of m out of n objects

B. Fewer than the number of combinations of m out of n objects

C. Equal to the number of combinations of m out of n objects

D. Sometimes fewer and sometimes greater than the number of combinations of m out of n objects

Answer: A. Greater than the number of combinations of m out of n objects

Since the order of arrangement matters in a permutation but not in a combination of objects, for each combination there are several different ways in which the objects can be ordered. Hence, the number of permutations is always greater.

(Average) (Skill 13.2)

90. A school has 15 male teachers and 35 female teachers. In how many ways can they form a committee with 2 male teachers and 4 female teachers?

A. 525

B. 5,497,800

C. 88

D. 263,894,400

Answer: B. 5,497,800

The number of ways one can pick 2 male teachers out of 15 =

$$^{15}_{2}C = \frac{15!}{13!2!} = \frac{14 \times 15}{2} = 105$$

The number of ways one can pick 4 female teachers out of 35 =

$$^{35}_{4}C = \frac{35!}{31!4!} = \frac{32 \times 33 \times 34 \times 35}{2 \times 3 \times 4} = 52360$$

Hence, the total number of ways the committee can be chosen = 105 × 52,360 = 5,497,800.

(Average) (Skill 13.4)

91. The population of geese in a city is given by the difference equation:

$$p_{n+1} = p_n + 0.1p_n$$

where p_n is the population in the nth year since the counting was begun.

If the initial number of geese in the year $n = 0$ was 1000, what will the population be after 2 years?

A. 1200

B. 1210

C. 1100

D. 1150

Answer: B. 1210

After 1 year the population will be

$P_1 = P_0 + 0.1P_0 = 1000 + 0.1 \times 1000 = 1100.$

After 2 years the population will be

$P_2 = P_1 + 0.1P_1 = 1100 + 0.1 \times 1100 = 1210.$

(Easy) (Skill 13.4)

92. The scalar multiplication of the number 3 with the matrix $\begin{pmatrix} 2 & 1 \\ 3 & 5 \end{pmatrix}$ yields:

A. 33

B. $\begin{pmatrix} 6 & 1 \\ 9 & 5 \end{pmatrix}$

C. $\begin{pmatrix} 2 & 3 \\ 3 & 15 \end{pmatrix}$

D. $\begin{pmatrix} 6 & 3 \\ 9 & 15 \end{pmatrix}$

Answer: D. $\begin{pmatrix} 6 & 3 \\ 9 & 15 \end{pmatrix}$

In scalar multiplication of a matrix by a number, each element of the matrix is multiplied by that number.

(Easy) (Skill 13.4)

93. **Find the sum of the following matrices:**

$\begin{pmatrix} 6 & 3 \\ 9 & 15 \end{pmatrix} \begin{pmatrix} 4 & 7 \\ 1 & 0 \end{pmatrix}$

A. $\begin{pmatrix} 10 & 10 \\ 10 & 15 \end{pmatrix}$

B. $\begin{pmatrix} 13 & 7 \\ 9 & 16 \end{pmatrix}$

C. 45

D. $\begin{pmatrix} 20 \\ 25 \end{pmatrix}$

Answer: A. $\begin{pmatrix} 10 & 10 \\ 10 & 15 \end{pmatrix}$

Two matrices with the same dimensions are added by adding the corresponding elements. In this case, element 1,1 (i.e. row 1, column 1) of the first matrix is added to element 1,1 of the second matrix; element 2,1 of the first matrix is added to element 2,1 of the second matrix; and so on for all four elements.

(Rigorous) (Skill 13.4)

94. **Solve the following matrix equation:**

$3x + \begin{pmatrix} 1 & 5 & 2 \\ 0 & 6 & 9 \end{pmatrix} = \begin{pmatrix} 7 & 17 & 5 \\ 3 & 9 & 9 \end{pmatrix}$

A. $\begin{pmatrix} 2 & 4 & 1 \\ 1 & 1 & 0 \end{pmatrix}$

B. 2

C. $\begin{pmatrix} 8 & 23 & 7 \\ 3 & 15 & 18 \end{pmatrix}$

D. $\begin{pmatrix} 9 \\ 2 \end{pmatrix}$

Answer: A. $\begin{pmatrix} 2 & 4 & 1 \\ 1 & 1 & 0 \end{pmatrix}$

Use the basic rules of algebra and matrices.

$3x = \begin{pmatrix} 7 & 17 & 5 \\ 3 & 9 & 9 \end{pmatrix} - \begin{pmatrix} 1 & 5 & 2 \\ 0 & 6 & 9 \end{pmatrix} = \begin{pmatrix} 6 & 12 & 3 \\ 3 & 3 & 0 \end{pmatrix}$

$x = \frac{1}{3}\begin{pmatrix} 6 & 12 & 3 \\ 3 & 9 & 0 \end{pmatrix} = \begin{pmatrix} 2 & 4 & 1 \\ 1 & 1 & 0 \end{pmatrix}$

(Average) (Skill 14.1)

95. Mr. Sanchez is having his students work with one-syllable words, removing the first consonant and substituting another, as in changing *mats* to *hats*. What reading skill are they working on?

   A. Morphemic inflections

   B. Pronouncing short vowels

   C. Invented spelling

   D. Phonemic awareness

Answer: D. Phonemic awareness

Phonemic awareness is the acknowledgement of sounds and words; a child's realization that some words rhyme is one of the skills that fall under this category.

(Rigorous) (Skill 14.2)

96. Which of the following is not a primary way to differentiate instruction?

   A. Product

   B. Content

   C. Quantity

   D. Process

Answer: C. Quantity

Teachers can differentiate instruction by modifying content, process, or product. Differentiation does not distinguish differences in quantity of work for different students; it distinguishes differences in types of work.

(Average) (Skill 14.3)

97. To summarize a passage, a student should:

   A. Answer the key questions raised in the passage

   B. Paraphrase the main idea

   C. Create a list of key words in the passage

   D. State the main idea and supporting details

Answer: D. State the main idea and supporting details

To create a summary, a student should identify the main idea of a passage and the details that support the main idea.

(Easy) (Skill 14.3)

98. A Venn diagram is an example of which type of comprehension strategy?

   A. Text structure

   B. Graphic organizer

   C. Summarization

   D. Textual marking

Answer: B. Graphic organizer

Graphic organizers are graphical representations of content. Venn diagrams, a type of graphic organizer, show the similarities and differences between two concepts.

(Easy) (Skill 14.4)

99. **Which of the following is true about content-area vocabulary?**

    A. Content-area vocabulary should be taught by connecting new words to familiar ideas, words, and experiences.

    B. Content-area vocabulary should be taught beginning in middle school.

    C. Content-area vocabulary should be taught primarily in language-arts classes.

    D. Content-area vocabulary should be introduced once and then used occasionally for review.

    Answer: A. Content-area vocabulary should be taught by connecting new words to familiar ideas, words, and experiences.

    When teachers explicitly teach vocabulary, it is best if they can connect new words to ideas, words, and experiences with which students are already familiar. This will help to reduce the strangeness of the new words.

(Average) (Skill 14.5)

100. **According to Piaget, at which developmental level would a child be able to learn formal algebra?**

    A. Pre-operational

    B. Sensorimotor

    C. Formal operational

    D. Concrete operational

Answer: C. Formal operational

According to Piaget, it is only at the formal operational stage beyond age twelve that a child is able to understand abstract symbolic concepts as required in formal algebra. Basic algebraic ideas using concrete representations may be introduced in the previous stage.

CPSIA information can be obtained at www.ICGtesting.com

227361LV00001B/21/P